Shakespeare's queer children

Sexual politics and contemporary culture

Kate Chedgzoy

Manchester University Press

Manchester and New York

distributed exclusively in the USA and Canada by St. Martin's Press

Copyright © Kate Chedgzoy 1995

Published by Manchester University Press
Oxford Road, Manchester M13 9NR, UK
and Room 400, 175 Fifth Avenue, New York, NY 10010, USA

Distributed exclusively in the USA and Canada
by St. Martin's Press, Inc., 175 Fifth Avenue, New York, NY 10010, USA

British Library Cataloguing-in-Publication Data
A catalogue record for this book is available from the British Library

Library of Congress Cataloging-in-Publication Data
Chedgzoy, Kate
  Shakespeare's queer children : sexual politics and contemporary culture /
Kate Chedgzoy.
    p. cm.
  Includes bibliographical references.
  ISBN 0–7190–4657–2—ISBN 0–7190–4658–0 (pbk.)
  1. Shakespeare, William, 1564–1616—Political and social views.
2. Homosexuality and literature—England—History—16th century.
3. Homosexuality and literature—England—History—17th century.
4. Domestic drama. English—History and criticism.   5. Psychoanalysis and
literature—England—History.   6. Literature and society—England—
History.   7. Social isolation in literature.   8. Parent and child in literature.
9. Children in literature.   10. Family in literature.   11. Gays in literature.
I. Title
PR3024.C48   1995
822.3'3—dc20   95–21452
                                                                                       CIP

ISBN 0 7190 4657 2 *hardback*
      0 7190 4658 0 *paperback*

First published in 1995

99 98 97 96 95   10 9 8 7 6 5 4 3 2 1

Photoset in Great Britain
by Northern Phototypesetting Co Ltd, Bolton
Printed in Great Britain
by Bell & Bain Ltd, Glasgow

Contents

Acknowledgements

Shakespeare's queer children spent three years being a Ph.D. thesis, and nearly two becoming a book. During that time, many people helped me in many ways, and I wish I knew how to do justice to them all. Specific debts are acknowledged in footnotes: here, I want to act like an Oscar-winner for a moment, and express my gratitude to a long list of people without whom …

First, my family, who knew long before I did that I would sooner or later write a book, and did more than anyone else, for longer than anyone else, to make that possible.

The women in the Liverpool community of feminist academics who provided the immediate context for my thesis, especially Emma Francis, Elspeth Graham, Melanie Hansen, Janice Hoadley, Shirley Jones, Claire Martin, Val Pedlar, and Suzanne Trill.

Jonathan Bate and Kate McLuskie, examiners as generous and humane as any Ph.D. candidate could wish for.

The people who welcomed me into a new community when I moved to Warwick, particularly Bridget Bennett, Gill Frith, Tracey Potts, Julie Sanders, Sue Wiseman, and the members of the Lesbian and Gay Studies Group. And Peter Davidson and Jane Stevenson, who helped me find the place in which the thesis became a book.

Everyone who enabled me to test out drafts of the material by inviting me to give papers and lectures, or generously read and commented on drafts.

Anita Roy and Michelle O'Connell at Manchester University Press, for taking me on in the first place, and then helping me to see (finally) what I was trying to say. Special thanks to Anita for the title.

Margaret Burton, Cathy Rees, and Barbara Smith, and my students and colleagues in Liverpool, Chester, and Warwick.

Finally, there are two people I cannot thank enough: Ann Thompson, in every respect an exemplary supervisor, and a model for my own aspirations as a feminist academic, whose continuing support and friendship are worth more than I can say without embarrassing us both; and Claire Stevens, who knows that the past is our mirror and helped me find out how to reflect a future I wanted.

Acknowledgements and thanks are also due to Rogers, Coleridge and White for permission to quote extracts from Angela Carter's *Wise Children*; Janys Chambers for *Lear's Daughters*; Macmillan, for H.D.'s *By Avon River*; Suniti Namjoshi, for *Snapshots of Caliban*; and Keith Collins, for all permissions relating to the work of Derek Jarman.

Introduction

'This island's mine'

A young black man from Hackney, recently the victim of a queer-bashing at the hands of the Metropolitan Police, claims a place at centre-stage to declare, 'This island's mine by Sycorax my mother / Which thou tak'st from me'.[1] Uttered in the penultimate scene of *This Island's Mine*, a play written by Philip Osment for Gay Sweat-shop Theatre Company, what exactly is the weight, the signi-ficance, of Shakespeare's words in the mouth of Selwyn/Caliban? What right does the 'I' that speaks here have to claim these words – let alone this island – as his own, and whom does he represent? The many possible answers to these questions lead us directly to two further, intertwined questions: who may speak of/for Shake-speare? and for/to whom may Shakespeare be made to speak? This book offers some answers to all these questions; answers which sometimes question the received wisdom of Shakespeare studies, or challenge cultural givens, but which will also, I hope, do justice to the extraordinary aesthetic, emotional and political resonance of Selwyn/Caliban's heartfelt cry.

As it appears towards the end of Gay Sweatshop's play, the dec-laration, 'This island's mine by Sycorax my mother / Which thou tak'st from me', functions not as an assertion of exclusive, con-trolling possession, but as a claim to entitlement and belonging, to membership of a diverse and many-voiced culture, in the face of forces which would deny Selwyn/Caliban such entitlement. Selwyn, as I said, has been queer-bashed; a small child is taunted at school because his mother shares her life with another woman; a middle-aged miner is made redundant from the only job he has ever known; and an elderly Jewish refugee lives in fear of a resur-gence of the intolerance which made her an exile in the first

[1]

place. The island in which Osment's characters are making their lives is presented in the play as hostile to the choices they have made, the hopes and desires they live out. In the introduction to the volume in which *This Island's Mine* was published, Osment notes that the idea for the play was born out of a desire to forge links between actual exiles, and people who feel like exiles in their own country, as he himself did when he began work on it in the midst of the hysterical homophobia which marked the late 1980s.[2] *This Island's Mine* appropriates Shakespeare to insist that the history and culture of this island, which Caliban shares with the play's audience as much as with its other characters, are not merely monolithic and exclusive, but are also composed of, and belong to, the diverse voices of the exiled, marginal, dispossessed and oppositional individuals who populate it. *The Tempest*, it suggests, can belong to Miranda, Caliban, Sycorax and Claribel, as much as to Prospero.

In its appropriation of Shakespeare's cultural authority to enable a critique and re-evaluation of the patterns of power and desire which shape cultural entitlement in the late twentieth century, *This Island's Mine* engages movingly with the questions of exclusion, entitlement and opposition which this book will explore. The play creates a microcosmic world in which people who are marked, by virtue of their gender, race, sexuality or class, as 'other', are constantly obliged to negotiate with the dominant culture which produces this marginalised and stigmatised status. The high cost of this enforced negotiation is made clear; but so, too, are the pleasures of community, resistance, and the appropriation of the very substance of the dominant culture – in the form of *The Tempest* – to enable this pleasurable opposition. Similarly, this book will argue that Shakespeare is not the exclusive possession of any one social group or cultural formation, but has provided an enabling and empowering resource which has allowed 'other' voices to make themselves heard, to stake a claim to cultural centrality, often in the face of those forces which would consign them to internal exile. I attend here to a few of the ways in which Shakespeare's works have been re-created in different historical moments and contexts, to answer a variety of aesthetic, emotional and political needs. If Shakespeare comes nearer than any other English playwright to satisfying all the competing demands and desires to which the theatre is subject, it is surely not because his works succeed in reconciling or obliterating these differences, but because they offer a cultural space where conflicting desires – aesthetic, social and erotic – can be staged, explored and transformed through the medium of art.

Present in the audience at Gay Sweatshop's meta-theatrical rendition of *The Tempest* is a motley assortment of people, whose lives have become intertwined over the course of the play as the result of a series of baroque coincidences, manipulated perhaps by the hand of an invisible Ariel. For Philip Osment, the play's central achievement is its exploration of 'the idea of families and how we create alternative families for ourselves based not on blood ties but on a community of interest and ideas – pretended families, if you like' ('Finding Room', p. lxi). The term 'pretended families' is borrowed from the Conservative Government's 1988 attack on lesbian and gay rights in Section 28 of the Local Government Act, which stigmatised households headed by lesbians or gay men as 'pretended family relationships'. I take up the question of Section 28's implications for contemporary cultural politics in Chapter 5; here, I am more immediately concerned with the critique and refashioning of the Shakespearean family which *This Island's Mine* performs, and which is the central topic of Chapters 1 and 2.

The families which coalesce briefly out of a series of shifting, provisional alliances in Gay Sweatshop's play are many and various, and it is true that some of them do involve pretence, whether in the form of denial of a child's homosexuality, or a father's refusal to acknowledge the child born – in a scathing inversion of the scenario sketched in *The Tempest* – of his sexual coercion of a black servant. Marianne/Miranda has refashioned the family in her marriage of convenience to Martin, a middle-class, middle-aged solicitor and her relationship with her lover Debbie, a working-class Londoner; yet she is still trying to make good her escape from her father Stephen, a beloved but controlling Prospero figure whose uncanny power is eventually revealed to have its source in unscrupulous exploitation, when she discovers that he is in fact the father of her childhood friend Jody. And Jody is the daughter of Berta, the black maid who offered Marianne the love which was not forthcoming from her biological mother: 'sitting in her lap / Face pressed to her bosom, / listening to the words resonating in her chest / As Berta told stories, / The smell of dough mingling with her perfume and sweat. / Sometimes / In the arms of a lover, / The memory – so sweet – / Returns to choke her with emotion' (p. 89). Chapters 1 and 2 of this book trace the patriarchal abjection and feminist redemption of the Shakespearean mother, while the demonising of Sycorax is addressed in Chapters 3 and 5. Berta reinscribes Sycorax – and with her all the missing Shakespearean mothers – as a figure of warmth and security: the home from which Marianne/Miranda is excluded in a state of patriarchal exile.

Absent from the party who go to see Selwyn's performance in *The Tempest* is Miss Rosenblum, Martin's elderly Jewish landlady, who forty years earlier had refused Stephen's offer of marriage and a new life in the USA, quoting Miranda's celebrated words, 'Oh, brave new world that has such people in't!' as a sardonic comment on his vision of the free-enterprise future (p. 107). Stephen is bewildered by her remark, and she has to explain, 'That's Shakespeare, / The greatest writer in the English language, / Your language'; to which he responds with a comment which may be hostile, patriotic, or simply uncomprehending, 'I speak American'. When Selwyn is being harassed by the precious director of *The Tempest*, who wants him to speak Caliban's lines with a strong West Indian accent, he concedes, relinquishing his power to claim and define the culture in which he participates: 'Who is Selwyn to argue with England's greatest playwright?' (p. 91). Stephen is an affluent white man, his self-confidence bolstered by his sense of himself as a pioneer, the maker of a new world – 'We're on the edge of a new age / My country will lead the way forward / And I'm gonna be part of that' – and is stymied when Shakespeare, in many ways traditionally held to be the *genius loci* of the old world Stephen is rejecting, is used to query his dream. Selwyn, in contrast, working-class, black and gay, occupies one of the most stigmatised and oppressed positions this island can allot a man; but he too finds himself baffled by Shakespeare's cultural power. In Chapter 3, I address the body of work which has traced the exclusionary and oppressive uses which have historically been made of Shakespeare in the sphere of colonial encounters and the assertion of national identity; but I hope to show that Shakespeare *can* speak to both Stephen and Selwyn in a language they will understand – and moreover, that Selwyn has the right to speak back.

[4]

The actors who play Marianne and Stephen also play Miranda and Prospero in the scenes where *The Tempest* is being rehearsed or performed; in an Author's Note, Osment stresses that this doubling is a crucial element of his appropriation of Shakespeare's play (p. 83). And Marianne/Miranda is also Maggie, Martin's sister, from whom he has been alienated since she and her miner husband Frank accidentally saw him at a gay pride parade, which caused them to prevent him from seeing his nephew Luke. Martin sees it as rough justice, then, when Luke comes to find him in London, displaying a certain 'family likeness' (p. 92) when he turns up on his uncle's doorstep demanding support as he learns to accept and act on his own gay identity. The question of class is crucial in shaping the possibilities which are open to Luke – indeed, this is true of all the gay men in the play. Yet in the unlikely and strictly provisional alliance which the 1984–85 miners' strike brings about between Luke's father Frank and the members of a lesbian and gay support group, the possibility of renegotiating the boundaries of class and sexual difference is affirmed. In Chapters 4 and 5 I trace the complex role, both problematic and liberating, which class difference has often played in the construction of gay identities. Literary culture has played a crucial part in creating a world of meaning in which men like Martin and Selwyn can make sense of their desires, and these chapters show that the validation which Luke so desperately needs has repeatedly been provided by appropriations of Shakespeare which demonstrate that love between men need be neither sordid nor secretive.

This Introduction represents a second attempt. Initially, I tried to do everything in the strictly conventional way, setting out my theoretical stall in considerable and polysyllabic detail, and decking it with my various wares, described chapter by chapter. But it didn't work; it was leaden and inert, and worse, it stood in direct contradiction to everything the book itself tries to do. This is a book about diversity and multiplicity; about the subversion of the fantasied monolithic icons of a culture which believes itself to be uncontestably dominant by a polyphonic choir, in which by no means all the voices are in harmony with each other. It makes no sense to me to try and impose a single, fixed way of reading upon it. I have no wish to produce a new appropriation of Shakespeare in the service of a particular ideological or personal project. Rather, my aim is to convey some sense of how many, and how various, are the personal and political uses to which his works have been put. My subject, then, is the pleasure and empowerment which the dispossessed and marginalised can derive from the appropriation of Shakespeare, and writing this book has been an intensely pleasurable, varied and empowering experience. I hope the same may be said for the experience of reading it.

Notes

1   *The Tempest*, I.ii.332–46. All references to Shakespeare's plays are to the relevant Arden edition. Here, though, Caliban's words are quoted from Philip Osment, *This Island's Mine* (1988) in Philip Osment (ed.), *Gay Sweatshop: Four Plays and a Company* (London, Methuen, 1989), pp. 81–120 (p. 119).
2   'Finding Room on the Agenda for Love: A History of Gay Sweatshop', in *Gay Sweatshop*, pp. vii–lxviii (p. lxi).

Chapter 1

Successors to his name:
Shakespearean family romances

Wise Children,[1] Angela Carter's last novel, is the tale of Dora Chance, superannuated vaudeville star and illegitimate daughter of the twentieth century's greatest Shakespearean actor, Sir Melchior Hazard. The novel offers a vision of some of the key icons of modern English society and culture which comes from outside the mainstream: that it comes from the wrong side of the tracks, as Dora herself says, is underscored by the location of the significantly titled Bard Road, her life-long home, on 'the left-hand side … the *bastard* side of Old Father Thames' (p. 1). A fabulous transformation of the Shakespearean family is the novel's central vehicle of cultural critique: 'mother is as mother does' and 'a father is a moveable feast' (p. 216) in a text where the politics of legitimacy are inseparable from deconstructive play, and the cultural power of Shakespeare is appropriated, made benign and lavished open-handedly on theatrical knight and game-show hostess alike. Dora's life-story undoes many of the fantasies and assumptions which help to secure Shakespeare's place as the embodiment and guarantor of a certain powerful version of English culture, and in telling her tale, she draws together several themes which have played shaping roles in the cultural reproduction of Shakespeare since the Restoration. The novel's deployment of textual and structural allusions to Shakespeare collapses comedy and tragedy together in a complex web which makes it impossible to ascribe originary authority to a single pre-text. *Hamlet* looms large, however, both at the level of allusion, and because for the late twentieth century it constitutes – however anachronistically – the paradigmatic Shakespearean representation of the nuclear family which Carter's novel deconstructs. In

Wise Children, Hamlet's most celebrated soliloquy, one of the iconic moments of English culture, becomes a dance routine for identical twin sisters, dressed as bellhops and wondering whether a parcel should be delivered to '2b or not 2b' (p. 90). The collision of high and low cultures and the substitution of not one but two daughters for one of literature's most famous sons offers a light-hearted means of asking a genuinely significant question about cultural address and entitlement – to whom, and for whom, can Shakespeare be made to speak in the twentieth century? *Wise Children* demonstrates the value of appropriating Shakespeare's culturally powerful texts creatively in order to show, as the book's jacket asserts, 'how thoroughly the legitimate and illegitimate worlds are entangled … in a country whose cultural life continues to be crippled by false distinction between "high" and "low"'. Carter's novel challenges these hierarchies by means of a carnivalesque celebration of illegitimacy and low culture, and at the same time exposes the damaging falsity of the categories and practices which make such terms meaningful.

Carter's revisions of Shakespeare frequently flirt with or are refracted through the work of other writers and artists who have engaged in the same enterprise, including Brecht, Mendelssohn, Joyce, Marx and Freud – in *Wise Children*, for instance, Dora enjoys a Hollywood liaison with a certain *émigré* German script consultant, himself known for his appropriations of Shakespeare.[2] And the novel's flirtation with the hypothesis of paternity evokes James Joyce's exploration of the same issue in the 'Scylla and Charybdis' episode of *Ulysses*, where Stephen Dedalus mediates his own encounter with Shakespeare via multiple literary fathers, and considers the possibility that '*Amor matris*, subjective and objective genitive, may be the only true thing in life. Paternity may be a legal fiction.'[3] Nevertheless, in Stephen's speculations on the 'apostolic succession, from only begetter to only begotten', it is the mother who is eliminated from the family, which is reconstructed as an exclusively masculine space where the capacity for procreation and literary creation are coextensive, as Buck Mulligan parodically notes: 'Himself his own father, Sonmulligan told himself. Wait. I am big with child. I have an unborn child in my brain. Pallas Athena! A play! The play's the thing! Let me parturiate! He clasped his paunchbrow with both birthaiding hands' (p. 208).

[8]

One of the epigraphs to *Wise Children* quotes Shakespearean actress Ellen Terry's wistful comment, 'How many times Shakespeare draws fathers and daughters, never mothers and daughters.' Carter transforms the patriarchal family romance which provokes such an anxiety of origins in Stephen Dedalus by making the daughter's subjectivity central. Conversely, another of the key themes of the novel, signalled by a further (semi-Shakespearean) epigraph, 'it's a wise child that knows its own father, but a wiser father that knows his own child', is contained in the realisation that paternity can never be more than a problematic hypothesis, or as *Ulysses* calls it, a legal fiction. *Wise Children* is full of idealisations and misrecognitions of the relationship between father and child: misconceptions of authenticity and legitimacy which can offer a metaphor of Shakespeare's position as cultural father, source and guarantor of all that is finest in English literary history, which is both secure and ambivalent, unchallengeable yet grounded in the shakiest of foundations.

Wise Children enacts a playful and profound study of the reproduction and subversion of the Shakespearean family, shifting on to the terrain of fiction a debate which has flourished in academic Shakespeare studies for some time now. In the critical project of delineating and critiquing the continuing emotional resonance of Shakespeare's representations of families which has blossomed in the last decade or so, many critics, particularly in the USA, have been inspired by psychoanalysis, a discourse which C. L. Barber characterised as 'a sociology of love and worship within the family'.[4] Conversely, feminist critics have also used psychoanalytic theory to expose the intricate and often painful entanglement of love with fear, hostility and rage within the family, revealing that Shakespeare's families are endowed with a psychic and social power which is not always entirely benign. Rather than applying psychoanalytic theory to the analysis of Shakespearean texts, my concern will be to explore the significance both of the recursive relationship which the twentieth century has set up between psychoanalysis and the Shakespearean family – mythologies which together have provided twentieth-century Western culture with its key images of what it means to belong to a family – and of recent feminist critiques which have prompted revision of the meanings of Shakespearean and Freudian families. In particular, I will argue that the Freudian construct of the family romance offers a way of making sense of the structures of authority and desire which shape both Shakespeare's enduring social and psychic significance as a cultural father figure, and our willingness to continue to be his children. Shakespearean families have provided such powerful metaphors for cultural production and entitlement that it is hard to resist the desire to belong to that mythic community – although the price that has to be paid for inclusion within the 'traditional' family is often a high one. But feminist reinscriptions of Shakespearean families have shown that the cost of such membership does not always have to be submission either to the patriarchal strictures of Freudian psychoanalysis, or to the social and religious underpinnings of the family. In the utopian space of literature, the power relationships which shape real-life families in both Shakespeare's time and our own are suspended, so that the family can belong to, and be defined by, daughters as well as fathers, mothers as well as sons. This act of redefinition involves a multiple effort: memorialising the enduring emotional and aesthetic power of the Shakespearean family; critiquing its negative and oppressive aspects; and envisaging its potential future meanings. In Chapter 2 I will discuss some feminist revisions of Shakespeare which critique and subvert the patriarchal family. In this first chapter, though, I begin by tracing some of the ways in which Shakespearean familial metaphors have both accrued and been productive of the exceptional emotional and cultural power which made that feminist critique necessary.

Wills and power: the transformations of Judith Shakespeare

Edward Bond's controversial play *Bingo* tells the sorry tale of the last years of William Shakespeare, successful playwright, property-owner, and family man.[5] In the play, Shakespeare's daughter Judith voices the claims of the community on the individual; claims which are resisted or ignored by a man drifting free of social and familial ties. The family is represented as primarily an economic unit, incapable of sustaining the emotional burdens associated with it, so that Bond's political agenda operates dramatically as a problem in human communication: when Judith berates her father for his failure to care about the misery of his wife and their old female servant he merely says, 'Stop it, Judith. You speak so badly. Such banalities. So stale and ugly' (p. 18). Her reply, 'I can only use the words I know', is a mixture of defiance, accusation and resignation. Language is the currency of emotion within the family, and it is scarcely surprising that Judith's words are less valuable than her playwright father's. But the main reason her speech counts for nothing is that for Bond's Shakespeare, the exchange of property is the only meaningful form of communication, and it is a bitter and perilous one; as he tells his daughter, 'I loved you with money. The only thing I can afford to give you now is money. But money always turns to hate' (p. 42). He makes his scorn for Judith and her mother clear when he shoves his will under a door for them to read, with the contemptuous words, 'It's all there. Your legal share. And the bed' (p. 47). As the play – subtitled 'Scenes of money and death' – ends, Shakespeare lies dying, self-poisoned, while Judith ransacks his room in a fruitless search for a further will which might treat her more kindly.

Judith's desperate search for an alternative will elicits a certain emotional investment from the spectator of Bond's play; yet this theatrical response is countered by attention to the historical evidence which tells us that her efforts were futile, for in reality no such will existed. The fragmentary documentary records which deal with the real Judith Shakespeare's life, mainly by way of her relationship with her father, do not of course constitute points of origin which can be used to secure or refute the conjectures offered by Bond, or by other writers who have re-created 'Judith Shakespeare'. They are themselves textual traces which require interpretation: Judith Shakespeare's identity is constituted in the act of deciphering them, and in the light of the desires which have always already attached themselves to the figure of her more famous father. Shakespeare's actual will was drawn up within a few months of Judith's marriage in 1616 to Thomas Quiney, her inheritance being a marriage portion of £150, plus the interest on a further £150 – she was only to have access to the capital if her husband endowed her with land of equivalent value.[6] E. K. Chambers notes that 'some students have thought that the will indicates displeasure with Judith herself, either at her marriage or at its accompanying excommunication'.[7] Other scholars see the will's differential treatment of Judith and her sister Susanna as an unexceptional attempt to secure the family's property, in the absence of a male heir, through the sons of the eldest daughter – although these plans were thwarted by intransigent biology, and the entire Shakespeare direct line, male and female, died out by 1670.[8] In either case, the distribution of wealth decreed in Shakespeare's will may be seen as illustrating the extent to which, in a patriarchal society, women's social identity is constructed with reference to their husbands and fathers, and their value is not intrinsic to them, but is dependent on their ability to bear sons, thereby safeguarding the family's material and symbolic investment in posterity.

In a recent study of the significance of Shakespeare's will, Richard Wilson argues that we can make sense of this fascinating but enigmatic document by attending to the ways in which it diverges from the testamentary practices typical of Shakespeare's society.[9] According to Wilson, such an analysis reveals a Shakespeare who is concerned less with leaving behind a material acknowledgement of the ties of kin and community than with ensuring the transmission of his private property to selected lineal descendants, and thereby reflecting 'the extent to which recognition of kinship had already lost out to recognition of property in his society' (*Will Power*, p. 187). Shakespeare's real motives must remain opaque, of course; but what the subsequent history of his will unequivocally reveals is that how he chose to dispose of his property has consistently been perceived as a legitimate matter of cultural concern – and not only to professional scholars, as the hoary controversy (and hoarier jokes) over his bequest of the second-best-bed to his wife testifies. Private property or shared heritage, Shakespeare's name and works represent a uniquely valuable cultural legacy, and one strand of the contest for cultural authority has shaped itself as the struggle to claim the right to be called his heir.

Edward Bond's play, written nearly twenty years ago, gains added point at the present moment from the government-sponsored popularisation of the notion of 'heritage', of which Stratford-upon-Avon's tourist trade is only one of the more egregious examples – a notion which smoothly conflates property, 'wealth-creation' and culture.[10] The struggle over a material Shakespearean inheritance represented so dramatically by Bond offers a potent image for the various processes involved in the transmission and appropriation of Shakespeare's cultural heritage. Like *Bingo*, most work on these themes has focused on questions of class and economics, failing to consider the significance of the fact that only women survived to carry on the Shakespeare name. Taking the various tales of 'Judith Shakespeare' as a starting-point, I want now to explore the gendering of these processes of cultural inheritance in relation to Shakespeare.

The image of a Shakespearean cultural patrimony from which the playwright's daughter is excluded is a resonant one. While there is a long and complex tradition of male writers claiming an Oedipal affiliation to Shakespeare – albeit one which is often problematic – the figures of Shakespeare's silent female relatives have been emblematic of cultural exclusion. Since the late Victorian period, various writers have made the shadowy figure of Shakespeare's sister or daughter central to meditations on women's uneasy relationship to male-dominated literary culture. In all these accounts, Judith's gender and sexuality both stand in the way of her literary success; but the metaphors of exclusion and impoverishment which have been used to place women in relation to the central cultural heritage embodied by Shakespeare are incorporated, challenged and revised in a variety of ways, reflecting and responding to changing cultural and historical contexts.

Shakespeare's younger daughter was an utterly obscure figure until the popular novelist William Black published a novel entitled *Judith Shakespeare* in 1883. The eponymous heroine of this romantic tale is a high-spirited, strong-willed girl, whose reluctance either to settle down with one of her numerous suitors, or to behave in a suitably maidenly manner, gets her into trouble. Judith's problems begin when she shows one Leofric Hope, a Londoner on a surreptitious visit to Stratford, manuscript pages from her ageing father's most recent play – it is of course that romance of the father–daughter bond, *The Tempest*. Judith herself is illiterate (as, probably, was the real Judith Shakespeare), and is modestly lacking in any aspirations to literary endeavour. Instead, her filial pleasure in her famous father's writing, and frustration at being unable to read it for herself, are presented in mitigation of her indiscretion. The gravity of this misdemeanour only emerges later, when it transpires that Hope has copied the play and tried to sell it in London, while spreading scurrilous gossip about the nature of the innocent Judith's attentions towards him. Judith's mishandling of her father's property thus becomes inseparable from the question of her own chastity and reputation; as one of her most persistent suitors, the right but repulsive Puritan Master Blaise says, 'Your father may regain possession of his property ... but can he withdraw the name of his daughter from the ribald wit of the taverns?'[11] Judith's plight exemplifies the dangers of transgressing the commonplace Renaissance injunction to women to be both chaste and silent, which meant that unruly speech could all too easily be construed in terms of illicit sexuality and concomitant loss of reputation. Patricia Parker has pointed out that the inscription of this double injunction to silence and chastity on the privatised, enclosed female body enables it to function as a sign and seal of property.[12] Thus Judith perceives herself as guilty of an immodest garrulousness which is also a crime against property, and in a gesture which makes her misdeed's connection with her sexuality clear, she pleads with her older sister Susanna to prevail on their father to take her brideprice in exchange for the damage she has done. However, Susanna points out that without a bride-price Judith will have no future on the marriage market, which will damage the family's fortunes still further. Eventually, she is forgiven anyway; having been punished by the favoured Victorian device of a 'brain-fever' which required that her hair be cut off, thereby enacting a metaphorical rebuke to her transgressive femininity, she is reunited with her childhood sweetheart. But the novel's conventional 'happy ending' can only serve to underscore the irony of Judith's confinement to domestic femininity; there is still no outlet for the frustrations and fantasies which caused the trouble in the first place.

Black's novel provides a remarkably unselfconscious demonstration of the assumptions about female creativity which Judith Shakespeare later came to symbolise in the hands of more politically sophisticated writers. It is surely no coincidence that this mythic Judith Shakespeare began to take on a life of her own at just the moment when modern feminism, with its interest in women's access to education, economic independence and creative expression, was emerging. The socialist feminist writer Olive Schreiner worked intermittently from 1883 (the year in which Black's novel was published) until 1920 on a feminist *roman à thèse*, *From Man to Man*, in which she makes the invocation of some mute inglorious female Shakespeare central to her elegy for every woman's thwarted creativity:

We have had Shakespeare; but what of the possible Shakespeares we might have had, who passed their life from youth upward brewing currant wine and making pastries for fat country squires to eat, with no glimpse of the freedom of life and action, necessary even to poach on deer in the green forests, stifled out without one line written, simply because, being of the weaker sex, life gave no room for action ... ?[13]

Schreiner here not only speaks of the deprivation and misery endured by women whose creativity could find outlet only in domestic service, but also points to the loss and impoverishment this has imposed on the culture as a whole. At the same time, the references to 'fat country squires' and to poaching – perhaps echoing the legend that Shakespeare was once caught poaching on Sir Thomas Lucy's Warwickshire estate[14] – underscore the restrictions which the English class system has often imposed on the 'freedom of life and action' of male as well as female writers.

Virginia Woolf called *From Man to Man* 'a stupendous work upon woman ... an unfinished masterpiece',[15] and a few years after Schreiner's death she too explored the causes and effects of the stultification of female creativity, in a version of the myth of Judith Shakespeare which has come to provide feminist criticism's most powerful metaphor of women's uneasy relation to literary tradition. Wondering 'why women did not write poetry in the Elizabethan age', Woolf identifies her archetypal frustrated female poet as 'Shakespeare's wonderfully gifted sister, called Judith ... [who was] as adventurous, as imaginative, as agog to see the world as he'.[16] It is of course significant that Woolf transforms 'Judith Shakespeare' from the playwright's daughter into his sister. The neatly alliterative phrase 'Shakespeare's sister' has a talismanic quality which both encapsulates feminist anger at the social forces Woolf blamed for crushing her mythical Judith's wonderful gifts, and also celebrates women's literary creativity in the most prestigious terms of the dominant culture, by asserting that Shakespeare *could* have had such a sister. By making her Judith a sister rather than a daughter, Woolf maintains a strict focus on the restrictions imposed by her gender, rather than her position as a dependent, juvenile family member with a duty of obedience to the father who provides for her economically, and has a stake which is more than merely economic in her future marriage. What this Judith does have in common with her predecessor in Black's novel, though, is that she is uneducated and worn down by domestic tedium. So she sets off to London, in the footsteps of her adored brother, to try her luck in the theatre: 'The birds that sang in the hedge were not more musical than she was. She had the quickest fancy, a gift like her brother's, for the tune of words. Like him, she had a taste for the stage' (*A Room of One's Own*, p. 47). Woolf here seems to echo the terms in which the later seventeenth and eighteenth centuries tried to make a virtue of Shakespeare's lack of formal education by celebrating his 'natural genius', a strategy which sometimes seemed to entail the invocation of a metaphorical femininity, since contemporary women who were struggling to write had to make a similar virtue of necessity, as one influential study puts it.[17]

When Judith finally arrives in London and presents herself at a theatre, a manager gifted with a sense of humour which uncannily anticipates Dr Johnson's bellows something about poodles dancing and women acting and 'hinted – you can imagine what' (p. 47). At last Nick Greene (who reappears as something of a scoundrel in *Orlando*, written at about the same time as *A Room of One's Own*)[18] takes pity on her, she finds herself pregnant by him with her dreams of success as a poet in tatters, 'and so – who shall measure the heat and violence of the poet's heart when caught and tangled in a woman's body? – [she] killed herself one winter's night and lies buried at some cross-roads where the omnibuses now stop outside the Elephant and Castle' (p. 47). Again, Judith's literary aspirations are explicitly represented as being in conflict with her sexuality, although Woolf revises the misogynous representation of female speech and sexuality as uncontrollable in order to show, in contrast, how successful predatory male sexuality has been in controlling women. In *A Room of One's Own*, Woolf demonstrates how lethal the combination of sexual harassment and the internalisation of patriarchal sexual ideologies can be for a woman who aspires to creativity:

> No girl could have walked to London and stood at a stage door and forced her way into the presence of actor-managers without doing herself a violence and suffering an anguish which may have been irrational – for chastity may be a fetish invented by certain societies for unknown reasons – but were none the less inevitable ... To have

lived a free life in London in the sixteenth century would have meant for a woman who was poet and playwright a nervous stress and dilemma which might well have killed her (p. 49).

Since the 1970s many feminist critics have explored Woolf's prescient analysis of the complex and historically specific interconnections between women's sexuality and creativity, and patriarchal attempts to regulate both.[19] This, however, is only one aspect of the challenge to the historical silencing of women which Woolf mounts in *A Room of One's Own*. Her famous declaration that 'we think back through our mothers if we are women' is embodied in her search in that text for an enabling lineage of literary foremothers, whose voices may break the silence enjoined by the more repressive kind of father. In a letter to the *New Statesman* in October 1920, Woolf had said:

> the conditions which make it possible for a Shakespeare to exist are that he shall have had predecessors in his art, shall make one of a group where art is freely discussed and practised, and shall himself have the utmost of freedom of action and experience. Perhaps in Lesbos, but never since, have these conditions been the lot of women.[20]

Throughout the twenties and thirties Woolf repeatedly argued that women need both a sustaining tradition behind them and the support of a community of interest around them in order to write. In a paper given to the Brighton Workers' Educational Association in 1940 she emphasised the essentially intertextual nature of writing by means of a familial metaphor: 'Books descend from books as families descend from families. Some descend from Jane Austen; others from Dickens. They resemble their parents, as human children resemble their parents; yet they differ as children differ, and revolt as children revolt.'[21] The faintly Oedipal overtones of this comment cast a shadow over Woolf's more usual insistence on the creative, enabling possibilities of relations between generations of writers and generations of books, underscored in her own writing practice by her copious revisionary use of literary allusion.

It has recently been suggested that Woolf did early modern women a disservice by exaggerating the extent of their silence; a silence which, Margaret J. Ezell argues, the powerful myth of

Shakespeare's sister has actually perpetuated.[22] In contrast, I would argue for the importance of the fact that in writing the story of Shakespeare's sister, Woolf breaks the long historical silence which stifled the voices of women writers, and incorporates the brother himself in a text which, by memorialising seventeenth-century women writers such as Dorothy Osborne, Margaret Cavendish and Aphra Behn, puts flesh on the dry bones of women's literary history. Despite Woolf's rather gloomy perception of the difficulties placed in the way of Renaissance women who wanted to write, which led her to overstate the sparseness of their literary output, it is ironic that until the burst of interest in early modern women's writing which has taken place in the last decade, *A Room of One's Own* provided many readers with their only glimpse, however unsatisfactory, of early modern women's writing. At the same time the book famously enjoins a prophetic duty on women of the future to ensure that 'the opportunity will come and the dead poet who was Shakespeare's sister will put on the body which she has so often laid down' (p. 108) – and Christine Froula argues that Woolf herself appropriated Shakespeare in order to do just that:

> though Woolf begins in anxiety about the daughter-artist's cultural dispossession, she ends by creating a Shakespeare to which she lays powerful claim on behalf of women writers – most immediately, herself. In practising the aesthetic theory that she draws upon Shakespeare to formulate, she herself strives to 'put on the body that [Judith Shakespeare] has so often laid down.'[23]

Woolf herself has become a uniquely central figure in the landscape of contemporary feminist writing, and in a loving but ambivalent act of homage to this literary foremother, novelist Ellen Galford has recently retold and amplified the tale of Judith Shakespeare.[24] Half a century on, things are looking up for Judith – not least, perhaps, because in Galford's lesbian–feminist version, she is no longer an entirely isolated figure battling against men to find a public voice, but is located amongst a community of vocal and independent women. The narrator, a herbalist and lover of Moll Cutpurse, is introduced to Judith Shakespeare by Mavis Jonson, mother of the more famous Ben, whom she had 'chivvied and scolded and bullied ... to be ever restless and ambitious', though he is, in Moll's opinion, 'but a pale shadow of his mother when it comes to spinning a tale' (p. 146). Mavis's literary bent is for gossip, traditionally perceived as a communal, female oral form which eludes both preservation in print and notions of authorship as ownership. In a gossip session convened by Mavis, this Judith becomes the first who gets to tell her tale in her own words:

> In my childish folly I had aped my brother's bookishness, and painstakingly practised my letters by a stolen candle-end at nights ... My parents chided me: they said that maids must stitch up seams instead of sonnets, and lie in a man's bed instead of in his bookcase (p. 150).

Galford follows Schreiner in using the figure of a thwarted female Shakespeare to expose the construction of women's domestic and sexual duties in opposition to their literary desires, emphasised here by the sardonic use of zeugma. And like Woolf, she sends her Judith off to London to try her luck as a writer in emulation of her brother.

Raped and assaulted on the way, Judith takes refuge with a young housewife in the liberties, then goes in search of her brother; but 'the only news I could get of him, delivered with a leer, was that he was "away with my lord in the country"' (p. 153). The inversion here is quietly ironic; the brother free to drift temporarily away from his career as a writer and return to the country for sexual pleasures which, though illicit, are winked at, while his sister has to battle her way on the reverse journey, fending off unwanted sexual assault. Picked up by one Nick Parry who claims to be a friend of her brother, Judith becomes his lover, but eventually realises that he is not fulfilling his promise to present her work to the managers at the playhouses where he has acted. She tries to get on with her writing, but in a new twist on the connection between unruly sexuality and female public utterance discovers that 'for some reason the sight of me bent over my papers seemed to excite his lust, and all such efforts on my part led me nowhere but back to bed' (p. 157). William Shakespeare eventually finds her and complains that 'the jest had gone round all the playhouses, that now I'd come to London to write plays, my illustrious brother had gone down to the country to sew and spin', implying that writing is a doubly dangerous activity for women, sexualising the woman herself and emasculating any man associated with her who fails to gain control over her sexuality. Driven to despair by the frustration of her creativity, Judith tries to drown herself in the Thames, but turns out to be more fortunate than her Woolfian predecessor: she is rescued and tended by a fisherman's wife, with whom she forms a partnership to sell ballads, concluding, 'let those jeer who will, for I do what I set out to do – I earn my bread through poesy' (p. 163).

The form in which this Judith finally succeeds in asserting a public voice is apt in the light of Woolf's use of the ballad 'The Queen's Maries' as a leitmotif in *A Room of One's Own*. Considering the ballad to be, like gossip, a popular oral form aptly associated with women, Alice Fox suggests that by weaving 'The Queen's Maries' into the fabric of her own book, Woolf effectively endows her fictional Judith with a voice grounded in women's historical participation in popular culture, so that she stands as a representative of anonymous female ballad makers and a 'mother' of contemporary women writers.[25] Woolf's assertion that 'Anon.' was often a woman is not, however, a romantic attempt to redeem the silent past. Rather, *A Room of One's Own*, as we have seen, closes with an exhortation to contemporary women to take up the cultural and political responsibilities laid on them by the past and work to create the conditions in which 'the dead poet who was Shakespeare's sister will … find it possible to live and write her poetry' (p. 108). Discussing American women writers' uses of Shakespeare, Elaine Showalter turns this injunction on its head; rather than seeing it as an exhortation to women to write, she perceives Woolf's re-creation of Shakespeare's sister as the semi-magical invocation of 'the Dark Lady, the feminist messiah, the tenth muse' who will automatically validate women's literary and intellectual production.[26] Although her discussion illustrates some of the numerous empowering and creative ways in which American women writers have used Shakespeare's works as a source of inspiration and validation, Showalter's conclusion is that such self-authorising strategies have now become 'self-defeating and obsolete'; and she implies that 'Shakespeare's sister' can only ever be a dutiful daughter of the white cultural fathers. To back this up, she quotes the admonition of Afro-American critic Henry Louis Gates that 'We must resist the description of the works of women and the works of persons of color as … shadowy fragments of a Master Text that we, somehow, have been unable

to imitate precisely, or to recite correctly, or to ventriloquise elo-
quently enough.'[27] However, the enduring vitality of the myth of
Judith Shakespeare and the creative energies embodied in the
numerous ways in which it has been reworked demonstrate that
even in writing out of or about the cultural dispossession and
oppression for which Shakespeare's life and work have furnished
apt metaphors, writers have also found in the figure of Shakespeare a source of inspiration and strength which authorises their
own work. Against the pessimistic analysis offered by Showalter
and Gates, my contention throughout this book will be that this
construction of a relation of domination and subjugation to a
Shakespearean master text is belied by the creative confidence of
the many writers and artists from culturally oppressed or marginalised groups who have succeeded in plundering Shakespeare's
texts to their own ends.

'We acknowledge them our fathers in wit': literary sonship

I want now to elaborate on the androcentric model of cultural
inheritance with which writers like Woolf have negotiated, by
turning from the more or less miserable and inarticulate fates
shared by Shakespeare's fictional female relatives to the putatively
more central tradition claimed by writers who have sought to cast
themselves as Shakespeare's literary sons. Since the Restoration,
Shakespeare's pre-eminence in English-speaking culture has
entailed representations of the playwright as a benignly powerful
father-figure. Yet Shakespeare is explicitly excluded from the most
famous father–son model of literary heritage, that offered in
Harold Bloom's influential book *The Anxiety of Influence*.[28] In
Bloom's view, Shakespeare was exempt from the anxiety of influence because he was the outstanding instance of 'the complete
absorption of the precursor' (p. 11), in that his chief precursor,
Marlowe, was a lesser figure. Moreover, Bloom's theory margin-
alises drama, constructing lyric poetry as the central vehicle of literary patrimony.[29] It is curious, though, that Bloom excludes
Shakespeare from his model by considering him only as a literary
son, not a father. I want to explore the possibility that Shakespeare has indeed been a crucial literary father-figure, for artistic
daughters as well as sons, but that, nevertheless, Bloom is right to
exclude him from his own agonistic schema, in that Shake-

spearean paternal/poetic power has most often been experienced as benevolent and enabling. While it is true that male writers have sometimes claimed to suffer Oedipal anxieties in relation to Shakespeare, I shall argue below that this is primarily a rhetorical strategy designed to secure the legitimacy of their literary sonship. And the women writers I discuss in Chapter 2 are not subjugated by Shakespeare's cultural power, but rather succeed in appropriating it in the service of a feminist critique of the patriarchal family – even though the latter has often sought its emotional ratification and cultural legitimisation in the reproduction of Shakespearean images of the family.

With or without Bloom's sanction, Shakespeare could have been seen as a disablingly powerful Oedipal precursor. Yet since the Restoration his literary sons have demonstrated a remarkable ability to negotiate with his cultural power and appropriate it to their own ends. The actor-manager and playwright Sir William Davenant, for example, did nothing to quash – and may have fostered – rumours that he was Shakespeare's illegitimate son. Indeed, he used his dubious parentage to give his production of *Hamlet* an authority supposedly grounded in authenticity, converting illegitimate parentage into a sign of cultural legitimacy.[30] His career is paradigmatic of the empowering and troubling dimensions of male writers' figurations of Shakespeare as a literary father, in which *Hamlet* figures as a key symbol of the transmission from father to son of a cultural authority and continuity which are underwritten by Davenant's sustained commitment to theatrical production throughout the upheavals of the mid-seventeenth century.

William Davenant had succeeded Jonson as Poet Laureate in 1638, and remained loyal to the royalist cause throughout the revolutionary period, occasionally staging private performances of plays for the exiled court. At the Restoration, his company, the Duke's men, was one of the two recognised by Charles II. The rival company, the King's men, led by Thomas Killigrew, included many veterans of the pre-1642 stage, while Davenant's men were younger. He compensated for what might have been perceived as a disadvantage by deploying the trope of artistic sonship in order to capitalise on his company's belatedness. We cannot know how much credence was attached to it, but the rumour that Davenant was Shakespeare's illegitimate son was still in circulation as late

as 1778, which suggests that, whether or not it was believed to be
true, it was certainly felt to hold some significance or interest. The
earliest written version of the rumour is to be found in a manuscript note by John Aubrey, dating from about 1681, which states
that Davenant's father kept a tavern in Oxford. Shakespeare supposedly stayed there on his annual journey to Stratford, and 'was
exceedingly respected' – particularly, it would seem, by the
innkeeper's wife. According to Aubrey, Davenant would claim
'that it seemed to him that he writt with the very spirit that Shakespeare, and was *seemed* contentended [*sic*] enough to be thought
his Son: he would tell them the story as above [in which way his
mother had a very light report, whereby she was called a
whore].[31] Convinced of his spiritual sonship, Davenant is happy
to sacrifice his mother's good name for the sake of his own literary reputation; the idealisation of the father, and the vicarious
glory with which it endows the son, more than compensates for
the degradation of the mother. Joseph Spence's *Anecdotes,
Observations and Characters* (compiled *c.* 1736, published 1820)
cites a similar comment supposedly made by Pope, that the
'notion of Sir William Davenant being more than a poetical child
only of Shakespeare, was common in town; and Sir William himself seemed fond of having it taken for truth'.[32]

As well as allowing the rumour of his descent from Shakespeare
to go unchecked, Davenant stressed the continuity of artistic succession, which contemporaries saw as an element in the Duke's
men's success, as this well-known account of their production of
Hamlet indicates:

> Sir *William* having seen *Mr. Taylor* of the *Black-Fryars* Company Act
> it, who being Instructed by the Author *Mr. Shakespear* taught Mr.
> *Betterton* in every Particle of it; which by his exact Performance of
> it, gain'd him Esteem and Reputation, Superlative to all other Plays
> … No succeeding Tragedy for several Years got more Reputation, or
> Money to the Company than this.[33]

The virtue of Betterton's performance lies in the precision of his
reproduction of the role as it was taught him by his artistic men-
tors, and as Gary Taylor points out, 'the questionable accuracy of
such accounts matters less than the evident importance of
authenticity' (*Reinventing Shakespeare*, p. 14). The notion that
an artistic son's highest glory lies in memor(ial)ising his father

echoes Hamlet's repeatedly enjoined responsibility to remember his father, and to act on this memory – a commitment which is itself imaged in literary terms:

Remember thee?
Ay, thou poor ghost, whiles memory holds a seat
In this distracted globe. Remember thee?
Yea, from the table of my memory
I'll wipe away all trivial fond records,
All saws of books, all forms, all pressures past
That youth and observation copied there,
And thy commandment alone shall live
Within the book and volume of my brain,
Unmixed with baser matter.

(I.v.95–104)

While Hamlet swears to make his mind a *tabula rasa*, inscribed only by his father's desires, Davenant's Shakespearean sonship is constructed as a palimpsest of mutually supportive genealogies. In a recent essay on *Hamlet* and history, Francis Barker has warned that stressing the psychic work of mourning and recuperation may serve to erase the historical difference and political valency involved in remembering the dead:

Hamlet must remember his father: this is recognisable from within more or less modern liberal humanist perspectives where the emphasis on the authenticity of the personal and the familial both masks and counters the social. It may be the *project* of the text to remember the king, that major sign, still, in the play's world, of historical power. But the mourning of fathers … becomes its dominant articulation.[34]

Barker's formulation seems to imply that the personal and familial are somehow other than social, denying their imbrication in what he calls historical power – as if history were the province only of kings, warriors, lawmakers. In contrast, I would argue that one of the reasons so many later writers have felt obliged to negotiate with their Shakespearean patrimony by way of *Hamlet* is precisely because the play offers such an uncannily accurate revelation of the interwoven psychic and political structures by means of which our culture makes sense of the experience of being beholden to a father-figure.

The extent to which Shakespeare could, none the less, represent a distinctly anxiety-producing father-figure is illustrated by the case of Dryden, who, *pace* Bloom, appears to have suffered from a classic version of the anxiety of influence, triangulated via Davenant, with whom he collaborated on *The Enchanted Island*, an adaptation of *The Tempest*. In the preface to their version, published after Davenant's death, Dryden notes that the play 'was originally *Shakespear*'s: a Poet for whom [Davenant] had particularly a high veneration, and whom he first taught me to admire.'[35] In the verse prologue to the play Dryden expresses how Shakespeare as artistic precursor entirely pre-empted and absorbed his followers:

> Shakespear, *who (taught by none) did first impart*
> To Fletcher *Wit, to labouring* Johnson *Art.*
> *He Monarch-like gave those his subjects law,*
> *And is that Nature which they paint and draw ...*
> *If they have since out-writ all other men,*
> *'Tis with the drops which fell from* Shakespear's *Pen ...*
> *But* Shakespear's *Magick could not copy'd be,*
> *Within that Circle none durst walk but he.*
>
> (*Works*, X, p. 6; italics present in original)

Davenant coped with this potentially disabling pre-eminence by appropriating it via the trope of reproduction: Dryden, seeking in *All for Love* to move beyond Shakespeare, is in a more imperilled position, comically signalled for a post-Freudian reader by the creative force attributed to the '*drops which fell from* Shakespear's *Pen*'. This passage is curiously ambivalent about Shakespeare's poetic power, however, invoking the image of the untaught Shakespeare, a passive conduit for Nature's creative forces, at the same time as registering anxiety about his pre-emptive excellence. This neoclassical version of Shakespeare which stresses his 'native genius' while decrying his ignorance may itself be a way of dealing with the Oedipal threat.[36] This, perhaps, is what is at stake when Dryden, in the Preface to *All for Love*, says

> I hope I need not to explain myself, that I have not Copy'd my
> Author servilely: Words and Phrases must of necessity receive a
> change in succeeding Ages: it is almost a Miracle that much of
> [Shakespeare's] Language remains so pure; and that he who began

Dramatique Poetry among us, untaught by any, and as *Ben Johnson* tells us, without Learning, should by the force of his own Genius perform so much, that in a manner he has left no praise for any who come after him.[37]

Dryden as playwright constantly returns to Shakespeare, and in the context of the repertoire of the Restoration theatre there are good pragmatic reasons for this. Nevertheless, the terms in which Dryden expresses his sense of cultural succession do seem to suggest that there is something more at stake; that, like Hamlet, he is haunted by the ghost of his precursor. Shakespeare, according to Nicholas Rowe, gave 'the top of his Performance [as] the Ghost in his own *Hamlet'*.[38] In the prologue to his adaptation of *Troilus and Cressida*, Dryden has the ghost of Shakespeare – played by Betterton, the greatest Hamlet of his age, and thus evoking the tradition that Shakespeare himself played the role of Old Hamlet's ghost – say

> *Now, where are the Successours to my name?*
> *What bring they to fill out a Poet's fame?*
> *Weak, short-liv'd issues of a feeble Age;*
> *Scarce living to be Christen'd on the Stage!*
> 　　　　　　　　(*Works*, XIII, p. 249; italics present in original)

It is ironic that this assertion of unassailable Oedipal mastery is spoken by such an intangible, contradictory figure as a ghost – the insubstantial embodiment of present absence. A similar sense of paternal disappointment and filial frustration gives point to a passage from the essay *Of Dramatick Poesie*:

> But it is to raise envy to the living, to compare them with the dead. [Jonson, Fletcher and Shakespeare] are honor'd and almost ador'd by us, as they deserve ... Yet give me leave to say thus much, without injury to their Ashes, that not onely we shall never equal them, but they could never equal themselves, were they to rise and write again. We acknowledge them our Fathers in wit, but they have ruin'd their Estates themselves before they came to their childrens hands.[39]

There may be a general sense of cultural belatedness at work here, such as afflicted many of Dryden's contemporaries, given that this statement is made in the context of a dialogue which works through the competing claims of the Ancients and Moderns. However, the image of the son dispossessed by the father is surely significant. In 'To the Right Honourable My Lord Ratcliffe', prefixed to *Examen Poeticum* in 1693, Dryden was still expressing his sense of the age's inferiority and belatedness *vis-à-vis* Shakespeare and Jonson.[40] And since Shakespeare, in both these instances, is one of a multiplicity of fathers, it seems relevant to invoke Marjorie Garber's analysis of the proliferation of fathers in *Hamlet*:

> The more the father is idealised, the more problematic is the presence of doubt, the gap in certainty that instates paternal undecidability ... Hamlet finds both too many fathers and too few – he is too much in the son, but where is paternity, where is the law? ... As in the case of the Medusa, where a multiplicity of penises is imagined to cover the unimaginable horror of no penis, of castration, so here the multiplicity of fathers covers the fact of lack.[41]

I want now to examine in more detail these psychic structures of idealisation and uncertainty which have shaped the cultural image of Shakespeare as a simultaneously absent and omnipotent father.

Family romances

The fantasies of Shakespearean artistic succession which haunt Restoration playwrights correspond to the Freudian concept of the family romance, in which the child casts into question the authenticity of his parentage, in order to be free to select parents who correspond more closely to his own idealised self-image.[42] The antagonistic nature of the child's struggle to construct an identity in relation to his parents generates feelings of ambivalence, which in turn find expression in the form of day-dreams in which the child replaces his parents with others of higher birth. When the child eventually discovers the truth about sexual reproduction and realises that, in Freud's words, '"*pater semper incertus est*", while the mother is "*certissima*"' ('Family Romances', p. 223; italics present in original), the family romance is transformed. Henceforward the child exalts the father, but no longer casts doubt on the maternal origin which is regarded as unalterable. If anything, the child's image of the mother is revised downwards, as he tries to picture situations which might have given her the opportunity for infidelity. The consequent overvaluation of the father and degradation of the mother – of which Shakespeare's supposed seduction of Davenant's mother is an intriguing example – is a formulation which crops up repeatedly in Freudian contexts.

So far, I have called the child 'he' – as does the Standard Edition of Freud's works in English, the authorised version, one might say, for the English-speaking world. In the original German, though, the word used for the child – 'das Kind' – is neuter, and since possessive pronouns are determined by the object of the phrase, not the subject, the gender of the child remains neutral. Yet when Freud introduces the notion that the family romance is motivated by a certain hostility or resentment towards the parents, immediately the form and intensity of this emotion are inflected by gender differentiation. He notes that the boy's hostility is primarily directed towards his father, remarking, 'in this respect the imagination of girls is apt to show itself much weaker'. Significantly, lack of antagonism is construed as typically feminine weakness, while Freud fails to consider that the mother–daughter relationship might have an entirely different structure. Later, I will suggest how a materialist feminist revision of the family romance can both expose and challenge the over-determinations of this structure, and show that women writers have used Shakespeare's plays to revise or analyse the abjected position of the mother within the family, to critique paternal power, and to enquire into the possibility of benevolent, enabling father–daughter relationships.[43] Misogynous though this framework may be, it is important because it is capable of offering such a precise diagnosis – if the pathologising term may be permitted – of the familial structure of Shakespearean artistic succession. So Marjorie Garber argues that the version of cultural authority instantiated by the myth of Davenant's exalted parentage and Dryden's defensive invocation of Shakespeare's ghost remains the essential form of the modern preoccupation with Shakespeare:

> The Ghost is Shakespeare. He is the one who comes as a revenant, belatedly instated, regarded as originally authoritative, rather than retrospectively and retro-actively canonised, and deriving increased authority from this very instatement of authority backward, over

time ... Shakespeare is for us the superego of literature, that which calls us back to ourselves, to an imposed, undecidable, but self-chosen attribution of paternity (*Shakespeare's Ghost Writers*, p.176).

Samuel Schoenbaum has suggested that Freud's own bizarre belief in the Oxfordian authorship of the plays of 'Shakespeare' could be seen as a version of the family romance; given the crucial role played by Shakespearean texts, especially *Hamlet*, in the formation of some of his most influential theories, bourgeois Freud may have found it difficult to accept his intellectual father's humble origins.[44] This seems plausible; it is a curious fact that Freud's construction of Hamlet as a prototypically Oedipal figure is always secured by a biographical reference which traces the character's origin to the author's neuroses, regardless of whether he is attributing the authorship of *Hamlet* to William Shakespeare, as in *The Interpretation of Dreams* (1900), or to the Earl of Oxford, as in *An Outline of Psychoanalysis* (1949). In the earlier work, Freud conflates *Hamlet* with *Macbeth*, assuming that both plays were written at about the same time (in 1601), and identifying them as neurotic symptoms connected with the deaths of both Shakespeare's father and his son, Hamnet, and thus with his anxieties about his own identity as father and son – 'For it can of course only be the poet's own mind which confronts us in Hamlet.'[45] Yet, adding a dizzying footnote to *The Interpretation of Dreams* in 1930, Freud casually remarks, 'Incidentally, I have in the meantime ceased to believe that the author of Shakespeare's works was the man from Stratford' (p. 368). And it is telling that he later elaborates on his conversion to the Oxfordian camp in another footnote,[46] which, while providing an ostensibly biographical origin for the psychic complexities of *Hamlet*, may also speak volumes about the tenacity of his own infantile repressions:

> The name 'William Shakespeare' is most probably a pseudonym behind which there lies concealed a great unknown. Edward de Vere, Earl of Oxford, a man who has been regarded as the author of Shakespeare's works, lost a beloved and admired father when he was still a boy, and completely repudiated his mother, who contracted a new marriage soon after her husband's death.[47]

Madelon Sprengnether, a pioneering psychoanalytic feminist critic of Shakespeare, has recently explored the role of Freud's own childhood in overdetermining the directions taken by his theoretical and clinical work.[48] Arguably, Freud's fascination with the Shakespearean family, with relation first to the plays and later to the question of authorship – a fascination which over many years proved generative for his own work – is just one exceptionally powerful instance of the larger phenomenon whereby Shakespeare has long embodied the idealised father of Western culture's collective family romance of its own past, which provides the structuring myth of the literary institution.

Freud represents the family romance as an antagonistic and conflict-ridden process, in which the child's idealisation of its parents could be interpreted as a displacement of a competitive desire to emulate them. As wider experience of life causes the child's idealisation to decrease, he or she begins to feel a dissatisfaction which Freud attributes to sexual jealousy:

> There are only too many occasions on which a child is slighted, or at least feels he has been slighted, on which he feels he is not receiving the whole of his parents' love, and, most of all, on which he feels regrets at having to share it with brothers and sisters ('Family Romances', pp. 221–2).

The child's belief that his/her love is not fully reciprocated finds expression in the compensatory fantasy of the family romance: that the people who embody the parental role are not really his/her parents, because they are not worthy to be so. Yet Freud makes the vital point that the family romance does not represent utter 'faithlessness and ingratitude' on the part of the child, but rather indicates a transformation of positive feelings for the parents, which the child experiences as having been spurned: 'indeed the whole effort at replacing the real father by a superior one is only an expression of the child's longing for the happy, vanished days when his father seemed to him the noblest and strongest of men and his mother the dearest and loveliest of women' (p. 225). Centrally, then, the family romance is an attempt to come to terms with a sense of loss and exclusion, which Freud images in terms of the child's exile from the fantasied plenitude of infancy. Contact with the real world forces the recognition that the parents are not the perfect, all-powerful figures they once seemed, and the family romance is the attempt to play out the frustration and disappointment born of this realisation. Essentially, it is the child's attempt to manage the horrible revelation that not all desires will be satisfied. To the extent that it offers a gendered account of exclusion, frustration and familial power-relations, then, the theory of the family romance can offer one way of constructing a map of the terrain occupied throughout history by Judith Shakespeare and her dispossessed sisters.

The term 'family romance' is sometimes used in a different and larger sense, to denote the narrative of love and loss which Freud constructed to account for the child's psychosexual development. This is the sense in which it is employed by Sandra Gilbert and Susan Gubar in *No Man's Land: The Place of the Woman Writer in the Twentieth Century*, where they echo Virginia Woolf's turn towards the mother as creative source, offering an alternative model of literary production/history as a familial, inter-generational process, centred on women's experience of their creative potential in relation to their 'powerful aesthetic foremothers'.[49] Gilbert and Gubar argue that the historically specific relevance of the Freudian model to modern women writers enables the identification of a *'female affiliation complex'* (p. 168; emphasis present in original), which implies a range of possible responses to literary influence, so that individual women writers are inevitably caught up in 'oscillating between their matrilineage and their patrilineage in an arduous process of self-definition' (p. 169).

While the theory they offer here is more flexible either than Bloom's strenuously masculinist account or the woman-centred revision of Bloom offered in their own earlier work,[50] Gilbert and Gubar continue to pose the writer's relation to masculine and feminine forebears as a choice between two phenomena which have single, fixed, but asymmetrical meanings. Feminist theories which depend on familial metaphors frequently fall into the trap of ascribing an entirely positive value to the mother–daughter relationship, while depicting the father–daughter relation as dangerously seductive if not downright abusive; whereas strong fathers are seen as essential role models for their sons, and the fate reserved for mothers' boys is notorious. In practice, of course, both male and female writers may respond in much more complex and varied ways to writers of either gender, and the range of responses available is not monolithically determined by gender, but is also subject to cultural and historical variation. Considering Shakespeare's use of his own literary forefathers, for example, Claire McEachern has argued against Bloom that 'Shakespeare is not, by some quirk of literary history, free of anxiety, but rather he frees himself from it ... [by] interrogating the power of patriarchy instead of guilelessly imitating it'.[51] Conversely, it is clear that Virginia Woolf found important creative models in many works by male writers, Shakespeare above all. The feminist fictions to which I return in Chapter 2, written out of dialogues with both the male-dominated literary past and the contemporary women's movement, create reinscriptions of the Shakespearean family which make possible an interrogation of the very terms of this debate.

M/othering Shakespeare

In analysing male writers' preoccupation with Shakespeare as a literary father-figure in terms of the Freudian concept of the family romance, I have perpetuated the valorisation of the idealised father at the expense of occluding that degradation of the mother which has constituted the historically recurrent obverse of this process. I want now to correct this imbalance by re-examining the Freudian notion of the family romance with reference to Carolyn Steedman's materialist–feminist revision of it in *Landscape for a Good Woman*.[52] Steedman argues that the essentialising cast of the Freudian account of loss and exclusion has the ideological function of mystifying and concealing the extent to which these experiences, and the emotions of envy, frustration, disinheritance which are concomitant with them, are historically and politically specific. Locating the family romance in the context of her own project to construct an autobiographical account of working-class childhoods, she demands that Freud's construction of this myth should itself be subjected to historical and political scrutiny, arguing that 'the first loss, the first exclusion, will be differently reinterpreted by the adult who used to be the child, according to the social circumstances she finds herself in, and the story she needs to relate' (*Landscape*, p. 111). Historically and politically, she points out, 'exclusion is the promoter of envy, the social and subjective sense of the impossible unfairness of things' (*ibid.*). In

Western culture, envy has long been held to be either a sin, or
alternatively a negative and destructive emotion, inimical to the
development of a politically usable class-consciousness. Steedman argues that the Freudian theory of the family romance adopts
this negative valuation of envy and ratifies it by essentialising it,
reinforcing the perception of envy as characteristic of the least
significant members of society: women, children, the poor.

Freud's own account of the family romance holds the seeds for
this recognition of the political overdetermination of the fantasy,
but not surprisingly he never articulated this insight himself.
Instead, his text maintains a hypostatising and unselfconscious
paternalism. Steedman notes that Freud was patronisingly
amused by a servant in his household who dreamt of replacing his
wife, and saw this as an adult version of the family romance. The
structure of this fantasy is interpreted by Freud solely in terms of
unsatisfied sexual desire; but as Steedman points out, 'it did not
escape the notice of either the children whom Freud observed for
the writing of "Family Romances" or of his domestic servants, that
the figures of fantasy who replace the reality are actually the pos-
sessors of material goods in the material world' (p.112). She
notes that the family romance

> operates like the fairy-tales which say to children: here are some
> kings and queens, a lost kingdom: use these figures to think about
> what you know. That children do use these items of romance, and
> that the psychoanalytic framework can be used across the barriers
> of class in spite of the actual and historical differences between an
> imposed ideology of the family and working-class family arrange-
> ments, is to do with the desire to be part of a story, even if it is some-
> one else's (p. 77).

To a unique extent, Shakespeare's plays, for our culture, provide
the materials for a collective family romance, which enables us to
think about what we know and tell ourselves a story of power, idealisation, love and belonging, of which we are all part – albeit one
which has different meanings for sons and daughters, mothers
and fathers.

I have spoken, so far, of fathers, daughters and sons; and I have
spoken of the occlusion of the maternal. What, then, *is* the
mother's role in the family romance of Shakespearean reproductions? I will complement the attention I gave to *Hamlet* as a

father–son narrative above by taking what some psychoanalytic critics have considered to be Hamlet's unresolved pre-Oedipal attachment to his mother as a symptomatic instance of the issues I wish to discuss. In Freud's earliest account of the Oedipus complex, in *The Interpretation of Dreams*, Hamlet is almost as central to the concept as Oedipus himself. Here the main emphasis is placed on Hamlet's violent rivalry with his father, although Freud unwittingly signposts the path the psychoanalytic interpretation of Hamlet was later to take when he comments that 'if anyone is inclined to call [Hamlet] a hysteric, I can only accept the fact as one that is implied by my interpretation' (p. 367). Freud's disciple Ernest Jones shifted the focus on to this imputation of a psychic condition often associated with femininity more decisively when he suggested that Hamlet's excessive devotion to his mother 'impart[s] a strikingly tender feminine side' to his character.[53] Later, Ella Freeman Sharpe, a colleague of Jones at the London Institute of Psychoanalysis, traced Hamlet's unconscious 'feminine identification' to textual metaphors.[54] She points to Gertrude's description of the ostensibly melancholic Hamlet as being 'as patient as the female dove' (p. 209), and notes that Hamlet himself dates the origins of his (suspiciously homoerotic) friendship with Horatio to the time when 'my dear soul was mistress of her choice' (pp. 204, 209). For Sharpe, a crucially symptomatic text is Hamlet's self-castigation for preferring effeminate words to masculine action:

> this is most brave,
> That I, the son of a dear father murdered,
> Prompted to my revenge by heaven and hell,
> Must, like a whore, unpack my heart with words
> And fall a-cursing like a very drab,
> A stallion!
>
> (II.ii.585–590)

The Signet edition notes that 'stallion' means 'male prostitute', adding the anxious parenthesis '(perhaps one should adopt the Folio reading, scullion = kitchen wench)'.[55] Since Hamlet has already likened himself to a whore and a drab, this is one stable door which hardly seems worth shutting. Hamlet here represents himself as effeminised and degraded by his failure to fulfil his responsibilities to his father. Ella Freeman Sharpe makes a connection between this passage and another key text for the psychoanalytic account of Hamlet when she comments, 'the "prostitute", male and female, is rooted at the oral level, where mother and father are merged into one figure. "My mother: father and mother is man and wife; man and wife is one flesh: and so, my mother"' (p. 212).

The associations established here between negation of the Oedipal father's role and the degradation of female sexuality are key themes in recent psychoanalytic readings of the play. 'Man and wife is one flesh' is the title of the chapter on *Hamlet* in Janet Adelman's recent book of psychoanalytic feminist readings of Shakespeare, *Suffocating Mothers*, where she argues

> the character of Gertrude as we see it becomes for Hamlet – and for
> *Hamlet* – the ground for fantasies quite incongruent with it … This
> [incongruence] is, I think, the key to her role in the play and hence
> to her psychic power: her frailty unleashes for Hamlet, and for
> Shakespeare, fantasies of maternal malevolence, of maternal spoil-
> ing, that are compelling exactly as they are out of proportion to the
> character.[56]

Adelman concurs with the argument advanced in Jacqueline Rose's influential essays on *Hamlet* in locating Gertrude at the heart of the dynamic which makes the play's representation of familial structures at once so compelling and so troubling.[57] The twentieth-century fascination with the Oedipal drama of *Hamlet* has become more preoccupied with the ambiguities of Hamlet's relationship with Gertrude than his presumed rivalry with his father, and thus has enabled feminist psychoanalytic criticism to intervene in the exclusively masculine model of cultural inheritance which I sketched earlier.

For Adelman and Rose, *Hamlet* typifies a key trope of patriarchal culture: the construction of masculine subjectivity over against the desired and feared maternal body. In their accounts, what gives the play its unique authority is its capacity to embody, while failing to diagnose or contain, this most powerful and troubling fantasy. *Hamlet* becomes a drama of liminality; of the inability to maintain boundaries between male and female, mother and son, self and not-self, life and death. Rose has been criticised by humanist feminist critics for evacuating female subjectivity from the representation of Gertrude, and reconfirming her status as a blank screen on to which masculinist fantasies are projected – a critical gesture which, in Carol Neely's view, conforms to a recent trend in historicist and post-structuralist readings of Renaissance culture in which 'women matter insofar as they stand for something else'.[58] Yet a diagnosis and critique of this process of androcentric reproduction is precisely what Rose's essay achieves, in an account of *Hamlet* which puts the mother–son rather than father–son relationship centre-stage.

The danger remains, however, that in emphasising the extent to which *Hamlet*'s representations of maternal sexuality are defensive fantasies which reveal the discontents of Oedipal masculinity, this project may serve to reinscribe the mother as a troubling *locus* of cultural unease, and thus reproduce the idealisation of the father and disgusted repudiation of the mother, in a re-enactment of the family romance which has characterised the cultural history not only of *Hamlet*, but also of the society which has enjoyed such a long fascination with it. The Oedipus complex, in the words of Madelon Sprengnether, 'formalises a conflict internal to patriarchy between paternal authority and maternal priority',[59] and in doing so it risks inscribing what is, after all, only a heuristically formulated theory within a narrative which has acquired the timeless, incontrovertible status of myth. Discussing Adelman's work, Karen Newman warns that the use of psychoanalytic paradigms runs the risk of excising the social and historical from the processes whereby subjective identity is formed, and naturalising hostility towards women as 'a part of every child's development, a product of "the infant's long dependence on female figures felt as all powerful"'.[60] Psychoanalytic theories offer a powerful way of analysing the sex/gender systems of Western societies; but a reliance on concepts which focus on the psychic power of the mother, while neglecting the social power of the father, may entail a profound complicity with the very discourses and structures which are being critiqued.

I conclude this chapter with a discussion of a Shakespearean appropriation which critically examines and revises precisely this formation. Gus Van Sant's 1991 film *My Own Private Idaho* patchworks together a narrative which is not quite a gay love story, and an ultimately unsuccessful quest for a lost mother, with a reworking of elements of *Henry IV*, parts 1 and 2 and *Henry V* set among the street kids of Portland and Seattle. The criticism is often made that these Shakespearean elements are not adequately integrated into the film, but I would suggest that this resistance to harmonious integration is precisely the point; the film collages together fragments of the Shakespearean texts with shards of modern culture in order to image the late twentieth-century family as the site of dislocation and misrepresentation, of messages which miss their target and codes best left undeciphered. *My Own Private Idaho* self-consciously traces the patterns of desire and loss which shape familial relations in a post-Freudian world, and appropriates Shakespeare's plays in order to demonstrate that while families of origin may offer their children little more than pain and confusion as the ground of their lives, a family which is chosen, however ramshackle and unorthodox it may appear, may nevertheless offer its members a kind of love and security unfindable elsewhere. Ultimately, though, someone who fills the place of the father is seen to be essential to the construction of any kind of family, while the maternal figure remains both elusive and highly problematic.

The film's narrative is structured through the relationship between Mike Waters (played by the late River Phoenix), the street kid in search of a mother he remembers only within the frame of grainy, out-of-focus, home movies which play time after time in the cinema of his memory; and Scott Favor (Keanu Reeves), son of one of the most powerful local businessmen, who re-enacts the Shakespearean friendship between Prince Hal and Falstaff within the context of the street culture he is temporarily inhabiting in order to play out his complex and conflictual relationship with his father. Mike's quest for the absent, idealised mother whose psychic power for him is in inverse proportion to her social marginality and insignificance is juxtaposed with Scott's rebellion against a wealthy and powerful but emotionally impotent father. These paired narratives of the son's attempt to make sense of family also provide the arena in which Mike and Scott fashion for themselves sexual and social identities which inscribe transgression as a mode of desire and a longing for love; a form of resistance to the normative; a strategy for achieving success within the realm of the normative; and, quite simply, a way of life born of material necessity. That Mike's family romance has no connection with the *Henriad*, whereas Scott's drama is self-consciously structured as an appropriation of it, is consonant with the Shakespearean exclusion of the maternal which I am tracing in this and the succeeding chapter. Shakespeare, it seems, offers sons a text which enables them to rewrite the script of their relations with their fathers, but not with their mothers.

Gus Van Sant's appropriation of parts 1 and 2 of *Henry IV* and *Henry V* is significant for a number of reasons. First, it uses a group of key English texts which are centrally concerned with a young man's accession to adult masculinity in order to problematise the construction of masculinity in relation to the family, sexuality and the material world. By sexualising the underworld in which Scott/Hal plays out his transition to manhood, Van Sant creates a social realm in which passion between men – in a variety of forms – is central, and foregrounds the complex, troubled relations between the homoerotic and the homosocial, between the subculture of rent-boys and the patriarchal world dominated by Scott's father. Second, the film marks and queries the absence of women from the script of masculine self-actualisation, not by reinserting them, but by making a feature of their absence and marginality. Visually, Mike's mother is present only in the wobbly, grainy home movie sequences, and in narrative terms she is equally elusive, having always just disappeared from each place they look for her. Scott's mother, although referred to once or twice, is entirely absent; his female significant other is Carmilla, a young Italian woman who barely speaks English and initially occupies the very distant, other social space of a ramshackle Italian smallholding. Carmilla's otherness is less, I think, a fantasy of the appropriation of the exotic feminine, than a sign of her exclusion from the symbolic realm of homosocial America in which most of the film's action takes place. Finally, the film places Shakespeare's plays in a context which takes love between men for granted, without either engaging anxiously with the question of his own sexual identity, or appropriating the name of Shakespeare in order to argue for the legitimacy of homosexuality. In Chapters 4 and 5 I will want to argue that at certain moments, such an appropriation has in fact constituted an important and powerful intervention into modern sexual and cultural politics; but it seems to me important that it should also be possible to make a film which is aesthetically and politically at ease with the juxtaposition of Shakespeare and homoeroticism – a coupling which is still too often seen as troubling or implausible.

The film opens on a deserted road in the wilds of Idaho, a territory which in its placelessness is to recur in the film as a significant location for the lost, displaced Mike, who sees in the landscape a strangely comforting and familiar human face. As he stands there, Mike succumbs to his first attack of narcolepsy – a condition in which, according to the title sequence, moments of stress make him fall asleep – in which a vision of a snowy white mountain rising from a plain turns into an image of a woman, dressed in white clothes which recall the down-market fashions of the early seventies, smiling tenderly at the adolescent boy whose head she cradles in her lap and murmuring, 'Don't worry. Everything's gonna be all right. I know. It's OK. I know.' The shabbiness of her dress and her prematurely aged face visually mark a disjunction between the assertion of maternal omnipotence in her words, and her capacity to fulfil the promise that everything will be all right. On a first viewing, one is likely to draw the inference that the woman is Mike's mother, though since the boy she is caressing is clearly not Mike, an element of mystery is coded into the hazy, wistful dream-image. Later, the film discloses that this boy is both Mike's brother and his father, so that whereas Scott reduplicates the paternal role by placing himself in relation to both his biological father and Bob, the Falstaff figure, Mike is effectively a son without a father.

We next see Mike apparently rousing from sleep, intercut with footage of salmon leaping upstream, in one of the surreal juxtapositions by means of which the film elliptically explores the nature of the search for love and home. As the camera pulls back from Mike's face and pans slowly down his naked torso, it becomes clear that he is no longer on that road in Idaho, but is being fellated by a male client, who contemptuously tosses a handful of bills into the fly of his jeans when he's finished. Leaving, Mike sees across the road a woman dressed like his mental image of his mother, prompting a reprise of the first 'home movie scene'. Money, sexuality and the maternal are intertwined for Mike, and all three are located in the place where he abdicates control, an asocial space of fantasy and disease. Mike's narcoleptic absences from himself literalise the familiar Renaissance sexual puns on 'spending' and 'dying'. Sex is one of the key factors which trigger his attacks and which thus enable him to find the place in his unconscious where his mother dwells. At the same time, sex for Mike is not itself a matter of love, desire or longing, but of money – it is the way he makes a living. His next client is a woman, and Scott is there too, reiterating the triad which inhabits his earliest memories, so that he again enters a fugue state in which he sees his mother embracing a small child, evidently the young Mike, though ominously dressed in girlish pastel pink. In the street outside the client's smart suburban home, Scott watches protectively over Mike's unconscious body, musing on the dynamics of his own family, particularly his father, who is in love with the sense of his own power: 'You have to be as good as he to keep up; you have to lift as great a weight', laments Scott. 'My dad doesn't know that I'm just a kid. He thinks I'm a threat'. Van Sant's direction plays off the verbal and visual elements of the film, as the son's resistance to the Oedipal scenario is spoken over the pietà-like image of him cradling his unconscious friend.

Scott's father is in one sense not unlike Mike's mother in that he is an ambivalent figure, the film crudely deploying physical disability – he uses a wheelchair – to signal the personal impotence which clashes with his social power. Here again, though, the parent's psychic power for the child is unmistakable, however fraught the interactions in which it is played out. Like Prince Hal, Scott's apparent refusal of the Oedipal masks a secret plan both to fulfil the parental desire for a good son which he appears to repudiate, and to go beyond his father. In fact, he is manipulating his father, eliciting a desire for the good son, which he intends to satisfy eventually on his own terms, precisely in the act of casting himself as a bad son. Scott paraphrases Hal's soliloquy at *1 Henry IV* I.ii.190–212 ('I know you all, and will awhile uphold / The unyoked humour of your idleness …'), focusing on achieving the desired end of startling his mother and father. But this never really happens: his mother remains entirely absent, and instead of the reconciliation, however fragile, achieved by Prince Hal and Henry IV, Scott continues to elude or resist the role of good son until after his father is dead – there is no scene of meeting and acceptance. What we do see, though, is Scott's rejection of his other father, Bob, the Falstaff figure. Like Hamlet, Scott multiplies his father-figures in order to compensate for the lack which structures his relationships with each of them – his father is emotionally wounded, Bob socially marginal. Although the desire both to please and to compete with his father clearly motivates Scott's behaviour, the film gives more screen time and attention to his relationship with Bob, a seedy and ramshackle affair which, like the friendship between Hal and Falstaff, seems to consist essentially in the playing out of scenarios designed to deceive, test or humiliate. To the elements of asocial play, deception and highly charged emotional tension which he found in Shakespeare's texts, Van Sant adds a thwarted, aggressive eroticism typical of a film whose depiction of sexual desire, heterosexual as well as homosexual, is unremittingly bleak, stylised and distancing. The fun and affection with which some productions of *1 Henry IV* in particular endow the friendship between Hal and Falstaff are hard to detect here; if warmth and pleasure exist in this underworld, it is principally in the camaraderie among the young hustlers.

This curious absence of affect is, I think, attributable to the fact that Bob's significance to Scott seems to be primarily symbolic, being described in terms which deliberately resist straightforward definition at the same time as they collapse together a number of diverse qualities. Thus before Bob ever appears, Scott and Mike discuss him in a conversation in which – as in another crucial confessional moment in the film, when Mike declares his love for Scott – their difficulty in finding words to articulate what is at stake is precisely the point. So Mike asks, 'Didn't you two have this, uh – I kinda remember you having, like, this real heavy, uh ...' – 'Thing', supplies Scott as Mike trails off, using a word which can refer to a sexual liaison in the lexis of slang but here appears to be deployed precisely as a way of resisting such straightforward definition. Scott goes on to elaborate on the nature of their relationship with increasing eloquence: 'He was fucking in love with me. He taught me better than school. I love Bob more than my father. I'd say I love Bob more than my mother and my father.' On their first encounter in the film, as Bob returns from a mysterious exile, Scott anoints him with a can of Coca-Cola (once advertised as 'the real thing'), calling him 'the sewer, the lecher ... and the listener – and more than that, my real father' – a statement which seems to combine the scathing criticism of Falstaff which Hal delivers in the mock court scene with a more direct avowal of his real importance to the younger man than Shakespeare's play offers. Later Bob will acknowledge Scott as his 'true son'; and the anointing of the father by the son is an inversion of ritual which coheres with both the film's resistance to conventional patriarchal relations, and its delight in the carnivalesque. From this meeting, the film is relatively faithful to the Shakespearean development of the relationship. Hal's rebuke to Falstaff when he asks the time (*1 Henry IV* I.ii.1–12) becomes 'You wouldn't even look at a clock unless hours were lines of coke, dials the signs of gay bars and time itself was a fair hustler', the robbery and its aftermath are virtually identical to their originals, while Scott is obliged to go through an interview with his father which recreates that between Hal and Henry IV at *1 Henry IV* III.ii down to the paternal fear that 'heaven is punishing me for my mistreadings', and the comparison between Scott and a more successful, dutiful and conventionally masculine cousin which prompts him to assert that 'a time will come when I will make this northern youth trade his good deeds for my indignities'.

This time does indeed come: news of his father's death prompts Scott to abandon Mike in Italy and return to Portland to move confidently among his father's business associates with Carmilla on his arm, marking a definitive break both with the homoerotic in favour of the homosocial, and more specifically with Mike and Bob. Whereas in both parts of *Henry IV* Hal's emotional world is peopled entirely by men, for Scott heterosexual desire intervenes to enable the accession to adult masculinity. Scott explicitly affirms his new identity by taking upon himself the task of perpetuating his father's existence – 'we live on with his memory' – and subjecting Bob to a humiliating public repudiation which restages Hal's rejection of Falstaff. Yet this gesture is tempered by a declaration of love which also holds open the possibility of a social and subjective mobility not available to Hal: 'although I love you more than my dead father,' Scott tells Bob, 'I had to turn away. Now that I have, and until I change back, don't come near me.' These words seem to indicate that Scott's newly achieved patriarchal status is fragile, easily disrupted by the challenge or temptation which Bob represents, so that the latter must be held firmly at bay. This choice between worlds, between forms of masculinity and ways of being a son, is sharply imaged by the juxtaposition of Mr Favor's formal, high-society funeral with the wild, carnivalesque rite which the street kids enact over Bob's corpse in the wilderness on the edge of the cemetery. From their places in these two different worlds, Mike, forced to be author of himself, and Scott, successor to his father's name, gaze at each other across a social and emotional divide which clearly marks the material and symbolic power of paternal authority – even where that authority is effectively founded in lack and impotence.

Scott and Mike each pass through a sort of family romance of their own, in that they are seeking to construct a fictional alternative to the families they were actually born into. But the reality of the name of the father continues to shape what is materially and emotionally possible for them, consigning them respectively, without possibility of appeal, to the legitimate and illegitimate spheres of society. Yet I would argue that the film ultimately withholds the kind of aesthetic closure which would endorse this reassertion of the power of the patriarchy to define and control its children's lives. The pleasures of *My Own Private Idaho*'s disjunctive, associative, often surreal construction are in excess of and disrupt its somewhat pessimistic narrative; while the juxtaposition of Shakespeare's *Henriad* with these marginal lives at least offers a space where the son's place in culture can be re-imagined.

Notes

1 London, Chatto & Windus, 1991.
2 On the function of intertextuality in Angela Carter's fiction, see Elaine Jordan, 'The Dangers of Angela Carter', in Isobel Armstrong (ed.), *New Feminist Discourses: Critical Essays on Theories and Texts* (London, Routledge, 1992), pp. 119–31. In a review of *Wise Children* which emphasises its intertextuality, Delia Sherman argues that it is principally indebted to the writings of Charles Dickens ('Grand Illusionist', *The Women's Review of Books*, July 1992, 33). However, Carter herself preferred to stress the Shakespearean elements, claiming that she had tried to include references to all of his plays in *Wise Children*. Her Dickensian novel is surely *Nights at the Circus* (London, Chatto & Windus, 1984).
3 James Joyce, *Ulysses* (Harmondsworth, Penguin, [1922] 1985), p. 207.
4 'The Family in Shakespeare's Development: Tragedy and Sacredness', in Murray M. Schwartz and Coppélia Kahn (eds), *Representing Shakespeare: New Psychoanalytic Essays* (Baltimore, Md, Johns Hopkins University Press, 1980), pp. 188–203 (p. 199).
5 Edward Bond, *Bingo* (London, Eyre Methuen, 1974).

6 Samuel Schoenbaum, *William Shakespeare: A Documentary Life* (Oxford, Clarendon Press, 1975), pp. 238–61. Although it is impossible to establish precisely what Shakespeare's estate would have been worth, Judith's portion is small even in relation to the most conservative estimates.

7 E. K. Chambers, *William Shakespeare: A Study of Facts and Problems*, 2 vols (Oxford, Clarendon Press, 1930), II, p. 176.

8 It has been suggested that Shakespeare's anxiety about securing both his substantial property and Judith's economic independence may have been motivated by lack of trust in the apparently feckless Quiney. See Carol Thomas Neely, 'Constructing Female Sexuality in the Renaissance: Stratford, London, Windsor, Vienna', in Richard Feldstein and Judith Roof (eds), *Feminism and Psychoanalysis* (Ithaca, NY, Cornell University Press, 1989), pp. 209–29 (p. 216).

9 See 'A Constant Will to Publish: Shakespeare's Dead Hand', in Richard Wilson's *Will Power: Essays on Shakespearean Authority* (Hemel Hempstead, Harvester Wheatsheaf, 1993), pp. 184–237.

10 See Graham Holderness, 'Shakespeare and Heritage', *Textual Practice*, 6 (1992), 247–63.

11 William Black, *Judith Shakespeare* (London, 1885), p. 298.

12 *Literary Fat Ladies: Rhetoric, Gender, Property* (London, Methuen, 1987); see especially Chapter 2, 'Literary Fat Ladies and the Generation of the Text', (pp. 8–35), and Chapter 6, 'Motivated Rhetorics: Gender, Order, Rule', (pp. 97–125).

13 *From Man to Man* (London, Virago, 1982), p. 219. Schreiner worked on the novel intermittently from 1883 almost until her death in 1920; it was published, still unfinished, in 1926 – hence the slight incoherence of this passage.

14 Chambers, *Facts and Problems*, I, 18–21; Schoenbaum, *Documentary Life*, pp. 82–7.

15 'Olive Schreiner', in Virginia Woolf, *Women and Writing*, ed. Michèle Barrett (London, Women's Press, 1979), pp. 180–3 (p. 182).

16 *A Room of One's Own* (London, Grafton, [1927] 1977), pp. 45–6. Sandra Gilbert and Susan Gubar suggest that Woolf may have read Black's novel in their *No Man's Land: The Place of the Woman Writer in the Twentieth Century*, 2 vols (New Haven, Conn., Yale University Press, 1988) I, *The War of the Words*, p. 93.

17 Elaine Hobby, *Virtue of Necessity: English Women's Writing 1649–88* (London, Virago, 1988). The argument that this may have made Shakespeare a sympathetic figure for aspiring women writers is advanced in Marianne Novy's 'Women's Revisions of Shakespeare 1664–1988', her Editor's Introduction to *Women's Revisions of Shakespeare* (Urbana, Ill., University of Illinois Press, 1990), pp.

1–15 (p. 2).

18 The relations between these two texts as revisions of Shakespeare are discussed by Christine Froula, 'Virginia Woolf as Shakespeare's Sister: Chapters in a Woman Writer's Autobiography', in Marianne Novy (ed.), *Women's Revisions of Shakespeare*, pp. 123–42 (pp. 129–38).

19 The doyenne of this branch of Woolf studies is Jane Marcus; see for example *Virginia Woolf and the Languages of Patriarchy* (Bloomington, Ind.: Indiana University Press, 1987), and *Art and Anger: Reading Like a Woman* (Columbus, Ohio: Ohio State University Press, 1988).

20 'The Intellectual Status of Women', reprinted in *The Diary of Virginia Woolf*, ed. Anne Olivier Bell, 5 vols (Harmondsworth, Penguin, 1981) II, *1920–24*, Appendix III, pp. 339–42 (p. 341).

21 'The Leaning Tower', in *The Moment* (London, Hogarth Press Uniform Edition, 1952), p. 106.

22 Ezell offers an iconoclastic account of the profound influence Woolf's tale has had on feminist literary research and teaching in 'The Myth of Judith Shakespeare: Creating the Canon of Women's Literature in the Twentieth Century', in her *Writing Women's Literary History* (Baltimore Md, Johns Hopkins University Press, 1993), pp. 39–65. Another alternative slant on the myth of Shakespeare's sister is proposed by Margaret W. Ferguson, who notes that Elizabeth Cary was, like Woolf's Judith, barred from participating in the London theatrical world, but nevertheless *did* manage to become the only female contemporary of Shakespeare to write plays. Ferguson argues that in *Mariam* (written *c.*1603, published 1613), Cary unravels the 'chaste, silent and obedient' topos which was used to deter women from writing. See her 'Running On with Almost Public Voice: The Case of "E.C."', in Florence Howe (ed.), *Tradition and the Talents of Women* (Urbana, Ill., University of Illinois Press, 1991), pp. 37–67.

23 'Virginia Woolf as Shakespeare's Sister', pp. 123–4.

24 *Moll Cutpurse* (Edinburgh, Stramullion, 1984). The figure of Mary ('Moll') Frith, who dressed in men's clothing and worked as a petty criminal in the London underworld at the turn of the seventeenth century is immortalised in Thomas Dekker and Thomas Middleton, *The Roaring Girl* (1608), ed. Paul A. Mulholland (Manchester, Manchester University Press, 1986, The Revels Plays).

25 'Literary Allusion as Feminist Criticism in *A Room of One's Own*', *Philological Quarterly*, 63 (1984), 145–61 (155–6).

26 *Sister's Choice: Tradition and Change in American Women's Writing* (Oxford, Clarendon Press, 1991), p. 41.

27 *Ibid.*: Gates is quoted from an unpublished paper, 'The Master's Pieces: On Canon-Formation and the Afro-American Tradition', presented at Princeton University in 1989.

28 Oxford, Oxford University Press, 1973.

29 In contrast, Jonathan Bate argues that the Bloomian schema is relevant to Shakespeare, but that his chief precursor is Ovid, in 'Ovid and the Sonnets: or, Did Shakespeare feel the Anxiety of Influence?', *Shakespeare Survey*, 42 (1989), 65–76.

30 See Gary Taylor, *Reinventing Shakespeare* (London, Hogarth Press, 1990), pp. 13 ff., to which my discussion of Davenant and Dryden's careers is indebted.

31 Quoted in E. K. Chambers, *Facts and Problems* II, p. 254. The bracketed phrase is scored through in the MS.

32 *Ibid.*, p. 277. Chambers cites four other eighteenth-century references to the tale.

33 John Downes, *Roscius Anglicanus, Or an Historical Review of the Stage* (New York, Garland Facsimile, [1708] 1974), p. 21; italics present in original.

34 'Which Dead? *Hamlet* and the Ends of History', in Francis Barker, Peter Hulme and Margaret Iversen (eds), *Uses of History: Marxism, Postmodernism and the Renaissance* (Manchester, Manchester University Press, 1991), p. 50.

35 *The Works of John Dryden*, 20 vols (Berkeley, Calif.: University of California Press, 1970–89), X (1970), ed. Maximillian E. Novak *et al.*, p. 3.

36 If Marianne Novy is right to argue that in contrast it is precisely this quality which made Shakespeare accessible to Dryden's female contemporaries, this confirms the gendering of the Oedipal model offered by Bloom.

37 *The Works of John Dryden*, XIII (1984), ed. Maximillian E. Novak *et al.*, p. 18.

38 Quoted in Brian Vickers (ed.), *Shakespeare: The Critical Heritage*, 6 vols (London, Routledge & Kegan Paul, 1974–81), II (1974), p. 192.

39 *The Works of John Dryden*, XVII (1984), ed. Samuel Holt Monk *et al.*, pp. 72–3.

40 See *The Works of John Dryden*, IV (1973), ed. A. B. Chambers *et al.*, 366. Similarly, in 1696 John Oldmixon called Shakespeare 'the Father of our Stage'. Quoted in Vickers, *Shakespeare: the Critical Heritage*, II, p. 3.

41 *Shakespeare's Ghost Writers: Literature as Uncanny Causality* (London, Methuen, 1987), p. 134.

42 Sigmund Freud, 'Family Romances' (1909), in *On Sexuality*, Pelican Freud Library vol. 7 (Harmondsworth, Penguin, 1977), pp. 217–26.

43 See Chapter 2 below. It has been argued that an empowering father-figure often plays a key role in daughters' creative achievements; see Lynda E. Boose and Betty Flowers (eds), *Daughters and Fathers* (Baltimore, Md, Johns Hopkins University Press, 1987).

44 *Shakespeare's Lives* (Oxford, Clarendon Press, 1971), pp. 612–13.

45 Sigmund Freud, *The Interpretation of Dreams*, Pelican Freud Library, vol. 4 (Harmondsworth, Penguin, 1976), p. 368.

46 Freud's copious and idiosyncratic use of the footnote to both autho-rise and problematise the arguments advanced in the body of his text is notorious. See particularly the discussion of the function of footnotes in the Dora case-study in Charles Bernheimer and Clare Kahane (eds), *In Dora's Case: Freud, Psychoanalysis, Feminism* (London, Virago, 1986).

47 *An Outline of Psychoanalysis* (London, Hogarth Press and the Insti-tute of Psychoanalysis, 1949), p. 61.

48 See 'Anticipating Oedipus', Chapter 1 of her *The Spectral Mother: Freud, Feminism and Psychoanalysis* (Ithaca, NY, Cornell University Press, 1990), pp. 13–21.

49 I, *The War of the Words*, p. 167.

50 Sandra Gilbert and Susan Gubar, *The Madwoman in the Attic: The Woman Writer and the Nineteenth-Century Literary Imagination* (New Haven, Conn., Yale University Press, 1979).

51 'Fathering Herself: A Source Study of Shakespeare's Feminism', *Shakespeare Quarterly*, 39 (1988), 269–90 (289). I am less per-suaded than McEachern that Shakespeare's transformations of his source material invariably have the effect of making it more 'femi-nist': see my discussion of the relations between the anonymous *True Chronicle History of King Leir* and Shakespeare's *King Lear* below, Chapter 2.

52 *Landscape for a Good Woman: A Story of Two Lives* (London, Virago, 1986). Steedman makes eclectic and revisionary use of Freud, Lacan and the British school of object-relations psychoanaly-sis indebted to Melanie Klein and Donald Winnicott. I return to the question of the relations between these discourses, and their rele-vance to feminist literary criticism, in Chapter 2.

53 Ernest Jones, *A Psychoanalytic Study of Hamlet* (London, Essays in Applied Psychoanalysis, 1922), p. 48.

54 Ella Freeman Sharpe, 'The Impatience of Hamlet', in her *Collected Papers on Psychoanalysis* (London, Hogarth Press and the Institute of Psychoanalysis, 1950), pp. 203–14.

55 William Shakespeare, *Hamlet*, ed. Edward Hubler (New York, New American Library, 1963), p. 90.

56 Janet Adelman, *Suffocating Mothers: Fantasies of Maternal Origin*

in Shakespeare's Plays (London, Routledge, 1992), p. 16.

57 '*Hamlet* – the Mona Lisa of Literature' in Jacqueline Rose, *Sexuality in the Field of Vision* (London, Verso, 1986), pp. 123–40, and 'Sexuality in the Reading of Shakespeare', in John Drakakis (ed.), *Alternative Shakespeares* (London, Methuen, 1985), pp. 95–118.

58 'Constructing Female Sexuality', in Feldstein and Roof (eds), *Feminism and Psychoanalysis*, p. 210.

59 Sprengnether, *The Spectral Mother*, p. xi.

60 *Fashioning Femininity and English Renaissance Drama* (Chicago, Ill., University of Chicago Press, 1991), p. 62. Newman's final phrase is quoted from Janet Adelman, '"Born of Woman": Fantasies of Maternal Power in Macbeth', in Marjorie Garber (ed.), *Cannibals, Witches and Divorce: Estranging the Renaissance* (Baltimore, Md., Johns Hopkins University Press, 1987), pp. 90–121 (p. 97).

Chapter 2

Wise children and foolish fathers:
carnival in the family

I concluded the previous chapter with a consideration of the son's place in the Shakespearean family. I want now to explore the ramifications of various attempts – theoretical, critical and creative – to analyse and critique the relations between Shakespearean fathers and daughters, and to recover the absent Shakespearean mother. I begin by addressing some aspects of the multiple histories of Shakespearean representations and reproductions of the family, via a consideration of the relations between gender and sexuality in psychoanalytic readings of Shakespeare, and an exploration of the narratives of the pain and dispossession inflicted by the patriarchal family on its own members, which feminists have reconstructed from the texts of *King Lear*. Works like the Women's Theatre Group's play *Lear's Daughters*, and Jane Smiley's Pulitzer Prize-winning novel *A Thousand Acres*,[1] record the pain inflicted on daughters by the Shakespearean family at its most patriarchal; but Angela Carter's *Wise Children*,[2] to which I return in the last section of this chapter, offers a carnivalesque feminist revision of the entire Shakespearean canon which both celebrates the pleasure his plays can offer fathers, daughters and others in even the most adverse circumstances, and holds out the possibility of healing and transforming the family.

Meditating on the always-thwarted human desire to recapture the bliss most of us experienced as infants, Julia Kristeva speaks of the abject, which she defines as 'the violence of mourning for an "object" that has always already been lost'.[3] It is tempting to relate this evocative phrase to the massive investments of yearning and desire which cultural history has cathected on to the semi-mythical aesthetic bounty represented by the figure of Shakespeare. It precisely evokes the insatiable longing for aesthetic self-presence and plenitude which Shakespeare's plays seem somehow more able than other texts to offer the possibility of recuperating, but nevertheless always elude. This ambivalent fascination is perhaps one reason why they constitute such an inexhaustible storehouse of resonant myths and images, endlessly open to appropriation and reproduction. It is a notion which is particularly relevant to theatre, the most evanescent of art forms. A performance is always irrecoverably lost once it is over, even though tantalisingly inadequate traces of it may remain in the form of scripts, audience response or audio-visual records; yet it is this fundamental loss, this constant slipping away which is built into drama, which motivates its constant re-creation – the mounting of new productions and the re-creation of dramatic texts in new forms constitute both an attempt to master the loss and a glorying in the pleasures of transience.

In using Kristeva's phrase to designate the pleasures and pain of theatrical impermanence, however, I am dragging it a long way from its original context and meaning. In Kristeva's own work, it refers primarily to the looming figure of the pre-Oedipal mother, who, as we saw in Chapter 1, has often been culturally significant in so far as she is absent or degraded in relation to the father. Some psychoanalytic work on Shakespeare proposes that all attempts to master loss essentially derive from that first loss which is associated with separation from the mother – a notion which offers a different take from the family romance theory on the problem for the child of the contradiction between the mother's apparent omnipotence so far as the child is concerned, and her social powerlessness and marginalisation relative to men. Kristeva's theorisation of abjection focuses on this ambivalent status of the maternal presence: its key themes are the construction of subjectivity over against the desired and feared maternal body, which can never be fully repressed, but always returns to haunt the fragile, vulnerable subject; and the subject's experience, consequent on this inadequately achieved repression, of those liminal states in which the boundaries of the body and of the self are blurred, transgressed and refigured. Kristeva offers an account of the construction of desiring subjectivity which stresses the fault lines, tensions and difficulties of achieving a stable identity as the embodied subject of an unproblematic desire, and her description of the world of abjection sounds uncannily like the characteristic Shakespearean scenario:

> a universe of borders, seesaws, fragile and mingled identities, wanderings of the subject and its objects, fears and struggles, abjections and lyricisms. At the turning point between social and asocial, familial and delinquent, feminine and masculine, fondness and murder (*Powers of Horror*, p. 135).

At this point, I want to introduce the Bakhtinian notion of carnival in order to provide an alternative, more positive and materialist account of bodily and social liminality. Kristeva has been a prominent advocate of Bakhtin in the West, and there are important intertextual relations between the two *œuvres*. Indeed, Toril Moi argues that Bakhtin's work played a significant role in enabling Kristeva to develop some of her most important theoretical concepts: 'working from Bakhtinian terms such as "dialogism" and "carnivalism", Kristeva turns them into allusions to the kind of textual play she was later to analyse through concepts such as "the semiotic", "the symbolic" and the "chora"'.[4] As Moi suggests here, Kristeva's appropriation of Bakhtin marks a turn away from the latter's interest in the social and political dimensions of the concept of carnival to a focus on its more purely textual, and later psychic, aspects. Putting both carnival and abjection into play together is therefore a productive gesture, in that each can compensate for the lacks of the other. Carnival politicises and historicises abjection; abjection restores the psychic dimension to carnival. The universe of abjection is profoundly ambivalent, a space of pleasure and danger, and this co-presence of non-exclusive oppositions makes it intrinsically carnivalesque. Moreover, Kristeva's own definition of carnival emphasises its abject qualities:

> The carnival first exteriorises the structure of reflective literary productivity, then inevitably brings to light this structure's underlying unconscious: sexuality and death. Out of the dialogue that is established between them, the structural dyads of carnival appear: high and low, birth and agony, food and excrement, praise and curses, laughter and tears.[5]

In one sense, then, the laughter of carnival and the horror of abjection can be seen as different responses to similar manifestations of liminality. Using both together to read culture thus keeps the focus on the crucial element of ambivalence, providing a way of accounting for phenomena of disruption, liminality and resistance.

In a polemical critique of *Powers of Horror*, however, Jennifer Stone argues that the theory of abjection is dangerously reactionary, in so far as it 'exchanges history for carnival and stamps on memory'.[6] The question of the relation between psyche and history is always a problematic one, of course, and it is foregrounded by a consideration of Shakespearean family images, in which their undoubted continuing emotional resonance is often appropriated to shore up a transcendent, conservative notion of the timeless family. However, this makes the need for feminism to develop a historically sensitive method of analysing these images all the more urgent, and a number of recent works have demonstrated that the theories of Kristeva can usefully be deployed in the service of such a historically informed, materialist reading of culture, by means of a critical process which 'translocate[s] the issues of bodily exposure and containment, disguise and gender masquerade, abjection and marginality, parody and excess, to the field of the social constituted as a symbolic system'.[7] The experience of embodiment and the workings of desire cannot be disentangled from social relations which are effects of hierarchical structures of power, gender and wealth; and so combining the notion of abjection with the politically motivated discourse of carnival may enable the construction of an account of desire which meshes the psychic with the social. The concept of carnival redeems abjection by exposing its horror as a misogynous projection, and by providing access to a framework in which women can reinscribe the political and social elements of the ways their bodies have been hystericised, idealised, or rendered grotesque. Arguably, then, the theories of abjection and carnival can enable the production of an account of Shakespearean representations of sexual and social liminality which is attentive to both the psychic and material dimensions of the processes by which gendered identity is constructed and lived in history.

Absent mothers and desiring daughters: *King Lear*'s women

The crucial role of the maternal in abjection constitutes an unpredictable but fruitful development of a theme which recurred in Kristeva's work during the seventies and eighties.[8] She is fascinated by the way that what is ostensibly consigned to the oblivion of the asocial pre-Oedipal realm manages to return insistently to haunt the culture which seeks to repress it. In Kristeva's theory, the pre-Oedipal mother is conceived as exercising an ambiguous power over the subject, epitomised in the French phrase 'corps à corps', used in *Pouvoirs de l'Horreur* to describe the 'pre-objectal relationship' between mother and child,[9] but elided in the English translation. Literally 'body to body', the phrase evokes both an intimate embrace and a mortal combat, symbolising the fatal attraction which the mother's body holds for the emergent subject; an attraction which constitutes that body as abject. Kristeva's fascination with this unsettling return of the repressed pre-Oedipal mother chimes interestingly with recent attempts to excavate what Coppélia Kahn has characterised, in a Freudian metaphor, as the 'dim Minoan regions' of repressed maternity in Shakespeare's plays:

> In the history of psychoanalysis, the discovery of the Oedipus complex precedes the discovery of pre-Oedipal experience, reversing the sequence of development in the individual. Similarly, patriarchal structures loom obviously on the surface of many texts, structures of authority, control, force, logic, linearity, misogyny, male superiority. But beneath them, as in a palimpsest, we can find what I call 'the maternal subtext', the imprint of mothering on the male psyche, the psychological presence of the mother whether or not mothers are literally represented as characters.[10]

Earlier, Kahn had analysed Shakespeare's plays in terms of the Oedipal process by which the child – notably the male child – separates from the mother in order to achieve an individuated identity, and the psychic and social ramifications which this process has. So her own return to the maternal which is thereby abjected or repressed also enacts a gesture of reversal like the one she describes here. As such, it is metonymic of larger patterns in the most prominent and influential Shakespeare feminist criticism, away from attempts at accommodation with the patriarchal bard or straightforward rebukes of him for not being more feminist, towards a recognition of the subtleties and ambivalences of Shakespearean constructions of gender and sexuality.

The critical project of unearthing the Shakespearean maternal subtext was inaugurated by a review essay in which Coppélia Kahn discussed Adrienne Rich's *Of Woman Born* (1976), Dorothy Dinnerstein's *The Mermaid and the Minotaur* (1976), and *The Reproduction of Mothering* (1979) by Nancy Chodorow.[11] These three books have exercised an extraordinary influence over Anglo-American feminist thought; in particular, Chodorow and Dinnerstein, psychologists by profession, were instrumental in the revisionary appropriation of the British school of object-relations psychoanalysis which was indebted to Melanie Klein and D. W. Winnicott, and which, in combination with a distinctively American form of ego-psychology, became the principal theoretical influence on feminist psychoanalytic criticism of Shakespeare.[12] Object-relations critics have been scolded by Lacanian feminists for assuming too unproblematic and unified a notion of subjectivity, reifying the mother as idealised/degraded object, and positing categories of gender identity as if they were fixed and self-evident. Certainly, very little attention is paid by critics like Kahn and Janet Adelman to the work of theorists like Kristeva who offer a more problematised understanding of subjectivity. Yet as feminist psychoanalytic criticism matures, there are signs of a pragmatic rapprochement between the two schools, at least as they are used in literary criticism. Recently, Janice Doane and Devon Hodges have given a twist to the conventional view of Kristeva as a post-Lacanian, locating her work as a version of object-relations theory at the same time as arguing that both Lacan and Winnicott were profoundly indebted to Melanie Klein.[13] And Valerie Traub has made convincing use of Lacan to theorise figurations of the maternal in the *Henriad*, arguing that

> despite significant differences in family and social structure between late-sixteenth-century England and twentieth-century Vienna and Paris, Shakespearean drama and psychoanalytic theory share in a cultural estimation of the female reproductive body as a Bakhtinian 'grotesque body', and ... repress this figure in their narratives of psychic development.[14]

Indeed, Mary Beth Rose has gone so far as to argue that attending to early–modern theorisations of the mother–child relationship may show that the cultural distance between Shakespeare's
England and Freud's Vienna – or Lacan's Paris – is not as great as
we habitually assume. Offering a detailed reading of Juan Luis
Vives's strictures on motherhood and child-rearing in *The Instruc-
tion of a Christian Woman* (translated into English in 1529), Rose
suggests that

> in Vives' analysis we can discern the outlines of what feminist and
> psychoanalytic criticism have identified as the oedipal plot: the
> essential separation from the mother (and consequent identifi-
> cation with the father) that proves the enabling condition for a full
> … adult life. That the desirable adult society should be construed as
> motherless helps us to understand the absence … of mothers from
> Shakespeare's romantic comedies.[15]

Rose's emphasis on the comedies is unusual; previously, as the
accounts of *Hamlet* I discussed in Chapter 1 demonstrate, psychoanalytic feminist critics like Kahn and Adelman have tended to
focus on the repression and abjection of the maternal in the
tragedies and romances, using the notion of the maternal subtext
both to relocate women in the plays and to expose the misogyny
of their sexualised rhetoric. The stress may fall differently; earlier,
I cited Coppélia Kahn's essay 'The Absent Mother in *King Lear*',
while Adelman's account of that play, using the more ominous
and ambiguous phrase which is the key to her argument and also
provides the title of her book, is entitled *Suffocating Mothers in*
King Lear.[16] The difference between these two titles does betoken
differences of emphasis and approach. But both critics agree in
stressing the significance of the change Shakespeare made to his
source play, *The True Chronicle Historie of King Leir*, whose starting-point is the king's grief for his recently deceased queen and
anxiety about the impact her death may have on his daughters,
since they are left

> … wanting now their mothers good advice,
> Under whose government they have receyved
> A perfit pattern of a vertuous life …
> Although our selves doe dearely tender them,
> Yet are we ignorant of their affayres:

For fathers best do know to governe sonnes;
But daughters steps the mothers counsell turnes.[17]

The contrast with the opening of Shakespeare's play is striking: as Adelman says, '*Leir* starts with the fact of maternal loss; *Lear* excises this loss, giving us the uncanny sense of a world created by fathers alone' (*Suffocating Mothers*, p. 104). The erasure of the mother and assertion of the father as the only begetter of his own children circumvents paternal anxieties about legitimacy and the unknowability of the female reproductive capacity, but at a high cost: as both Kahn and Adelman demonstrate, the repressed returns pervasively in the language of the play.

For a psychoanalytic feminist reading, one such return, Lear's self-diagnosis of hysteria – 'O! how this mother swells up toward my heart! / *Hysterica passio*! down, thou climbing sorrow! / Thy element's below' (II.iv.54–6) – poses a curious irony, since it was treating hysterical daughters, rather than fathers, that gave Freud the opportunity to undertake his analyses of unhappy families and, in forcing him to confront the apparent frequency of incest in the best-regulated homes, formed the basis of his revolutionary theories.[18] It is perhaps surprising, then, that feminist critics such as Coppélia Kahn, who begins 'The Absent Mother in *King Lear*' with a discussion of hysteria, have not related the association of hysteria with father–daughter incest to the play. Exploration of that subtext has instead been left to scholars interested in the origins of the Lear story in folklore – Ann Thompson notes that the 'Love Like Salt' folk-tale which lies behind the play is widely associated with incest and adultery,[19] while Barbara Melchiori pointed out the similarity of Lear's image of 'those pelican daughters' (III.iv.74) to the incest riddle in *Pericles* – 'I am no viper, yet I feed / On mother's flesh, which did me breed', arguing that the incest theme which is overt in the later play is already latent in *King Lear*.[20]

These matters are taken up by the American novelist Jane Smiley in her recent book *A Thousand Acres*, a re-imagining of *King Lear* from the point of view of Goneril – Ginny in the novel. The novel's title signals its concern with the difficulty of disentangling love, identity and ownership – 'paternal care, / Propinquity, and property of blood' (I.i.112–13) – within the patriarchal family. Smiley's realist fiction is a precise translation of Shakespeare's plot and characters into contemporary terms, using the Shakespearean framework to engage with social issues such as the tension between individual desires and social conventions which have the force of traditions; difficult relationships between adult children and elderly parents; and sexual abuse within the family. Her modern-day Lear, Larry Cook, is a Mid-Western farmer who hands his land over to his two older daughters, Rose and Ginny, and their husbands, so that he can retire; the youngest daughter, Caroline, has broken free of the family and gone to work as a lawyer in Des Moines. Ginny struggles to hold the family together and resolve the tensions caused by her father's sudden renunciation of responsibility for his farm, playing a quasi-maternal role in relation to him and both her younger sisters. But she herself is not a mother; she has miscarried five times. The king's mild comment on Gonorill in *Leir*, 'poore soule, she breeds yong bones, / And that is it makes her so tutchy, sure' (l. 844) escalates, in Shakespeare's play, into Lear's violent cursing of Goneril's own 'young bones' (II.iv.160) and her fertility (I.iv.273–9). In Smiley's novel, the emotional force of the curse is literalised: Ginny's inability to carry a child to term is caused by her father's use of nitrates on the farm, which has poisoned their drinking water. Her childlessness frees her to provide the semi-maternal care he demands; and when, towards the end of the novel, she remembers the repeated incestuous rapes she had to endure as a teenager, she realises that sexually, too, he had forced her to replace her own dead mother. Rose/Regan, who never lost the memory of her own sexual abuse, secretly nurtures her rage against her father for decades, and gloats over his dissolution into madness and dependency on the favoured youngest daughter, Caroline. But from the beginning of the novel, family damage is gouged into her body too, in the form of a cancer which demands a mastectomy and finally kills her.

In an important and controversial reading of *King Lear*, Kathleen McLuskie argues that the play makes its theatrical pleasures available only to those who collude with its misogyny and endorse the final restoration of patriarchal relations and reappropriation of Cordelia by her father, warning that 'a feminist reading cannot simply assert the countervailing rights of Goneril and Regan … Feminism cannot simply take "the woman's part" when that part has been so morally loaded and theatrically circumscribed'.[21] The compelling narrative pleasures of Smiley's fiction are secured by a revision of the plot which does take the women's part and which, despite Rose's premature death, refuses tragic closure: Larry Cook dies unobtrusively, 'off-stage' in Des Moines; after being defeated in a legal case which vindicates all of Rose's and Ginny's actions, Caroline fades out of their lives; and Ginny makes a new life for herself with Rose's daughters, acknowledging the weight of the past within her present, but no longer bound by it:

> my inheritance is with me, sitting in my chair. Lodged in my every cell, along with the DNA, are molecules of topsoil and atrazine … and diesel fuel and plant dust, and also molecules of memory … All of it is present now, here; each particle weighs some fraction of the hundred and thirty-six pounds that attaches me to the earth, perhaps as much as the print weighs in other sorts of histories (*A Thousand Acres*, p. 369).

Feminist revisions of Shakespeare entail the dual task of dealing with a patriarchal inheritance – coming to terms with the weight of history – and inscribing a feminist future by writing 'other sorts of histories'. Smiley's phrase exposes the ideological and emotional overdeterminations of the very notion of 'history'. Similarly, Lynda Boose has warned that since the concept of 'history' has often served as a rallying-point for the consolidation of conservative power, the turn to history which has been posited as characteristic of at least some forms of Shakespeare studies in the 1980s may not be without risks for feminists. Before marginalised groups endorse the (re)turn to history characteristic of much recent criticism of the Renaissance, Boose argues, 'history' needs to be rewritten to include them.[22]

In the last few years, much work which obeys this injunction has been published; feminist historians have transformed our understanding of the early modern period, while the increasing availability of writings by Renaissance women enables long silent voices to be heard again. This work – which often demonstrates that women's past is not merely a narrative of victimisation and exclusion – has been complemented by imaginative writing which re-evaluates the past and reinvents the present from a female perspective. Throughout the 1980s the Women's Theatre Group has extended this re-creation of culture to the theatre; their stated aim of restoring women to history and history to women has been achieved by the collective creation of plays like the 1987 production *Lear's Daughters*, which was explicitly conceived as a feminist revision of Shakespeare.[23] In the words of the editors of *Herstory*, a collection of Women's Theatre Group plays,

> 'History' tends to be understood in terms of knowledge based on facts for which there is documentary evidence … As regards *Herstory*, this concept has been widened to include a mythological and literary heritage from which women have been excluded or within which they have been marginalised, and which the women playwrights whose work is included here sought to 'revision'.[24]

Lear's Daughters provides an interesting contrast to most of the appropriations of Shakespeare I discuss here in that it is a collaborative work, collectively devised and written by Elaine Einstein with the Women's Theatre Group. Although many reviews of the original production indicate a certain discomfort on the part of critics with the notion of collectively authored work,[25] multiple authorship was, of course, a common enough procedure in Shakespeare's theatre; and in a sense, all theatrical performance is essentially collaborative, in that the author's script cannot be realised as performance without the participation of actors. Nevertheless, it seems particularly apt that collective authorship should be central to the public identity of this play, which allows each of Lear's daughters to tell her own story without reference to the rivalry which divides the sisters from each other in both Shakespeare's play and *A Thousand Acres*. *Lear's Daughters* foregrounds the emotional structure of the folk-tale which underlies *King Lear*, at the same time as offering a materialist critique of capitalism and women's place in it; as the editors of *Herstory* remark, 'this makes *Lear's Daughters* a play which speaks directly to audiences of the Thatcher years' ('Introduction', p. 13). The play is typical of much contemporary feminist theatre in that it is experimental in form and technique, using non-naturalistic, poetic speech and foregrounding movement and visual signification. The three daughters struggle to articulate their desires and experiences while Nanny – the only character who does not have an antecedent in Shakespeare's play, though she may owe something to the Nurse in *Romeo and Juliet* – and the Fool offer a sardonic commentary on the events and themes of the play.

The position of Nanny/Nurse as a paid surrogate mother-figure focuses questions of sexuality, maternity, wealth and class in so far as it echoes the historical practice of wet-nursing, common in Shakespeare's time, which sets up a complex and economically overdetermined relationship between biological motherhood and maternal care.[26] The Fool's function is to carnivalise the presentation of these issues, particularly the struggle with power and autonomy which is deadly serious for the sisters; in Scene 10, entitled 'Investment', she summarises and enacts a condensed version of a drama which is not quite *Lear's Daughters*, culminating in a performance of Scene 13 of that alternative drama – a scene in which the Fool talks about investment:

> Investment is … money, cash, dosh, lolly, crinks, ackers, makes the world go round, doubloons, duckets, crowns, pieces of eight, muck and brass. Money – Investment. (*puts coin down front of skirt. Mimes rubbing tummy*) Nest egg, pension, taken care of, rainy day, looked after, old age. (*smiles, waits, starts to wriggle as if eruption under skirt. Looks under skirt. Gasps with delight. Gasps. Reaches under skirt and pulls out fool doll. Cradles it as child*) Investment. Three princesses all grown older, thinking about their father and counting the cost (pp. 51–2).

In the Women's Theatre Group's performances the Fool, played by Hazel Maycock, was an androgynous figure with clown make-up and a costume which combined an evening gown, a man's dinner suit, and a grotesque pair of false breasts.[27] The published text does not specify that the Fool has to be portrayed in this way, leaving the script open to alternative interpretations. But the Fool's sexual liminality is emphasised in the dialogue:

CORDELIA: Are you a man or a woman?
FOOL: Depends who's asking.
REGAN: Well, which?
FOOL: Which would you rather? It's all the same to me.
GONERIL: How can you? (FOOL *looks at her*) How can you be so … accommodating?
FOOL: It's what I'm paid for.

(pp. 32–3)

As the Fool's caustic response to Goneril underlines, *Lear's*

Daughters is as preoccupied as *A Thousand Acres* or Edward Bond's *Bingo* with the impact of property and money on emotional relationships. Women's access to power lies in bearing a legitimate male heir, so when Regan becomes pregnant, in a desperate attempt 'to try and find something, to find me' (p. 60) Goneril forces her to get rid of a baby which would make her worthless on the marriage market. Following that feminist analysis which argues that women function as objects of exchange between men, and portraying marriage as a property transaction,[28] the play takes literally the question asked of the father of the bride, 'Who gives this woman?' (p. 63), and dramatises the struggles of Goneril, Regan and Cordelia to become something other than their father's chattels. As in Shakespeare's play, marriage provides the only possible way out; yet the image of Goneril ensnared in the lace of her veil demonstrates that it is only another form of imprisonment (p. 65).

While Lear's power looms over the action of the whole play, the elimination of the patriarch himself from the stage circumvents the problem, identified by Kathleen McLuskie, of the co-opting of the feminist spectator's sympathy for a character whose actions she may not wish to endorse. Lear is seen from the point of view of the women around him, and each voices her own perspective on the events which have made her family what it is. The irreconcilable contradictions of the characters' different memories of the same event, recalled polyphonically in Scene 5, 'Lear Returns Triumphant From a Sporting Tournament' (pp. 33–6), are smoothed over when Nanny retells the same story and the sisters reconstruct their memories and hers in order to achieve a version in which they can all share (Scene 7, 'The Nurse and the Sisters', pp. 40–2). The history of a family is a narrative, a story which its members tell itself; but real-life family romances rarely conclude with the happy endings characteristic of the fairy-tales which *Lear's Daughters* self-consciously recalls, and the women of Lear's family can only construct a version of the past which is acceptable to all of them at the cost of denying and distorting their own experiences.

Isolated by a spotlight at the beginning of the play, the Fool chants a ludicrous but somehow sinister limerick whose nonsensical babble foregrounds familial tensions:

There was an old man called Lear
whose daughters, da da da da, fear,
The Queen was their mum,
Da da da da son,
Da da da da da dada here.
(*she shakes her head*)

                                                                (p. 21)

Counting on her fingers like a child, she introduces the family: 'Three daughters, / Two mothers, / One father, / and the Fool' (p. 22). Whereas the mother is literally absent and figuratively over-present in *King Lear*, in *Lear's Daughters* her place is doubled: the Queen, the daughters' real mother, is dead, though she survives for them in the stories of their birth and childhood – 'fairy tales in the nursery' (p. 24) told by the woman who gave up her own child to work as their surrogate mother, the Nurse. As the Fool puts it, emphasising the shaping presence of economics at the heart of the family, 'Three daughters. With two mothers – one buying, one selling. One paying, one paid' (p. 27). In the Nurse's surreal and violent narratives, the Queen is nothing more than a fecund body, a physical presence devoid of agency in the births of her daughters: Goneril 'came out like a dart, head first, then body, all over scarlet, covered in blood' (p. 24); Regan 'dropped out onto the velvet plush like a ruby', while a volcano erupted (*ibid.*). The narrative of Cordelia's birth is at first whispered between her and the Nurse; then it is Cordelia herself who reports 'She said that the Queen was outdoors. And I grew like a red rose out of her legs. And there was a hurricane' (p. 26).

In the final scene of the play, the Nurse's reluctance to speak openly of Cordelia's birth is given new significance by a revelation which may or may not be true: that Cordelia is Nanny's own baby, exchanged at birth for Lear's son (p. 66). The enigmatic uncontrollability of female sexuality which always threatens to undermine the fiction of paternity and which shapes the rhetoric of Lear's rage in Shakespeare's play is here literalised by the Nurse's presence on stage, as she refuses to confirm whether this claim is true; maternity, the reason that the Nurse is as trapped at court as any of Lear's daughters, also provides her only means of resistance. She concludes the soliloquy in which her enigmatic revelation is offered with a shout of defiance – 'Lear! There are rats gnawing at your throne and I'll not be in it but I'll watch the spectacle from afar, smiling, knowing it is what I've always wanted to happen' (p. 66) – before marching off-stage and exiting through the audience. Lacking the courage or the means for such defiance, Lear's dutiful daughters are left on-stage in a tableau which forms a visual and structural rhyme with the start of the play and underscores the circularity of the action, the hopelessness of their attempts to escape their father's power, as each of them stretches out to grasp the crown which seems to them to offer their only hope of agency or autonomy. It is, as the Fool says, 'An ending. A beginning' (p. 69).

Disorderly women: carnival and gender

The psychoanalytic theorisation of the abjected maternal and the hopeless attempts of Lear's fictional daughters to resist similar subjection constitute the dark and violent side of the revolutionary semiotic carnival celebrated in Julia Kristeva's works of the early seventies. Kristeva once described carnival as 'a homology between the body, dream, linguistic structure and structures of desire',[29] a conceptualisation which had a certain currency among critics of what C. L. Barber called Shakespeare's festive comedies even before the translation of Mikhail Bakhtin's work popularised it as an epistemological and interpretative category. Taking a hint from Barber's diagnosis of 'the tendency for Elizabethan comedy to *be* a saturnalia, rather than to *represent* saturnalian experience',[30] this work has tended to focus on carnival under the aspect of licensed misrule, relating the carnivalesque qualities of Elizabethan drama to the festive social practices of early modern England.[31] Much of the work done in this area has been by scholars with a broadly radical or oppositional critical stance, and has circled round the desire – sanctioned by Bakhtin's idealistic populism – to locate early modern festive practices as a site of popular resistance to an oppressive, hierarchical social order. This is a highly problematic strategy, however, as it is clear that carnival actually served a wide range of political purposes, oppositional and reactionary, progressive and conservative.[32] In one of the most persuasive recent revisions of the notion of carnival, Peter Stallybrass and Allon White argue that 'the celebratory terms of

Bakhtin's formulation are unable to resolve the key dilemmas' of carnival:

> its nostalgia; its uncritical populism (carnival often violently abuses and demonises *weaker*, not stronger, social groups – women, ethnic and religious minorities, those who 'don't belong' – in a process of *displaced abjection*); its failure to do away with the official dominant culture, its licensed complicity.[33]

Moreover, there is historical evidence which suggests that far from constituting a free-spirited rebellion by the marginalised against the centres of power, carnivalesque practices were actively managed by the court and by local authorities as a way of maintaining their domination. Similarly, an alternative modern account of carnival, much more politically pessimistic than the one offered by Bakhtin, sees it primarily as authority's way of producing subversion precisely in order to contain it.[34] Terry Eagleton states this view in succinctly Shakespearean terms: 'carnival, after all, is a *licensed* affair in every sense, a permissible rupture of hegemony, a contained popular blow-off as disturbing and relatively ineffectual as a revolutionary work of art. As Shakespeare's Olivia remarks, there is no slander in an allowed fool.'[35] Analyses of the relationship between subversion and containment – usually in terms of fairly conventional notions of power relations, centred on state politics – have become a focus of considerable interest in Renaissance studies in recent years. Taking their cue from Natalie Zemon Davis's ground-breaking 'Women on Top', studies of the relation between carnival and early modern sexual politics have tended to centre on the issues of cross-dressing and gender masquerade.[36] I want now to explore a different angle by making the Bakhtinian notion of the grotesque body central to my account of carnival.

The grotesque body, introduced as part of Bakhtin's general theory of carnival in *Rabelais and his World*, is epitomised by liminality; by events and activities – eating, defecation, birth, death, sex – in which the boundaries between bodies, and between bodies and the world, are obscured, eroded and displaced. Bakhtin stresses the collective nature of the grotesque body; it is 'the collective ancestral body of all the people ... something universal, representing all the people ... The material bodily principle is contained not in the biological individual, not in the bourgeois ego, but in the people.'[37] This is a curious passage, on the one hand evoking a disconcerting air of the New Age in its cosmic, universalising populism; yet on the other, it seems to recognise that the body is the product of social formations. Despite Bakhtin's emphasis on the popular, collective nature of the grotesque body here, I believe that it is legitimate to use the concept heuristically to explore the processes by which individual instances of embodied subjectivity come to be formed and represented. However, the impulse towards the universal in the representation of the grotesque body needs to be countered by raising the question to what extent gender and sexuality are inscribed on that body. Bakhtin almost always speaks in very general terms of *the* body, regardless of factors like race and gender which might seem to contribute to differentiated constructions of bodiliness. And yet his descriptions of the grotesque body are replete with characteristics which have traditionally been coded as feminine, whereas the classical body to which it is opposed has certain conventionally masculine qualities. Woman is described, in a classically misogynous gesture, as the incarnation of the 'material bodily lower stratum' (p. 240), which is an essential principle of carnival. This would seem to indicate clearly that the female body has a special relation to the grotesque body, albeit one which offers questionable advantages to women; but Bakhtin never addresses this point directly, leaving to the reader the question of whether it is femininity as such which is to be identified with the grotesque, or merely particular, perhaps deviant, manifestations of it. In the work of both Bakhtin and Kristeva, and in early modern attitudes to the unruly woman, it does sometimes seem that it is femininity as such which is at stake: because of her inherently grotesque physiology, the female is taken to represent a destabilising force in society. One of Bakhtin's most vivid images of the grotesque body is his description of the terracotta figurines representing senile, pregnant hags which were found at Kerch:

> This is typical and very strongly expressed grotesque. It is ambivalent. It is pregnant death, a death that gives birth. There is nothing completed, nothing calm and stable in the bodies of these old hags. They combine senile, decaying and deformed flesh with the flesh of new life, conceived but as yet unformed (pp. 25–6).

Abject femininity thus constitutes the archetypal image of the grotesque body. This passage is strongly reminiscent of the moment in *Powers of Horror* when Kristeva invokes the ultimate of abjection:

> The scene of scenes is here not the so-called primal scene but the one of giving birth, incest turned inside out, flayed identity. Giving birth: the height of bloodshed and life, scorching moment of hesitation (between inside and outside, ego and other, life and death), horror and beauty, sexuality and the blunt negation of the sexual (pp. 155–6).

The disgust and horror conveyed by these abject representations of birth find an echo in the biblical taboos which, in the early modern period, enforced a view of childbirth as grotesque and defiled. Breaking a century's silence on the subject with the publication of his *Directory of Midwives* in 1651, Nicholas Culpeper recorded his disgust that conception and birth took place 'between the places ordained to Cast out Excrements, the very sinks of the body'.[38] Yet even this deeply misogynous view of the reproductive female body as a *locus* of filth can be nuanced with reference to the early modern rites which constructed childbed as a liminal, carnivalesque moment in the life of the mother, allowing her to benefit from a temporary reversal of the power-relations which normally shaped early modern marriages. The collective female rituals which surrounded the birth, the lying-in month, and the ceremony of churching thus served to turn the social and religious demand for the purification of a new mother to the woman's advantage.[39] This is the custom to which Hermione refers when she complains of being denied 'the childbed privilege, which 'longs / To women of all fashion', and forced to defend herself against Leontes' charges 'before / I have got strength of limit' (*The Winter's Tale*, III.ii.102–5).

Natalie Zemon Davis argues in 'Women on Top' that while, as in the childbirth rituals, women could sometimes use temporary inversion of social norms to their own ends, there were also negative consequences of the belief that the female reproductive capacity made women an innately disruptive, carnivalesque force in society. The implicit connection which the early modern period made between women's maternal role, social disorder and the grotesque body is illustrated by a popular broadsheet of 1566,

The True Description of a Child with Ruffes, which admonishes its audience,

> And ye O England whose womankinde
> in ruffes do walke so oft
> Parsuade them stil to bere in minde,
> This childe with ruffes so soft.[40]

This monstrous baby incarnates in its grotesque body both its mother's disorderly behaviour in wearing the excessive and inappropriate fashion of the ruff, and also her punishment for this transgression;[41] it constitutes a dire warning to women whose dress is inappropriate either to their gender or to their position in the socio-economic hierarchy. It was widely believed in early modern England that while the child was in the womb, its features were shaped by the mother's imagination and experiences, though deformity in the infant could also be a punishment for parental sin. Diane Purkiss suggests that the pun on the word 'conception' which links the mother's imagination and the child's appearance to explain monstrous births is particularly anxiety-producing because it reveals the extent to which the female reproductive capacity is ultimately outside male control: 'what is absent is the mark of paternity; the child fails to replicate the father, as patrilinearity demands, and becomes a mirror not even of the mother, but of the mother's imagination'.[42]

More generally, the assumption that women were the disorderly sex related to the belief that their possession of wombs made them more prone than men to suffer from hysteria. The womb was imaged almost as a creature with an independent existence; if it became dissatisfied with its normal location (because of insufficiently frequent sexual intercourse, or retention of menstrual fluids), it would wander its owner's body in search of satisfaction, overpowering her speech, senses and mental faculties. The woman's physiology therefore predisposed her to unruly behaviour. This historical conjunction of the discourses of carnival and hysteria is interesting in the light of the connections which a number of feminist works have recently made between the Bakhtinian notions of carnival and the grotesque body, and the Freudian account of hysteria. Clair Wills relates this connection to the depoliticisation of carnival as a social practice, suggesting that 'psychoanalysis ... corresponds to a sublimation of the social force of carnival into representation of carnival ... The hysteric's symptoms thus constitute a "staging" of the carnivalesque'.[43] Conversely, carnival can offer a way of reinscribing a historical dimension in the universalising discourse of psychoanalysis; for Wills goes on to stress that (unlike abjection), carnival should be seen 'not simply as the underside of the symbolic order but as engaged in a dialogic relation with it' (p. 137). If abjection and carnival meet on the site of the grotesque body, then a study of the historical restagings of that body in Shakespearean reproductions can enable the construction of an account of its representation which puts the psychic into a dialogic relation with history.

Resemblances between carnival and hysteria aside, it has been argued – for example by Natalie Zemon Davis – that there is a special relationship between women and carnival. But if this relationship exists, it is, like carnival itself, inherently and problematically ambivalent. For while carnivalesque practices undoubtedly sometimes offered women the chance to seize a temporary measure of liberation and social agency, women were also often the victims of ritual humiliation. On the positive side, Davis suggests that the image of the disorderly woman could operate both to extend behavioural options for women and to sanction riot and political disobedience for both men and women in a society which allowed the lower orders few formal means of protest.[44] Historical evidence indicates that, in this country at least, Davis is right in suggesting that women were able to use the figure of the unruly woman to legitimate their participation in social protest.[45] However, the figure of the unruly woman was so potent a symbol of and incitement to social disorder precisely because it was an inversion of the way things normally were and ought to be. Its power was enhanced by the fact that the absolute subordination of wife to husband, endorsed by Church and state, came to stand as an image of all forms of social subordination. In practice, women who violated the sexual and social norms of the community by resisting this subordination were often subjected to the carnivalesque punishments of the cucking-stool, skimmington rides, charivari, or being whipped through town wearing a scold's bridle.[46] It could therefore be argued that in this period, disorderly women were central figures in carnivalesque rites whose primary purpose, far from liberating them, was to punish their insubordination and deter them from protesting against an oppressive social hierarchy.[47] Nevertheless, it also seems clear that in material terms and at the level of signification, women were able to use the inversions and displacements of carnival to exercise a greater degree of social agency than was otherwise possible.

Discussing the representation of illegitimacy in seventeenth-century literature, Alison Findlay offers an alternative account of the connections between carnival's theorisation of transgression and post-Lacanian psychoanalysis. She argues that the bastard's body is a living embodiment of female transgression; illegitimacy binds the individual to the community by privileging the bodily link between mother and child rather than the verbal 'name of the father'.[48] This celebration of illegitimacy as incarnating the subversiveness of female sexuality is attractive but risky. Findlay is drawing on the Kristevan account of the Oedipal moment, whereby language acquisition is the means by which the subject is inserted into and internalises the structures of patriarchal society. This theory opens up a space for the romanticised representation of the sexualised maternal body as an asocial *locus* of resistance to the name of the father – a representation which, while undoubtedly appealing in many ways, is of questionable political value. I want now to turn to a reading of Angela Carter's *Wise Children*, where this understanding of female sexuality is both invoked and complicated by representations of female-centred, illegitimate, and alternative families which pose an explicit challenge to the structuring myths of psychoanalysis. As Carolyn Steedman notes in *Landscape for a Good Woman*, there is a problem in deploying the hegemonic bourgeois assumptions of psychoanalytic theory to interpret 'lives lived out on the borderlands, lives for which the central interpretative devices of the culture don't quite work' (p. 5). *Wise Children* puts such marginal lives at the centre of its fictional world, and tests out and appropriates the central icons and theories of the culture in the service of a revaluation of the illegitimate and marginal. But the subversive reinvention of Shakespearean families was a recurring theme in Carter's fiction long before she wrote *Wise Children*, and before discussing that novel I want to look briefly at some earlier texts.

In *Nights at the Circus*,[49] the American journalist Walser loses his memory – and thus his identity – as the result of a head injury when the circus train crashes in Siberia. Rescued by an escaped murderess and her lesbian lover, he is adopted by a homosexual shaman and reborn into language when he drinks his father/mother/lover's hallucinogenic urine and is inspired to declaim 'What a piece of work is man!' (p. 238) – a phrase which becomes an ironic and celebratory refrain for the novel. Shakespearean allusions weave through the text, supporting the alternative family networks which the characters patch together out of friendship, loyalty and need. As Lizzie, ex-prostitute, anarchist, and adoptive mother of navel-less trapeze artist Fevvers declares, 'We dearly love the Bard, sir … What spiritual sustenance he offers!' (p. 53).

In the collection *Black Venus*,[50] two stories revolve around similar themes. The juxtaposition of these two contrasting tales from Shakespeare both embodies the notion, commonplace in recent Shakespeare criticism, that the boundaries between comedy and tragedy are multiple and labile, and foreshadows Dora's realisation, in *Wise Children*, that 'comedy is tragedy that happens to *other* people' (p. 213). The role of Ophelia becomes a fatal reality for a struggling repertory actress in 'The Cabinet of Edgar Allan Poe', with the difference that this Ophelia is a mother, rather than a daughter, and her death precipitates the Shakespearean dissolution of her family:

> Lovers of the theatre plied her hearse with bouquets: 'And from her pure and uncorrupted flesh May violets spring.' (Not a dry eye in the house.) The three orphaned infants were dispersed into the bosoms of charitable protectors … When shall these three meet again? The church bell tolled: never never never never never (p. 55).

More cheerfully, the story 'Overture and Incidental Music for *A Midsummer Night's Dream*' is written from the point of view of the Golden Herm, better known as the 'changeling boy' who becomes the cause of dissension between Oberon and Titania in that play. Like the Chances, the Herm is an orphan, brought up by a surrogate female relative, who incarnates fertility even though she is not actually a biological parent:

> Titania, she, the great fat, showy, pink and blonde thing, the Memsahib, I call her, Auntie Tit-tit-tit-ania (for her tits are the things you notice first, size of barrage balloons) … She is like a double bed; or, a table laid for a wedding breakfast; or, a fertility clinic. In her eyes

are babies. When she looks at you, you helplessly reduplicate. Her eyes provoke engendering (pp. 65, 73).

To explain his unique origins, the Herm quotes *A Midsummer Night's Dream*:

For Oberon is passing fell and wrath
Because that she, as her attendant hath
A lovely boy, stolen from an Indian king

and adds petulantly, '"Boy" again, see; which isn't the half of it. Misinformation. The patriarchal version. No king had nothing to do with it; it was all between my mother and my auntie, wasn't it' (p. 66). This may just refer to the Herm's unique circumstances, but it seems to allude to a parthenogenetic female community complete in itself, which in this context may have a certain resonance in connection with the feminist dream of Amazon communities, compensating for Hippolyta's violent seduction into heterosocial arrangements; or it may speak to a more exclusively psychic fantasy of maternal omnipotence. At the very least, it seems to anticipate Grandma Chance's comment in *Wise Children*, that until she had the twins she had never known what men were for. Herm has occasion to complain about being called 'boy' more than once: '"boy" in the circumstances is pushing it a bit, she's censoring me, there, she's rendering me unambiguous in order to get the casting director out of a tight spot. For "boy" is correct, as far as it goes, but insufficient' (p. 65). This implies that androgyny is unrepresentable in theatrical terms, that no theatrical language adequate to express the multiplicity of the Golden Herm's identity is available. Yet in relation to Shakespearean comedy, it is precisely this androgyny, this disjunction between identities, which has been so erotically and theatrically fascinating in recent years. Echoing the pleasures and anxieties apparently provoked in theatrical performance and anti-theatrical discourse by the Elizabethan association of youth, effeminacy, and erotic attractiveness, the theatrical conventions of cross-gender casting and cross-dressing by female characters have contributed to an eroticisation of androgyny, resulting in the theatrical display of the disguised body as a polymorphous object of perverse desires.[51] And the point is that the instability or ambiguity of identity is not, as the Herm frets, problematic, but is the key to the

[71]

desirability of this liminal figure. The liberatory and pleasurable potential of the unfixing of identity, of the mobility and multiplicity of the human subject, is a theme which recurs in Angela Carter's fiction, but its treatment is not universally positive. I turn now to *Wise Children*, which explores both the pleasures of making oneself up as one goes along, and the pain and dispossession which lies in wait for those who – like the illegitimate Chance twins – find themselves at odds with the categories with which society seeks to fix and regulate the play of identity and difference.

'A genuine family romance': Angela Carter's *Wise Children*

Wise Children is a self-consciously Freudian and Shakespearean family romance, a playful deconstruction of the patriarchal nuclear family which Shakespeare's texts have often been used to ratify. It is the story of Dora Chance and, through her, of the four generations of parents and children which compose the doubled – and doubly fictional, doubly theatrical – Hazard and Chance families. Doubly fictional: because within the fictional world of the novel, the history of a family is represented as a fabulous romance which the participants tell themselves as they go along. Doubly theatrical: because the families are split between the legitimate classical theatre and the illegitimate, *déclassé* world of music-hall, song and dance, and the movies – although as the novel goes on it collapses the possibility of maintaining such a distinction between legitimate formal culture and illegitimate popular culture. Carter's text both explores and enacts the connections between femininity, popular culture and illegitimacy: 'our father was a pillar of the legit. theatre and we girls are illegitimate in every way – not only born out of wedlock, but we went on the halls, didn't we!' (p. 11). Dora even uses theatrical terms to note ruefully that far from being romantic in time-honoured literary style, their illegitimacy was 'at best … a farce, at worst, a tragedy, and a chronic inconvenience the rest of the time' (*ibid.*).

These theatrical overtones are foregrounded when, after an impromptu performance of 'Is You Is or Is You Ain't My Baby' on Brighton pier, the girls see a poster advertising their father's production of *Macbeth*: 'And here he was, treading the boards like billy-oh, in Shakespeare, and weren't we fresh from singing in the streets? We'd never felt quite so illegitimate in all our lives' (p. 69). The context of the Chances' lives rehabilitates the well-worn Shakespearean metaphor of life as a dramatic performance by defamiliarising it: so Dora mournfully thinks, as her chin skids across her bald husband-to-be's head while they dance at their engagement party and she contemplates a broken heart and the approach of war, 'replace the comic mask with the one whose mouth turns down and close the theatre, because I refuse point-blank to play in tragedy' (p. 154). Nora and Dora reach the low point of this cultural hierarchy in the dreary days of post-war Britain, appearing in 'a nude show-cum-pantomime in Bolton, *Goldilocks and the Three Bares* ... [W]e felt our art was swirling down the plughole and those were the days when high culture was booming, our father cutting a swathe with the senior citizen roles in Shakespeare' (p. 165).

In the novel, Carter twice explicitly invokes the notion of the family romance, in order to deconstruct the hegemony of the bourgeois nuclear family which founds its legitimacy in biological succession and the name of the father, replacing it with a family of elective affinities, a thing of shreds and patches which has to be constantly and lovingly reinvented by those who claim to be part of it. As Dora embarks on her tale, she reflects that 'Grandma Chance ... the grandma whose name we carry, she was no blood relation at all ... Grandma raised us, not out of duty, or due to history, but because of pure love, it was a genuine family romance, she fell in love with us the moment she clapped her eyes on us' (p. 12). The end of the novel brings the family Grandma Chance invented full circle, as Dora and her identical twin sister Nora at the age of seventy-five themselves become adoptive grandmas/mothers to twin foundlings, like them the illegitimate offspring of the Hazard line – to be precise they are, to Dora's satisfaction, the children of Father Gareth Hazard, SJ: 'given the history of fathers in our family, it seemed only right and proper we should have finally turned up a celibate one – a non-combatant, as it were' (pp. 199–200). The military metaphor here resonates uncannily with Grandma Chance's theory of war as a murderous attempt by old men to pre-empt the Oedipal threat from their sons.

It's as well that Carter appends a 'Dramatis Personae' to her novel in five acts: this Shakespearean proliferation of twins, siblings, parents and children creates ample room for confusion. As they push their newly acquired pramload home from their father's hundredth birthday party – at which he has finally acknowledged them as his children – Nora ponders the fictions of paternity:

> 'D'you know, I sometimes wonder if we haven't been making him up all along', she said. 'If he isn't just a collection of our hopes and dreams and wishful thinking in the afternoons. Something to set our lives by … We can tell these little darlings here whatever we like about their mum and dad … but whatever we tell them, they'll make up their own romance out of it' (p. 230).

Nora and Dora's longing for their father begins on the day when Grandma Chance takes them to the theatre for the first time, to see *Lady Be Good*, and Melchior walks in. On the way home she tells them the facts of life, to satisfy their newly aroused curiosity about fathers: 'She was a naturist, she was a vegetarian, she was a pacifist; when it came to sex education, what do you expect?' (p. 57). Once they know about their father, the family romance – and again, the term is Carter's – kicks in with a vengeance, and they each keep a postcard of Melchior in regal guise (Richard II for Dora, Prince Hal for Nora) tucked into their knickers. On the same day, they receive a gift of a toy theatre from their surrogate father Perry, and this seals their fate as performers, although 'we didn't know, then, how the Hazards would always upstage us. Tragedy, eternally more class than comedy' (p. 58).

Wise Children records the pain of cultural exclusion and exile from the legitimate family, but at the same time, it subverts the power structures which give rise to family romances by revealing that the exceptional psychic power which the father-figure holds may be in an asymmetrical and unstable relation to actual familial and social structures. Melchior Hazard's symbolic power in Dora's and Nora's eyes, as the guarantor of their uncertain origins and the embodiment of the legitimate culture from which they are excluded, is in excess of his representation as a largely absent and impotent figure. He is first introduced in his capacity as the unwitting donor of 'the only castrato grandfather clock in London' (p. 4). The image of the clock, a 'great, tall, butch, horny mahogany thing' with a 'funny falsetto ping' neatly disarms the power of the grandfather as origin of patrilineal authority. This is compounded by the 'horniness' of the clock; while this literally denotes the set of antlers which adorn it, the word must also evoke both the sexual desire for which 'horny' is currently a slang term, and, given the concatenation of infidelities which occur in the novel, the cuckoldry which it signified in Shakespeare's time.

Until the final reconciliation at his hundredth birthday party, Melchior refuses to support Nora and Dora either financially or emotionally, while Saskia and Imogen, the twin daughters he acknowledges as his, were actually fathered by his own twin brother Peregrine; the pregnancy which triggers his second marriage, to 'Hollywood harlot' Daisy Duck, turns out to be 'a twinge of indigestion' and the end of the honeymoon is the end of the marriage; his house burns down when a *Twelfth Night* party is all too appropriately sabotaged by his daughter's insatiable sexual desire, which unleashes a polymorphously perverse carnival subversive of all the hierarchies the event was supposed to maintain:

> A babble of agitated chorines cross-dressed in ruched knicks and hose had commandeered a crate of bubbly ... and now, pop! with a fusillade of small explosions, opened the bottles and hurled the contents into the fire ... while a row of chorus boys, in jester's garb ... unfastened their flies and added their own liquid contributions ... [B]eside the snow-caked sundial, a gentleman who'd come as Cleopatra was orally pleasuring another dressed as Toby Belch ... I spied with my little eye ... the lead soubrette who was grinding away for dear life in the woman-on-top position ... (p. 103).

In career terms, Melchior's glory is equally precarious: his successful Shylock, Richard III and Macbeth are all financed by his aristocratic wife; his attempt to make a Hollywood film of *A Midsummer Night's Dream* is a complete flop, although it later becomes known as 'a masterpiece of kitsch' (p. 200); and as 'the twentieth century's greatest living Shakespearean' he scores his biggest stage success, in an ironically apt collapsing of the high/low culture split, in a Shakespearean musical burlesque, 'personating, who else – the "Will", in *What! You Will!'* (p. 89). Eventually, the reconciliation with their father enables Nora and Dora to recognise to what extent he is the glorious but insubstantial creation of their own family romance, and to understand that for the orphaned Melchior his most cherished possession, the tattered cardboard crown which is the only memento of his own parents' Shakespearean success, fulfilled much the same purpose. In Dora's words, at the very moment when Melchior acknowledged his paternity, the moment which seemed to offer the twins a guarantee of cultural and personal legitimacy, he came to seem

> two-dimensional ... too kind, too handsome, too repentant ... he had an imitation look, even when he was crying, especially when he was crying, like one of those great, big, papier-mâché heads they have in the Notting Hill parade, larger than life, but not lifelike (p.230).

The transformations of embodied identity epitomised by Melchior's self-re-creation, Gorgeous George's tattoos, and the plastic surgery endured by 'the first Mrs Genghis Khan' typify the novel's representation of identity as artefact. Despite being, in the language of Shakespeare's time, 'natural' children, the twins are themselves works of art; twice the novel preoccupies itself with loving descriptions of their beautification, which in the precision of their references both elevate 'painting an inch thick' (p. 6) into an art, and evoke the cultural specifics of mid-twentieth-century Britain. The twins' celebration of feminine glamour, defiantly asserted against the ravages of time, offers a challenge to the morbid and misogynous associations of make-up and decay evoked by the reference to *Hamlet*, where 'painting an inch thick' is perceived as a desperate attempt to conceal the essential abjection of femininity.[52] Making-up takes on the status of an illusory, transformative art not unlike the popular theatre in which Nora and Dora have spent their lives, and in terms of which they reconstruct their past identities when they make themselves up for Melchior's party: 'From a distance of thirty feet with the light behind us, we looked, at first glance, just like the girl who danced with the Prince of Wales when nightingales sang in Berkeley Square on a foggy day in London Town' (p. 192). At the same time, as the very term 'make-up' implies, this activity stresses the extent to which femininity is always already a masquerade: '"It's every woman's tragedy", said Nora, as we contemplated our painted masterpieces, "that, after a certain age, she looks like a female impersonator"' (*ibid.*). The reference to Oscar Wilde meshes with a certain campness, a sense that life is always already a performance, a self-creating artefact, which runs right through the novel. Dora eventually realises, for instance, that 'the entire [hundredth birthday] party from first hello to last hiccup, was being taped for posterity; our father was bent on making an exhibition of himself until the bitter end' (p. 200). Not merely femininity but identity itself is a masquerade, and the desire to make a spectacle of oneself, which is more often associated with women, provides the explanation of Melchior's behaviour throughout his life.

This unreality is underlined when the twins realise that the curious outfit Melchior chooses to wear for his hundredth birthday party is the costume worn by his own father in the role of King Lear: 'he'd chosen to become his own father, hadn't he, as if the child had not been the father of the man, in his case, but, during his whole long life, the man had waited to become the father of himself' (p. 224). Reconstructing what they know of their grandfather, Melchior's father – a father who was 'wife-murderer, friend-murderer, self-murderer, "a little more than kin and less than kind"' – Nora wonders '"if the child is father of the man … then who is the mother of the woman?"' (*ibid.*). Dora's narrative responds with a teasing speculation which gently interrogates the repressions of the Shakespearean text: 'has it ever occurred to you to spare a passing thought as to the character of the deceased *Mrs* Lear? Didn't it ever occur to you that Cordelia might have taken after her mother while the other girls …' (p. 225; ellipsis present in original).

Wise Children comically encapsulates these and other anxieties about maternity, paternity and the Oedipal in Gorgeous George's music-hall act, the story of the father who tries to prevent his son usurping his prerogative by boasting about his own sexual ubiquity. In fact, the ultimate insecurity of the attribution of paternity and the uncontrollability of female sexuality enable the son and his mother to collude in having the last laugh, when the mother declares '"You just go ahead and marry who you like, son … 'E's not your father!"' (p. 65). Dora connects this anxiety about paternal power with her own ambivalence about the grotesque glorification of the British Empire with which George's act climaxes, as clad only in a Union Jack g-string, he reveals that his entire body is covered with a tattooed map of the world. Dora resists the enchantment shared by the rest of the audience: 'as regards the pink bits on his bum and belly, we knew already in our bones that those of us in the left-hand line were left out of the picture' (p. 67).

This disillusionment with the imperial project, which is conceived throughout Carter's fiction in exclusively patriarchal terms, is extensively explored by the sections of the novel which deal with the twins' journey to America to appear in their father's film of *A Midsummer Night's Dream*. In both *Wise Children* and *Nights at the Circus* Carter revises cultural hierarchy by re-evaluating the association of mass or popular culture with femininity;[33] and in both novels America features as a third term which both exposes and unsettles the binaries of mass/feminine and elite/masculine culture. In *Wise Children* there are two episodes where English elite culture, embodied by Shakespeare, is exported – with varying degrees of success – to the USA. In the earlier novel the process works in reverse, with Walser being absorbed into English cultural categories. The deconstruction of the hierarchy and the erosion of boundaries which maintain it is more complete in *Nights at the Circus*, which makes it harder to discuss in terms of spatial metaphors of import and export, although these structure the novel at many levels. In both novels, though, the connections between cultural imperialism and the real thing are made clear.

The bizarre incongruities of Melchior Hazard's cultural imperialist project are encapsulated by the grotesque spectacle of the twins as cultural ambassadors, entering America bearing a bust of William Shakespeare whose bald patch lifts off to reveal earth from the theatre at Stratford-upon-Avon, to be sprinkled on the set of the film before shooting starts. Although their Mexican maid believes that the bust must be a sacred relic and incorporates it into an impromptu shrine, it eventually emerges, in a thoroughly Bakhtinian assertion of the lower bodily stratum, that all through the train journey across America, it has served as the litter tray for Hollywood star Daisy Duck's pet cat (pp. 128-9). In a twist on the Shakespearean appearance/reality debate which is highly appropriate in the Hollywood setting, the twins find an ingenious solution to this indecorous problem: 'We filled the casket up again with soil from the Forest of Arden ("the residential motel of the stars"), from the facsimile Elizabethan knot garden itself; we thought that would make it more authentic' (p. 129). The authenticity of the simulacrum achieves its paradoxical apotheosis when Melchior walks on set bearing the pot on a crimson velvet cushion filched from the set of *Elizabeth and Essex* – Hollywood's Shakespeare incarnates the myth of an English golden age. But the solemn moment is broken by Genghis Khan's fury at Melchior's overly well-filled tights; this rare moment which foregrounds the potency of the paternal body does so only in order to make it ludicrous. In Dora's analysis, the situation stakes '*real* class', which should have led Melchior to stalk off the set, against 'his Hollywood future – that is, his chance to take North America back for England, Shakespeare and St George' (p. 133). When the show is on the road again, Melchior declares that the casket was 'borne hither as tenderly as if it were a baby by two lovely young Englishwomen, nymphs, roses, almost as precious to me as my own daughters'. As they go to his side, tearful at this renewed betrayal, Dora reflects bitterly on the fact that Melchior can't even tell them apart: 'he didn't even know us well enough to smell the difference, but he was well away, now it was family time' (p. 134). The myth of the Shakespearean family which Melchior uses Hollywood to promote is founded on his denial of the truth about his own family.

Throughout this misguided American expedition, Melchior represents himself as the true heir to his father's dissemination of Shakespeare across the continent, rhapsodising about Shakespeare as civiliser and cultural colonist of the globe – though a dark underside to these aspirations is hinted at by Dora's belief that Melchior saw the gendered alliance of English high culture and American popular entertainment enacted by his marriage to Daisy Duck as 'Shakespeare's revenge for the war of Independence' (p. 148). Such pretentions are smartly deflated when Dora debags Bottom, played by Gorgeous George, so that she can have a disguise to wear to her own wedding, at which she has been replaced by the groom's ex-wife who has made herself, with the aid of plastic surgery, into a precise replica of Dora:

> I inadvertently expose the British Empire, all that pink on his torso, not to mention the lesser breeds without the law. I didn't want our nation's shame out in the open for all to see so I rolled him under an imitation bush, picked off a handful of imitation leaves and covered him up. It felt like the end of something, when I did that, but there was no time to ponder as to the end of what (p. 157).

[79]

That this does indeed represent the end of all sorts of things is underscored when years later Dora is accosted by an ancient, filthy beggar as she's arriving at her father's hundredth birthday party, and recognises Gorgeous George:

> I'd got a twenty in my hand, ready to pay the cabby. Shakespeare, on the note, said: 'Have a heart.' 'Take that', I said and pressed his literary culture into the hand of he who once personated Bottom the Weaver. 'You can have it on the one condition, that you spend it all on drink … Go off and drink a health to bastards' (p. 197).

As a figure on a banknote, Shakespeare is commodified as a key symbol of cultural value; yet the droll image of him urging 'generosity to the undeserving poor' (p. 197) in the service of Englishness, popular culture and bastards has political implications which, behind the comedy, are of a piece with Carter's own heartfelt commitments as they are described in Marina Warner's tribute to her:

> *Wise Children* was born out of her democratic and socialist utopianism, her affirmation of 'low' culture, of the rude health of popular language and humour as a long-lasting, effective means of survival: her Shakespeare … isn't a poet for the elite, but an imagination springing out of folklore, with energy and know-how.[54]

Nora and Dora, like the resourceful heroines of one of the fairytales Carter collected, compensate for their own status as bastards, and for the inadequacies of their biological father, by doubling their family romance, appropriating their uncle Perry as a father-figure. The realisation that, in Freud's words, *'pater semper incertus est'* – or as mother-to-be Tiffany more succinctly puts it, 'there's more to fathering than fucking' – is what triggers, in the classical Freudian family romance, the overvaluation of the father and degradation of the mother. *Wise Children* reinstates mother and daughter as subjects of their own sexuality at the heart of the family by rewriting the two aspects of the classical Freudian family romance – the overvaluation of the father, and the degradation of the sexualised mother – and subverting them to create a more open and inclusive vision of the family. However, separating the assumption of the name of the father from biological paternity can cause more problems than it solves. The Oedipal anxiety which the family romance seeks to assuage is parodied by Melchior's reluctance to play Hamlet, for fear that 'the critics might think he wasn't half the man his mother had been' (p. 89) – it was his birth that had interrupted his mother Estella's dazzling career as a Shakespearean hero on the nineteenth-century American popular stage, since 'a female Hamlet is one thing but a pregnant prince is quite another' (p. 16).

Wise Children, in a sense, is *Hamlet* without the prince, in that Carter takes the structures of desire and loss which characterise that play's representations of familial dynamics from the point of view of the son, and makes the daughter's experience central to them. So Hamlet himself figures only as Melchior's and Peregrine's dead mother, inheritor of the alternative female tradition of theatrical succession embodied by Sarah Siddons, Charlotte Cushman *et al.*[55] As in the short story, 'The Cabinet of Edgar Allan Poe', it is Ophelia who takes centre-stage. Carter's Ophelia is Tiffany, 'the first Black in the family', whose own father was 'here today and gone tomorrow' (p. 35). Her mad scene is triggered by her unplanned pregnancy and rejection by her child's feckless father, Tristram Hazard (yes, one of those Hazards), host of the live game-show in which she unpredictably co-stars, appearing mad with misery, half-dressed and crowned with flowers picked from window-boxes and public parks. Like Ophelia, Tiffany sings distracted little songs which range from the meaningless to the indecent, distributes symbolic flowers, and speaks in disjointed phrases which say more than she knows. Unlike Ophelia, though, Tiffany is a mother-to-be as well as a daughter, and when she strips off the T-shirt Tristram had given her, an epiphanous revelation of maternal presence is generated by her temporary madness:

> It was a shock to see her breasts under the cruel lights – long, heavy breasts, with big dark nipples, real breasts, not like the ones she'd shown off like borrowed finery to the glamour lenses. This was flesh, you could see that it would bleed, you could see how it fed babies (p. 46).

In her representations of Tiffany and Estella, Carter inscribes the maternal subjectivity which Shakespeare's text occludes. Elaine Showalter has noted that Ophelia's 'visibility as a subject in literature, popular culture, and painting … is in inverse relation to her invisibility in Shakespearean critical texts' – and indeed her relative marginality in Shakespeare's text.[56] Carter eventually rewrites Ophelia to give her a way out of the madness caused by male rejection, representing her as a dungaree-clad, happily independent mother-to-be.

At the end of the novel, Tiffany, believed to have drowned herself in her madness, erupts into the middle of Melchior's centenary party, returning like Thaisa, reborn from a wooden trunk; like Marina, too, in that she collapses together the roles of both daughter and mother. Meanwhile, it is Peregrine who, like Hermione, returns apparently from the dead, and numerous other reconciliations are effected in a scene which, via a palimpsest of references, revises virtually the entire Shakespearean canon from *Hamlet* onwards. While 'Puck' alternately sings 'Oh my beloved father' and 'My heart belongs to daddy', Dora and Nora, 'like wizened children got up in our mum's clothes for a dare', go to Melchior who declares 'I am the one deserves to weep' (p. 217); and as Nora and Melchior dance together 'they were wreathed in smiles of foolish fondness for that which had been lost was found and so on' (p. 218). Evoking the reunions at the end of *Twelfth Night*, Dora calls Nora 'the other half of the apple' (p. 217). In Shakespeare, such family resemblances always serve to confirm identity and consanguinity – apart from Viola and Sebastian in *Twelfth Night*, think of the resemblance between Perdita and Leontes, Marina and Pericles. In Carter's novel the opposite is true, for Melchior resembles both the men who might have been his father, and Dora cherishes the fantasy that '*both* of them had a hand in it' (p. 22) – for the novel's preoccupation with the maternal body is countered by Dora's interest in the mysterious potency of the substance which she variously designates as 'come', 'seed' and 'jism'. Even at the moment of reconciliation, paternity and identity remain as insecure and elusive as ever.

Shakespeare's 'late plays' – *The Winter's Tale, Pericles, The Tempest, Cymbeline* – have been represented, in one strand of critical tradition, as valedictory romances of just such a reconciliation of the family. Psychoanalytic criticism has located the possibility for this reconciliation in a rewriting of the female body which serves to eliminate a sexuality imaged elsewhere in the Shakespearean canon as transgressive, excessive and disruptive. In C. L. Barber's much-quoted formulation, 'where regular comedy deals with

freeing sexuality from the ties of family, these late romances deal
with freeing family ties from the threat of sexual degradation'.[57]
The fantasied reconstruction of feminine sexuality which makes
this reconciliation possible is played out across the body of the
daughter. Janet Adelman has suggested that in this context 'maternal presence can be safely recovered in daughters because the
daughters are not mothers; virginal and unequivocally subject to
their fathers, the daughters protect against the sexualised maternal body, enabling the satisfaction of the desire for merger without its dangers'.[58]

Wise Children resists the temptation to counter the Freudian
degradation of maternal sexuality with a defensive idealisation.
The maternal body is represented as a complex and problematic
site inscribed with multiple social meanings. The body of Dora's
mother, herself an orphan who died in giving birth, is inscribed as
a powerful absence in the text. Dora tries to re-create her
mother's subjectivity at the moment of her own conception, and
fails – it is both too painful and too enigmatic, undecidable:

> I can imagine her stripping off in the cold room, turning towards
> the starving boy. How did she do it? Shyly? Nervously? Lewdly? Then
> everything fades to black. I can't bear to think any further. It hurts
> too much ... Was she scared? Or full of desire? Or half raped? (p. 24).

And so she rewrites the primal scene, which like *Wise Children*'s
version of the bed-trick,[59] happens the second time as farce:

> I'd like to think it went like this: She closed the door behind her,
> locked it. There he was on the bed, brushing up his Shakespeare.
> He looked up, hastily laying aside his well-thumbed copy of the *Col-
> lected Works*. She started pulling off her chemise. 'Now I've got you
> where I want you!' she said. What else could a gentleman do but
> succumb? Nine months later, her heart gave out when we were born
> (*ibid.*).

The maternal body disappears just as it is about to be unveiled,
vanishing in the collapse of seduction, conception, birth and
death into a single moment. And it is Grandma Chance who
becomes the embodiment of maternal presence: 'She lullabyed
us, she fed us. She was our air-raid shelter; she was our entertainment; she was our breast' (p. 29). For Dora, Grandma Chance
becomes the incarnation of her own maxim 'mother is as mother

does', definitively breaking the link between parenting and physiology: 'the older we grow, the more like her we become. Triumph of nature over nurture, ducky' (p. 28). That Grandma's role as good mother is capable of transcending the merely physiological is demonstrated by the fact that she is still protectively haunting the feminine household at 49 Bard Road, decades after her death:

> To this day I swear, sometimes, late at night, I hear a soft thump, thump, her bare feet on the stairs, coming down to make sure the gas is off in the kitchen, the front door is locked, us girls are safe home. And there's a smell of crushed mint that lingers in the breakfast room, sometimes, because her favourite tipple was crème de menthe frappé ... And that boiled cabbage of hers (p. 28).

Grandma Chance's body is represented here as the subject of its own, socially specific and deeply material history, inscribed by age, class, politics and diet as well as sex. In contrast, the body of Melchior's and Peregrine's mother, Estella, is a vivid and problematic presence, represented as 'a marvel and a mess' – refusing conventional, decorous feminine beauty, embodying a kind of semiotic uncontainability which exceeds its own boundaries:

> She was a will-o'-the-wisp, all air and fire ... Her hair was always coming undone, too, tumbling down her back, spraying out hairpins in all directions, her stockings at half-mast, her petticoat would come adrift in the middle of the street, her drawers start drooping (p. 12).

And yet one little scene suggests that Grandma Chance is not wholly subject to inscription by the material and historical realities of her life: that there is something more – something which escapes signification:

> She came into the bathroom once, she never dreamed of knocking, she hadn't got a stitch on. Me neither ... There we both were, captured in the mirror, me young and slim and trim and tender, she vast, sagging, wrinkled, quivering. I couldn't help but giggle ... 'That's all very well, Dora,' she said, 'but one fine day you'll wake up and find you're old and ugly, just like me.'
> Then she cackled (p. 94).

The grotesque mirroring of the bodies of mother and daughter constitutes a scandalous moment of misrecognition which can only find vent in this enigmatically doubled laughter. Feminist theorist Judith Butler has written of the 'shattering laughter' which

> seems quite literally to negate the categories of kinship and, by extension, of sex ... designates that excess that escapes conceptual mastery ... shatters the placid surface constituted by the petrifying gaze and which exposes the dialectic of Same and Other as taking place through the axis of sexual difference.[60]

The polyvalent laughter provoked by the daughter's encounter with the body of the mother serves to destabilise the social and familial structures of differentiation held in place by the family romance. Embarrassed, distressed, defiant and celebratory, this moment of laughter epitomises the contradictions of the sexualised maternal body from the point of view of the mother. Embarrassed and distressed, because in its flesh the mother's body inscribes the wounds of class and gender inflicted on the feminine subject who has lived out its material history. Defiant and celebratory, because this moment which incarnates what is excluded from discourse, the maternal sexuality which Freud and Shakespeare represented as unmanageable and threatening, also embodies what exceeds discourse: the mutual recognition of mother and daughter as subjects of their own bodies, their own histories, outside the sad and distorting fantasies of the family romance.

In her critique of the family romance, Carolyn Steedman speaks of 'the bourgeois household where doors shut along the corridor, hiding secrets that the actors in the drama have themselves created' (*Landscape*, p. 77). Melchior's house is a paradigmatic place of secrecy and denial; but at last, when it is flung open to the family carnival which holds out the promise of a shared future as well as a painfully intertwined past for the Chances and Hazards, it becomes the site for Dora's optimistic reinvention of the notion of the family home, prompted by the belated reunion of father and daughter: 'I placed the crown on his long, grey hair ... I was a touch long in the tooth for Cordelia but there you are ... They'd asked us on the stage and let us join in, legit. at last. There was a house we all had in common and it was called the past, even though we'd lived in different rooms' (p. 226). At the end of *Wise*

Children, as Dora celebrates the resolution of her own family romance by making love with Perry, the doors are blown open: 'all the dirty secrets hidden in the cupboards had come out at last, had come to fuck in his bed, in fact' (p. 219). For the second time, the daughter's sexuality shakes the father's house to its foundations, as Dora and Perry threaten to 'bring the house down, fuck the house down, come ("cum"?) all over the posh frocks and the monkey jackets and the poisoned cake and the lovers, mothers, sisters' (p. 220). But later, Dora reflects ruefully:

> Now I remember how everything seemed possible when I was doing it, but as soon as I stopped, not, as if fucking itself were the origin of illusion. 'Life's a carnival', he said. He was an illusionist, remember. 'The carnival's got to stop, some time, Perry', I said. 'You listen to the news, that'll take the smile off your face' (p. 221).

Wise Children's deeply pleasurable celebration of the carnivalesque is nevertheless scrupulous in embedding such moments of excess and transgression in a precise, socially specific material context, reminding the reader that they usually occur in response to deprivation and oppression. In the end, though, it is carnival that wins out: the last words of the book are 'What a joy it is to dance and sing!' (p. 232). The tensions and rivalries of the family romance are transformed into a family carnival open to all comers, and the question which implicitly structures the novel – 'if the child is father of the man ... then who is the mother of the woman?' (p. 224) – is answered by the multiple voices of the panoply of mothers who are also daughters, daughters who become – however belatedly or unconventionally – mothers. Margaret Whitford has pointed out that feminist accounts of the mother–daughter relationship have sometimes had difficulty dealing with the fact that it is necessarily a relationship which involves two points of view which may be in conflict, or even mutually exclusive.[61] Much work on the subject centres on the child rather than the mother, and Carter's novel – as the title indicates – is no exception. As I have suggested, the presence of mothers in the novel remains ghostly, ambivalent and elusive; the story ends just at the moment when the Chance twins belatedly accede to motherhood, and Dora's own maternal subjectivity evades representation.[62] *Wise Children* rescues the mother from her Shakespearean and psychoanalytic abjection, but its principal concern is with giving the daughter a voice to tell her own story. Leaving sons to fend for themselves, Carter puts the marginalised daughter's experiences and desires at the heart of the novel, and in the process subverts some of the more damaging myths of the family. This gesture in itself cannot counter the patrilineal tradition of reproductions of Shakespeare, which surely owe their influence at least partly to their androcentric focus on the Oedipal structures which Freud called one of the great myths of Western culture – Shakespeare's sons are still, after all, the gatekeepers of cultural centrality. Yet it is the very ambivalence of his representations of sexual and familial relationships which seems to have enhanced rather than diminished their cultural power – as the existence of the present work testifies. Nevertheless, Carter's challenge to the hegemonic accounts of cultural and familial legitimacy serves to clear a space for new voices, new visions of the family, which may offer the next generation of Chances a happier alternative to the tragi-comic histories of Shakespeare's family romances: '"We're both of us mothers and both of us fathers", [Nora] said. "They'll be wise children, all right"' (p. 230).

Notes

1 Women's Theatre Group and Elaine Feinstein, *Lear's Daughters*, in Gabrielle Griffin and Elaine Aston (eds), *Herstory: Plays by Women for Women*, 2 vols (Sheffield, Sheffield Academic Press, 1991), I, pp. 19–69; Jane Smiley, *A Thousand Acres* (London, Flamingo, 1992).

2 London, Chatto & Windus, 1991.

3 *Powers of Horror: An Essay on Abjection*, trans. Leon Roudiez (New York, Columbia University Press, 1982), p. 15.

4 Toril Moi (ed.), *The Kristeva Reader* (Oxford, Blackwell, 1986), p. 34.

5 'Word, Dialogue and Novel', in *The Kristeva Reader*, pp. 34–61 (p. 49).

6 'The Horrors of Power: A Critique of "Kristeva"', in Francis Barker *et al.*, (eds), *The Politics of Theory* (Colchester, University of Essex, 1983), pp. 38–48 (p. 43).

7 Mary Russo, 'Female Grotesques: Carnival and Theory', in Teresa de Lauretis (ed.), *Feminist Studies/Critical Studies* (London, Macmillan, 1988), pp. 213–29.

8 See for example 'Stabat Mater' (1974), in *The Kristeva Reader*, pp. 160–86; 'Motherhood According to Giovanni Bellini' (1977), in Julia

Kristeva, *Desire in Language*, trans. Thomas Gora (Oxford, Blackwell, 1984), pp. 237–70; and *Black Sun: Depression and Melancholia* (1986), trans. Leon Roudiez (New York, Columbia University Press, 1989). For an alternative way of reading Kristeva's theorisation of the maternal with Renaissance literature, see Elizabeth D. Harvey, *Ventriloquized Voices: Feminist Theory and English Renaissance Texts* (London, Routledge, 1992), chapter 3, 'Matrix as Metaphor: Midwifery and the Conception of Voice', pp. 76–115.

9 *Pouvoirs de l'Horreur: Essai sur l'Abjection* (Paris, Editions du Seuil, 1980), p. 20.

10 Coppélia Kahn, 'The Absent Mother in *King Lear*', in Margaret W. Ferguson, Maureen Quilligan and Nancy J. Vickers (eds), *Rewriting the Renaissance: The Discourses of Sexual Difference in Early Modern Europe* (Chicago, Ill., University of Chicago Press, 1986), pp. 33–49.

11 Coppélia Kahn, 'Excavating "Those Dim Minoan Regions": Maternal Subtexts in Patriarchal Literature', *Diacritics* (1982), 32–41. In this country Dinnerstein's book was published under the title of *The Rocking of the Cradle and the Ruling of the World*.

12 For a brief and lucid account of this appropriation and its consequences, see Marianne Hirsch, 'Object-relations Oriented Criticism', in Elizabeth Wright (ed.), *Feminism and Psychoanalysis: A Critical Dictionary* (Oxford, Blackwell, 1992), pp. 280–3.

13 Janice Doane and Devon Hodges, *From Klein to Kristeva: Psychoanalytic Feminism and the Search for the "Good Enough" Mother* (Ann Arbor, Mich., University of Michigan Press, 1992).

14 *Desire and Anxiety: Circulations of Sexuality in Shakespearean Drama* (London, Routledge, 1992), p. 51.

15 'Where are the Mothers in Shakespeare? Options for Gender Representation in the English Renaissance', *Shakespeare Quarterly*, 42 (1991), 291–314 (301–2).

16 See *Suffocating Mothers*, Chapter 5, pp. 103–29.

17 [Anon.], *The True Chronicle Historie of King Leir*, in Geoffrey Bullough (ed.), *Narrative and Dramatic Sources of Shakespeare*, 7 vols (London, Routledge & Kegan Paul, 1957–1973), VII (1973), pp. 337–402 (p. 337), ll. 12–14, 17–21.

18 Intriguingly, Freud's single discussion of *King Lear* bypasses the question of incest by taking Lear's desire for Death – represented by Cordelia – as the psychic mainspring of the plot; see 'The Theme of the Three Caskets' (1913), Pelican Freud Library vol. 14 (Harmondsworth, Penguin, 1985), pp. 233–48.

19 '*King Lear*': *The Critics Debate* (Basingstoke, Macmillan, 1988), p. 15.

20 Barbara Melchiori, 'Still Harping on My Daughter', *English Miscellany*, 11 (1960), 59–74. The quoted lines are from *Pericles* I.i.65–6. For my purposes, the fact that Shakespeare may well not have written these words is less significant than that such circulation as they have had has been authorised by his name. Unlike Melchiori's, my argument does not depend on speculation about Shakespeare's incestuous feelings for his own daughters.

21 'The Patriarchal Bard: Feminist Criticism and Shakespeare: *King Lear* and *Measure for Measure*', in Jonathan Dollimore and Alan Sinfield (eds), *Political Shakespeare: New Essays in Cultural Materialism* (Manchester, Manchester University Press, 1985), pp. 88–108 (p. 102).

22 Lynda E. Boose, 'The Family in Shakespeare Studies; or – Studies in the Family of Shakespeareans; or – The Politics of Politics', *Renaissance Quarterly*, 40 (1987), 707–42 (735).

23 For an account of the aesthetic choices which were shaped by the theatrical/political context in which the play was first produced, see Lizbeth Goodman, 'Women's Alternative Shakespeares and Women's Alternatives to Shakespeare in Contemporary British Theatre', in Marianne Novy (ed.), *Cross-Cultural Performances: Differences in Women's Re-Visions of Shakespeare* (Urbana, Ill., University of Illinois Press, 1993), pp. 206–26 (pp. 220–2).

24 Gabrielle Griffin and Elaine Aston, 'Introduction', *Herstory*, pp.7–18 (p. 8). For a feminist historian's perspective on these issues, see Judith Allen, 'Evidence and Silence: Feminism and the Limits of History', in Carole Pateman and Elizabeth Gross (eds), *Feminist Challenges: Social and Political Theory* (London, Allen & Unwin, 1986), pp. 173–89.

25 For an interesting discussion of the difficulties the company had in deciding how authorship of the play should be credited, and the influence of this uncertainty on its critical reception, see Lizbeth Goodman, *Contemporary Feminist Theatres: To Each Her Own* (London, Routledge, 1993), pp. 97–100.

26 The popular image of wet-nursing in the early modern period is of wealthy women farming their children out to lower-class women for reasons of medical or social fashion; but it was sometimes the case that orphans or very poor children, whose own mothers could not take care of them, would be wet-nursed at the expense of the parish. See Fiona Newall, 'Wet-nursing and Child Care in Aldenham, Hertfordshire, 1595–1726: Some Evidence on the Circumstances and Effects of Seventeenth-century Child-rearing Practices', in Valerie Fildes (ed.), *Women as Mothers in Pre-Industrial England* (London, Routledge, 1990), pp. 122–38.

27 Shakespeare's Fool is sometimes played by a woman, of course; when the role was restored by Macready in 1838, it was played by Priscilla Horton, and female Fools remained popular throughout the nineteenth century. See J. S. Bratton, *'King Lear' (Plays in Performance)* (Bristol, Bristol Classical Press, 1987), pp. 11–12.

28 For the classic articulation of this analysis, see Gayle Rubin, 'The Traffic in Women: Notes Toward a Political Economy of Sex', in Rayna Reiter (ed.), *Toward an Anthropology of Women* (New York, Monthly Review Press, 1975), pp. 157–210.

29 'Word, Dialogue and Novel', in *The Kristeva Reader*, pp. 34–61 (p. 48).

30 C. L. Barber, *Shakespeare's Festive Comedy: A Study of Dramatic Form and its Relation to Social Custom* (Princeton, NJ, Princeton University Press, 1959), p. 36.

31 Among the many works on this subject, see for example Robert Weimann, *Shakespeare and the Popular Tradition in the Theater* (Baltimore, Md, Johns Hopkins University Press, 1978); Michael D. Bristol, *Carnival and Theatre* (London, Methuen, 1985); and Leah S. Marcus, *The Politics of Mirth: Jonson, Herrick, Milton, Marvell and the Defense of Old Holiday Pastimes* (Chicago, Ill., University of Chicago Press, 1986).

32 Emmanuel Le Roy Ladurie's classic *Carnival at Romans* (Harmondsworth, Penguin, 1981) describes what happened when plans to use the carnival at Romans in France in 1580 as the springboard for a popular anti-authoritarian rebellion were discovered by the authorities, who turned the mutiny into a massacre. Further examples of the multi-faceted political potential of carnival can be found in Barry Reay (ed.), *Popular Culture in Seventeenth-Century England* (London, Croom Helm, 1985), and Anthony Fletcher and John Stevenson (eds), *Order and Disorder in Early Modern England* (Cambridge, Cambridge University Press, 1985).

33 *The Politics and Poetics of Transgression* (London, Methuen, 1986), p. 27.

34 On seventeenth-century political uses of carnival, see the essays collected in Reay (ed.), *Popular Culture*, and Fletcher and Stevenson (eds), *Order and Disorder*. Useful overviews of the subversion/containment debate and of the various possible assessments of the political effectiveness of carnival can be found in Marcus, *The Politics of Mirth*, and Jonathan Dollimore, *Sexual Dissidence* (Oxford, Oxford University Press, 1991).

35 *Walter Benjamin, or Toward a Revolutionary Criticism* (London, Verso, 1981), p. 148.

36 Davis's canonical 'Women on Top' is collected in her *Society and*

Culture in Early Modern France (Cambridge, Polity Press, 1986), pp. 124–51. For interesting examples of articles with a Shakespearean emphasis dealing with women, transgression and carnival, particularly in the context of cross-dressing, see Jean E. Howard, 'Cross-dressing, the Theatre, and Gender Struggle in Early Modern England', *Shakespeare Quarterly* 39 (1988), 418–40, and Valerie Traub, 'Desire and the Differences it Makes', in Valerie Wayne (ed.), *The Matter of Difference: Materialist Feminist Criticism of Shakespeare* (Hemel Hempstead, Harvester Wheatsheaf, 1991), pp. 81–114.

37 Mikhail Mikhailovich Bakhtin, *Rabelais and His World*, trans. Hélène Iswolsky (Cambridge, Mass., MIT Press, 1968), p. 19.

38 Quoted in Richard Wilson, *Will Power: Essays on Shakespearean Authority* (Hemel Hempstead, Harvester Wheatsheaf, 1993), p. 163.

39 See Adrian Wilson, 'The Ceremony of Childbirth and its Interpretation', in Fildes (ed.), *Women as Mothers*, pp. 68–107.

40 Quoted in Patricia Crawford, 'The construction and experience of maternity in seventeenth-century England', in Fildes (ed.), *Women as Mothers*, pp. 3–38 (p. 7).

41 This notion is reinflected in a more satirical way in *The Winter's Tale*, where Autolycus attempts to sell a broadside ballad about a usurer's wife who gave birth to twenty money bags (IV.iv.260–9). More prosaically, Alice Thornton recorded that due to a fright she experienced in pregnancy, when she was nearly cut with a penknife, her son Robert was born with 'a mark of a deep bloody colour upon [his] heart' (quoted in Lucinda McCray Beier, *Sufferers and Healers: The Experience of Illness in Seventeenth-Century England* (London, Routledge & Kegan Paul, 1987), p. 233).

42 Diane Purkiss, 'Producing the Voice, Consuming the Body: Women Prophets of the Seventeenth Century', in Isobel Grundy and Susan Wiseman (eds), *Women, Writing, History* (London, Batsford, 1992), pp. 139–58 (p. 154).

43 Clair Wills, 'Upsetting the Public: Carnival, Hysteria and Women's Texts', in Ken Hirschkop and David Shepherd (eds), *Bakhtin and Cultural Theory* (Manchester, Manchester University Press, 1989), pp. 130–51 (p. 134).

44 'Women on Top', p. 131.

45 For numerous examples of such actions, see Davis, 'Women on Top', Fletcher and Stevenson (eds), *Order and Disorder*, and Reay (ed), *Popular Culture*.

46 More details on these practices can be found in Lynda E. Boose, 'Scolding Brides and Bridling Scolds: Taming the Woman's Unruly Member', *Shakespeare Quarterly*, 42 (1991), 179–213, and Martin

Ingram, 'Ridings, Rough Music and Mocking Rhymes in Early Modern England', in Reay (ed.), *Popular Culture*, pp. 166–97.

47 Social historian David Underdown argues that such punishments increased dramatically between about 1560 and 1640, which he characterises as a period of intense anxiety about social disorder in general, and a time of particular concern about the maintenance of patriarchal power relations, in his article 'The Taming of the Scold: The Enforcement of Patriarchal Authority in Early Modern England', in Fletcher and Stevenson (eds), *Order and Disorder*, pp. 116–29. Underdown's analysis has recently been contested by Martin Ingram in his '"Scolding women cucked and washed": A crisis in gender relations in early modern England', in Jenny Kermode and Garthine Walker (eds), *Women, Crime and the Courts in Early Modern England* (London: UCL Press, 1994), pp. 48–80.

48 *Illegitimate Power: Bastards in Renaissance Drama* (Manchester, Manchester University Press, 1994), p.19.

49 London, Chatto & Windus, 1984.

50 London, Chatto & Windus, 1985.

51 There have been numerous discussions of this issue in the last few years; for a recent summary, see Laura Levine, *Men in Women's Clothing* (Cambridge: Cambridge University Press, 1994).

52 Laurie Finke, 'Painting Women: Images of Femininity in Jacobean Tragedy', in Sue-Ellen Case, (ed.), *Performing Feminisms: Feminist Critical Theory and Theatre* (Baltimore, Md, Johns Hopkins University Press, 1990), pp.223–36.

53 For an important critical account of this topos, see Andreas Huyssen, *After the Great Divide: Modernism, Mass Culture, and Postmodernism* (Basingstoke, Macmillan, 1988).

54 Marina Warner, 'Introduction', in Angela Carter (ed.), *The Second Virago Book of Fairy Tales* (London, Virago, 1993), pp. ix–xvi (p. xvi).

55 For a more detailed discussion of this topic, see my 'The (Pregnant) Prince and the Showgirl: Angela Carter's Revision of Shakespeare', in Mark Burnett and John Manning (eds), *New Essays on 'Hamlet'* (New York, AMS Press, 1994), pp.249–69.

56 'Representing Ophelia: Women, Madness and the Responsibilities of Feminist Criticism', in Patricia Parker and Geoffrey Hartmann (eds), *Shakespeare and the Question of Theory* (London, Methuen, 1986), pp. 77–94.

57 '"Thou that beget'st him that did thee beget": Transformation in *Pericles* and *The Winter's Tale*', *Shakespeare Survey*, 22 (1969), 59–68.

58 *Suffocating Mothers*, p. 197.

59 'I had brushed up my Shakespeare; I recognised for what it was the

game that Nora and I had played out once before as romance. And now we'd perform the "substitute bride" bit, as in *Measure for Measure* and *All's Well That Ends Well*, as farce' (p. 149).

60　*Gender Trouble: Feminism and the Subversion of Identity* (London, Routledge, 1991), p. 103.

61　Margaret Whitford, 'Mother–daughter Relationship', in Wright (ed.), *Feminism and Psychoanalysis*, pp. 262–65 (p. 264).

62　In one of Carter's last short stories, however, a quite literally ghostly mother finds an articulate voice and intervenes energetically in her daughter's life: see 'Ashputtle *or* The Mother's Ghost', in *American Ghosts and Old World Wonders* (London, Chatto & Windus, 1993), pp. 110–20.

Chapter 3

Rewriting the narratives of shame: women's transformations of *The Tempest*

Towards the end of Marina Warner's novel *Indigo*,[1] Miranda Everard journeys to the Caribbean island of Enfant-Béate which had been the home of Sycorax, Caliban and Ariel until it was colonised by her ancestor Kit (later Sir Christopher) Everard in the early seventeenth century. Nearly four hundred years later, Miranda is exploring the island's old churchyard when she finds, overshadowed by the tree in which the spirit of Sycorax is eternally imprisoned, a marble memorial which records and celebrates the triumphs of that first colonising ancestor:[2]

> First read then weep when thou art hereby taught
> That Everard lies interred here, one that bought
> With loss of Noble blood Illustrious Name
> Of a Commander Great in Acts of Fame:
> Trained from his youth in Arms, his courage bold
> Attempted brave Exploits, and uncontrolled
> By Fortune's fiercest Frowns, he still gave forth
> Large Narratives of Military worth.
> Unsluice your briny floods, what! Can ye keep
> Your eyes from tears and see the marble weep?
> Burst out for shame: or if ye find no vent
> For tears, yet stay, and see the stones relent.

(pp. 316–17)

Miranda is unaware that at the very moment when she comes face to face with this icon of the imperial power of her family and her nation, an anti-colonial riot is breaking out in the island's nearby capital. What she does perceive is that, symbolically, the island has already inscribed its own insurgent power across the colonising text; a recent hurricane has split the memorial stone asunder, making of it a very different testament to the effects of history: 'Weep ... blood ... in Arms ... uncontrolled ... Narratives of shame ...' (p. 317). The resonant cadences of the verse are reduced to verbal rubble, fragmentary phrases hinting at horrors which language can barely convey. The poem's warning that a failure to mourn will make the 'marble weep' and the 'stones relent' is enacted by this de-composition of its meaning; yet the new message clearly implies that the cause for grief and shame is not the death of Sir Kit Everard, but the terrible consequences of his 'brave Exploits' for the natives of the island – none of whom, except Sycorax, are privileged to be buried in this churchyard. The desires and anxieties which mark the encounter of the female subject with Shakespeare in the context of colonial discourse coalesce in this moment in which the daughter of the colonial project, unaware of the momentous historical events being played out elsewhere, strives to make sense of the fragmentary records of her own history and the ambivalence she feels towards her inheritance. In this chapter, I want to explore the aesthetic, political and subjective implications of some of the forms this encounter has taken in writings by women in the twentieth century.

Like *Indigo*, H.D.'s *By Avon River*³ and Suniti Namjoshi's *Snapshots of Caliban*⁴ re-create *The Tempest* in ways which cannot neatly be assimilated to the conflict between the political and the aesthetic which has recurred in recent academic work on the play. The questions which these texts use *The Tempest* to explore – questions about the relationships between politics, art, pleasure and identity – are precisely those which are at stake in the struggles for authority and the anxieties about change which are currently demarcating the contested terrain of literary and cultural studies. The re-visions of *The Tempest* which I discuss may be particularly productive in the context of this debate over cultural power, because they offer ways of exploring many dimensions of the play while problematising – and perhaps even beginning to heal – the antagonistic polarisations of aesthetics and politics, magic and colonialism, black male and white female, which in recent years have played a structuring role in theatrical production and student response as well as critical debate. *The Tempest*'s own stress on the apparently magical power of humans to transform their world, and their place in it, makes it an apt vehicle for the individual, cultural and aesthetic transformations depicted by H.D., Namjoshi and Warner. These reinscriptions of the Shakespearean text show that its pleasures and its ideological effects alike are neither univocal nor timeless, but culturally contingent and open to intervention and re-creation from a variety of perspectives.

Traps and complexes: feminist theorisations of colonialism

It is surely no coincidence that the current feminist critical project to re-evaluate the sexual politics of Shakespeare's plays is more or less coeval with the emergence of critical interest in the politics of colonialism in texts like *The Tempest*. Yet paradoxically, this development has often re-enacted a polarisation of sexual and racial issues, in that the numerous oppositional, anti-colonial revisions of the play which have emerged over the last few decades, from a variety of cultural contexts, almost all focus on Caliban as a figure of resistance.[5] Where they notice Miranda's existence at all, they usually take her to be complicit in Prospero's oppressive project, if only by virtue of her passivity and willingness to function as token of exchange between the empire-building patriarchal dynasties. Rob Nixon has shown that, just at the moment when new historicist and cultural materialist critics launched a massive exploration of the play's discourses of power from a Eurocentric perspective, the production of appropriations by post- or anti-colonial writers working in Africa and the Caribbean effectively dried up. He suggests that this may be partly because of 'the difficulty of wresting from it any role for female defiance or leadership in a period when protest is coming increasingly from that quarter'.[6] Discussing some exceptions to this claim, Diana Brydon has suggested that it is not surprising that they are to be found in white-authored Canadian texts, arguing that the largely absent, silent Miranda is 'a fitting representative of Canada's aspirations as a dutiful daughter of the Empire'.[7] The gendering of the territory which is presumed to acquiesce in its own colonisation is not, of course, beside the point, although in taking Canada as an exemplar of such acquiescence Brydon glosses over the differences between anglophone, francophone and Native Canadians. Brydon contrasts the focus on familial structures and the use of

Miranda as a symbol of the developing self of the artist which she finds in these texts with the more explicitly political, Caliban-centred appropriations which, according to Nixon, were only produced by male African and Caribbean writers. In a similar argument, Elaine Showalter explores American women writers' use of *The Tempest* as 'a metaphorical account of the woman artist or feminist intellectual', focusing on their interest in 'Miranda's role as the motherless daughter of the Father who falls in love with his language and power'.[8] Brydon and Showalter both conflate a number of very diverse texts by women writers; in doing so they appropriate the figure of Miranda in order to construct an allegory of the relations between gender, writing and colonialism which locates femininity as innately passive and reactionary, and attributes the possibility of rebellion solely to the masculine agency of Caliban.

For a feminist reading, the problem with Caliban-centred appropriations is precisely that their representations of the relations of colonial power do not leave a space in which women can locate themselves as anything other than tools or victims of that power. Attempts to re-create *The Tempest* to include an element of subversive or rebellious female agency have thus had to be located in alternative, supplementary or oppositional narratives. Listen, for example, to what Miranda has to say for herself when she is voiced by the North American feminist critic, Lorie Jerrell Leininger, at the end of an essay which seeks to expose the ideological biases of Shakespeare's text:

> I will not be used as the excuse for [Caliban's] enslavement ... I cannot give assent to an ethical scheme that locates all virtue symbolically in one part of my anatomy. My virginity has little to do with the forces that will lead to good harvest or to greater social justice ...
>
> Will I succeed in creating my 'brave new world' which has people in it who no longer exploit one another? ... I will at least make a start by springing 'the Miranda trap', being forced into unwitting collusion with domination by appearing to be a beneficiary. I need to join forces with Caliban – to join forces with all those who are exploited or oppressed – to stand beside Caliban and say,
>
> > As we from crimes would pardoned be,
> > Let's work to set each other free.[9]

In Leininger's polemical version of *The Tempest*, Miranda represents the self-image of the white feminist critic, striving to integrate the felt experience of victimisation which generated her feminism with the more ambivalent position she holds within the discourses of racial domination. Miranda is identified as a liminal figure: empowered by her whiteness, disadvantaged by her femininity, she is perfectly placed to mediate the complex interrelations of race, gender and sexuality in constructing and maintaining the patriarchal, imperialist power which Prospero wields in Leininger's vision of the play.

Although numerous writers, creative and academic, have discovered within the text of *The Tempest* both the means to lay bare the workings of colonial discourse and the seeds of a critique, Leininger does not believe that the play either has any such potential for ideological critique, or can be redeemed from its inherent sexism and racism. Rather, she steps outside the framework of the drama and performs an act of critical appropriation, creating a contemporary version of Miranda who refuses to be a pawn in the elaborate chess game which history has made of the elements of her play. In spirit, this assertive Miranda has much in common with the one who calls Caliban 'abhorred slave' – though many editors have denied that Prospero's daughter was capable of uttering such words, and have attributed them to him instead[10] – but she explicitly rejects the subject position and political stance implied in that outburst, in order to align herself with Caliban in struggle against what she perceives as their shared victimisation by the intertwined forces of patriarchy and imperialism. Recent histories of grass-roots activism demonstrate that this vision of a 'rainbow coalition' against oppression is not entirely sentimental. But in Leininger's formulation it remains problematic to the extent that it occludes the very different locations of the white woman and black man in relation to the power structures which oppress them both; and it makes it very difficult to construct a subject position from which the black woman can name and challenge her experience of oppression – in contrast with the political leadership frequently offered by black women in actual liberation struggles.

More recently, another white feminist critic, Laura E. Donaldson, has also made the figure of Miranda central to a reconsideration of the relations between gender and racial difference.

Where Leininger sought to prise open 'the Miranda trap', Donaldson invents the 'Miranda Complex' as a paradigm of the way the white feminist is constrained by her positioning within the discursive regimes of patriarchy and colonialism.[11] She contrasts this with the 'Prospero Complex', naming the structure which identifies Prospero with the colonising European male, and Caliban with the subjugated native other. Donaldson argues that by focusing on just one form of oppression, these paired schemas obscure the complex relations of racial and sexual domination which serve to maintain Prospero's power, preventing Caliban and Miranda from 'seeing' each other, and thereby recognising their shared oppression as 'victims of colonial Prosperity' (p. 16). Her solution to this stalemate is to shift the focus of her exploration of the genealogies of literary colonialism away from the Prospero/Caliban axis, and on to the relationship between Caliban and Miranda – more specifically, the accusation that Caliban attempted to rape Miranda.

Feminist historians of rape have recently shown that in Shakespeare's time, the dominant discourse which regarded it primarily as a crime committed by one man against another man's property was beginning to be displaced by an alternative account which perceived the raped woman as the injured party.[12] Although her account does not draw on potentially relevant historical sources, Donaldson similarly posits Caliban's attempt as a homosocial act, in which Miranda is merely the instrument of his revenge against Prospero: 'Caliban sees in Miranda only the distorted being of a woman whose possession not only would visit poetic justice upon the coloniser but also grant vicarious patronymic power' (p. 17). Donaldson does not enter into the historically fraught question of the relation of this imputed assault to the role actually played by rape, and by the myth of the black rapist, in maintaining the simultaneously sexist and racist power of the white male.[13] Her emphasis is on the way that the reactions of both parties to this accusation complicate a sentimental, idealistic identification of Miranda as the subject of white feminism, or of Caliban as the agent of indigenous rebellion. Rather, each is seen to be placed in an anomalous and uneasy position: Miranda disadvantaged by her gender, yet protected by and benefiting from colonialism; Caliban oppressed as the colonial subject, but empowered by his masculinity.

Donaldson uses these multiple anomalies to explore white women writers' various uneasy negotiations with the ideological and social structures of patriarchy and colonialism. Again, though, this paradigm is unable to consider the significance of the text's erasure of the 'other woman' – the black or native woman – as both subject and object of the colonial process. Although Sycorax is a native of North Africa and functions symbolically as 'black' by virtue of her magic, if not her ethnicity, she remains quite literally 'obscene' – both off-stage and demonised as grotesque and repulsive – throughout the play. Miranda's exemplary status in accounts of the play's colonialist politics is derived precisely from her isolation from all other women, regardless of race. Ania Loomba has shown that in constructing Sycorax as 'other' to both Prospero and Miranda, the text uses her to legitimise a colonial power which is specifically white and male (*Gender, Race, Renaissance Drama*, p. 152). The absent, obscene Sycorax thus turns out to be crucial to the play's regulation of racial and sexual difference. Just as the work I discussed in Chapters 1 and 2 has explored the implications of the repression or exclusion of women as mothers from many Shakespearean texts, and has traced some of the ways in which the maternal feminine constitutes the repressed which will always return to disrupt those texts; so also the very in-significance of the 'other' woman, the apparent difficulty of putting her into representation which characterises both Shakespeare's text and reproductions of it, comes to function as the repressed which returns to disclose what *The Tempest* cannot itself tell us about the histories of its meanings, pleasures and power.

'Shakespeare was a black woman'

This chapter had its origins in my reflections on the experience of teaching *The Tempest*, and I want now to consider the practical implications for cultural politics of the theoretical concerns outlined in the previous section by addressing the relations of gender, race, and the English literary curriculum. The tensions and anxieties condensed in the two different 'Miranda syndromes' proposed by Leininger and Donaldson are re-enacted by the gesture, recurrent in debates over the literary canon and its relation to the curriculum, which polarises Shakespeare and contemporary women writers – particularly, intriguingly, *black* women writers – as embodiments of opposing sets of cultural values. Shakespeare has come to function as the representative of a supposedly inclusive, humanist cultural tradition to which feminist writers and critics are presumed to be spitefully and destructively hostile. Hence the panic caused by reports that in some institutions of higher education, Shakespeare is being displaced from the literary syllabus, and thus by implication from the canon *per se*, in favour of writers like Margaret Atwood, Toni Morrison and Alice Walker, among others.[14] This anxiety produces a new version of the biographically secured allegory of *The Tempest*, which identifies Shakespeare with Prospero as both representative and guardian of a cultural heritage which, of its nature, is masculine, eurocentric, and elitist. Whether Alice Walker is to be identified with Miranda, Caliban, or Sycorax is less clear; what is certain is that she and Shakespeare are presumed to be mutually inimical. And the fact that the position of the woman of colour in this allegory is so problematic is by no means incidental. Ania Loomba quotes historian Gerda Lerner's comment that 'the myth of the black rapist of white women is the turn of the myth of the bad black woman' (*Gender, Race, Renaissance Drama*, p. 150) as a pretext to her own claim that in *The Tempest* 'we must read Caliban's rapacity as set against Sycorax's licentious black femininity and the passive purity of Miranda, whose own desire ... corroborates the will of the father' (p. 151). White women's loyalty to their fathers is – perhaps unwisely – assumed, and their occasional refusal of this alliance is marked as a shocking (and often sexualised) transgression; so when Miranda chooses to reject the values of the fathers, she is perceived as aligning herself with Caliban in rebellion. No loyalty to civilisation is expected of the black woman; hence an alliance between black and white women against white patriarchal power has the potential to be particularly threatening.

The anxieties about cultural authority which are condensed in this scenario were exposed in the furore which followed the publication in 1992 of a survey into the composition of English degrees at institutions which were members of SCEPCHE – at the time, the vast majority of polytechnics and colleges of higher education.[15] The survey was widely reported, particularly in the right-wing press, in ways which distorted both the balance of the original findings and the conviction of its author, Tim Cook, that 'the situation is encouraging, even for traditionalists, and the actual interests and need for intellectual stimulus and excitement of today's students are well catered for in the rich variety of literary experiences and critical approaches provided'.[16] While conceding that Shakespeare is compulsory in only about half of the institutions surveyed, Cook points out that he is on the syllabus in almost all of them, and remains a very popular option choice. In contrast, the *Sunday Telegraph* headlined its article, which ran across the top of the front page, 'Eng Lit students learn to get by without Shakespeare', and issued the dire warning that

> the findings provide further evidence of a decline in Shakespeare teaching, which will fuel concern among traditionalists about the way in which Shakespeare is being marginalised by modern teaching. The Prince of Wales has expressed concern at the decreasing interest in Shakespeare's plays (2 February 1992, 1).

In a manoeuvre which characterises the conservative position in this debate, the article subsequently represents Shakespeare as the embodiment and exemplar of 'our cultural inheritance', being forced to 'give way' to 'feminists and international writers' – the possibility that they too might participate in 'our cultural heritage' is not entertained.[17]

It is important to stress that there is nothing about the original survey which makes this prioritisation of a presumed antagonism between Shakespeare and feminist writers inevitable – the *Guardian*, for instance, clearly had other, equally contentious political issues on its mind when it pointed out that Seamus Heaney is taught at more institutions than Shakespeare. But it obviously suited conservatives like A. N. Wilson to use the survey as the pretext for an attack on feminism, claiming that 'the school of feminist clap-trap … has entirely taken a grip' of British universities, and declaring firmly that 'the thought police who masquerade as dons and lecturers in our benighted places of higher education' are doing the youth of the nation a grave disservice by denying that 'the Bard is especially enriching and ennobling – unlike the feminist writers who are ousting him'.[18] Wilson's article is a particularly effective intervention in the debate because it emphasises the pleasurable, inclusive and liberating qualities of Shakespeare's texts. He implies that it is their superiority in this respect which makes them preferable to the works of Margaret Atwood and Toni Morrison, which are presented as ideologically narrow and life-denying:

> To know and love Shakespeare is to become wiser and more genial. If you become wise and genial, you cease to become a feminist – or indeed an anything-ist. You learn to accept the strangeness and richness and variety of life, and to make up your own mind about it. You become more human (*ibid.*).

While the tone of his assault on feminism is perhaps unusually strident, in contrast with this remarkably mellow liberal–humanist celebration of Shakespeare, Wilson is nevertheless typical of a certain kind of opponent to changes in the literary curriculum in deploying an antagonistic scarcity model of the canon. This implies that only limited space is available in the pantheon of English literature, and that if feminists are to be admitted to it, this can only be done at the expense of excluding writers such as Shakespeare to whom they are assumed to be ineluctably hostile – an assumption which, it must be said, reveals a predictable ignorance of feminist Shakespeare criticism.[19]

An alternative, slightly more subtle, strategy represents women writers as superfluous, because they are always already subsumed by Shakespeare's humanist inclusiveness. Thus Lynn Cheney, right-wing Chair of the USA's National Endowment for the Humanities, approvingly quotes Maya Angelou's assertion 'I *know* that William Shakespeare was a black woman' as evidence that the traditional literary canon embodies 'truths that pass beyond time and circumstance; truths that, transcending accidents of class, race and gender, speak to us all'.[20] Quoting Cheney in a book which places Shakespeare and contemporary women writers in a dialogic and mutually enriching relation, Peter Erickson shows that although Angelou is undoubtedly a passionate Shakespearean and a forceful advocate of access to all forms of culture for people of all backgrounds, nevertheless the point of her appropriation of Shakespeare is precisely the opposite of the interpretation Cheney chooses to put on it. Taken in context, its effect is to illustrate the damage done by the imposition of cultural hierarchy, and to evoke the value of the coexistence of multiple cultural traditions (*Rewriting Shakespeare*, pp. 118–22).

Advocates of revision of the canon and the curriculum are

frequently accused by conservatives like Lynn Cheney and A. N. Wilson of wanting to cast aside the treasures of their literary heritage, such as Shakespeare, in favour of more fashionable, but perhaps transient, texts. I would suggest that a more accurate picture of the revisionist project is outlined by Peter Erickson's remark that 'the debate is not about Shakespeare's elimination from the canon but rather about the terms on which his work is to be included' (p. 5). Erickson offers two alternative frameworks for reconceptualising the canon: an additive and a transformative model. The additive model implies that the concept of the canon, and the criteria by which texts are deemed eligible for inclusion, remain intact, while the canon itself expands as new texts which meet these criteria are admitted to it one by one. In contrast, the transformative model entails, in Erickson's words, 'a fundamental change in the conventions by which we understand and organise canons ... [leading] to a more productive formulation of questions about the interrelationships among works in an expanded literary tradition' (p. 6). Similarly, Eve Kosofsky Sedgwick suggests that one of the most important gestures of the feminist challenge to the traditional canon has been to attack

> if not the empirical centrality, then the conceptual anonymity of the master-canon ... If it is still in important respects *the* master-canon it nevertheless cannot now escape naming itself with every syllable also *a* particular canon, a canon of mastery, in this case of men's mastery over, and over against, women.[21]

As the title of this chapter implies, I share Peter Erickson's project of working, by means of 'the continual reconstruction for the present of the cultural past' (p. 97), towards a transformation of the master-canon which re-evaluates its constitution in the light of the challenges proceeding from the feminist, black, and lesbian/gay communities; which acknowledges both Shakespeare's unique status and the frequently coercive processes by which it has been achieved; and which makes space for the revisionary and oppositional potential of the kinds of texts which have previously been denied canonical status. That such a transformation is already taking place *may* be signalled by the current advertising campaign for Toni Morrison's newly-canonical *Jazz*, which proudly declares 'This is Shakespeare singin' the blues!' – though a more cynical interpretation might be that market forces are already rushing in where political correctness fears to tread.

To exemplify this transformative project, I turn now to an analysis of three women's texts which remain faithful to Shakespeare's play in many of its details, while offering re-visions of it from the points of view of its marginalised or suppressed characters, in ways which make a re-evaluation of its colonial and patriarchal cultural uses more or less explicit. This shift of focus enables an integration of politically informed analysis with a sense of the magical and aesthetic pleasures of the text, and repositions the relations of margin and centre with the effect of opening up the possibility of a reconciliatory vision which is not only available on Prospero's terms. In this way, the texts themselves rewrite the narratives of shame which have become entangled with *The Tempest*'s histories. Naming this process 'revisionary myth-making', Liz Yorke sees it as central to the construction of a feminist poetics which involves both the reworking of old stories and the fabrication of new, living myths which project forward into the future, as well as drawing on the resources of the past: 'the revisionary task of reminiscence and retrieval [of women's experience] also involves re-inscription, a process in which the old narratives, stories, scripts, mythologies become transvalued, re-presented in different terms'.[22] Each of the texts I will consider in the rest of this chapter conforms to this model in offering both a transvaluation of *The Tempest* and a new myth which displaces the boundaries of Shakespeare's text by re-presenting it from a female perspective.

The earliest of these texts, H.D.'s *By Avon River* (1949) is a modernist tribute to Shakespeare, experimental in form in that it juxtaposes a lyric poem sequence and a scholarly essay. The latter is a work of cultural history which offers an account, based in the hermetic magical tradition which some commentators associate with Prospero,[23] of what made Shakespeare an exceptional cultural figure. In contrast, in the poem sequence, 'The Guest', which will be the focus of my account, the speaker's persona merges with that of Claribel, the King of Naples's daughter, in order to explore the situation of the woman struggling to achieve creativity and subjectivity within patriarchal culture. Although it is not an issue which H.D. addresses directly, Claribel's fate – an enforced, politically motivated marriage to an African king – is also pertinent to the question of the white woman's pivotal role in the imperial project. My reading of *By Avon River* will address this issue, but will also explore the text's representation of exile and alienation, and their magical, feminised transformation into the potential for reconciliation.

My second text, Suniti Namjoshi's *Snapshots of Caliban*, is also a poem sequence, but one which is post-modern rather than modernist, both in form and in the subjectivity it inscribes. Namjoshi is explicit and insistent in making the shifting, culturally-specific traces of her identity central to her self-presentation as a writer; as an upper-class diasporic Indian who has lived in Canada and England in the last few decades; and as a lesbian–feminist. Like H.D.'s, her text is not overtly concerned with what would conventionally be seen as the political, public realm. But the conjunction of her authorial self-inscription with her use of *The Tempest* to explore the war of egos between Prospero, Caliban and Miranda, from whose polyphonic and often hostile voices the poem is woven, powerfully emphasises the politics of the personal. And it is the politics of the personal – the question of who is to be master over Shakespeare's identity, yours, mine, Claribel's or Caliban's – that seems to me to be at the heart of what is at issue for our time in *The Tempest*.

This concern is explicitly taken up by Marina Warner's *Indigo*, the last text I shall discuss, which interweaves the story of the seventeenth-century colonisation of a Caribbean island legitimately inhabited by Sycorax, Ariel, Caliban and their kin, with the tale of a present-day Miranda who seeks for grace by returning to the emotional and geographical site of the long, painful 'narrative of shame' which she experiences as culminating in her own, racially ambiguous, politically oppositional identity. In my readings of these three texts, I will not be concerned to make an argument that they are somehow united, across time and place, by a shared feminist – or even feminine – investment in a given political and aesthetic agenda, or a certain way of transforming *The Tempest*. These texts are far too diverse for that to be a meaningful procedure. Rather, my focus will be on what is specific to each of them: by resisting teleology and unity, I hope to indicate the necessary particularity and empowering diversity of women's creative responses to patriarchal and colonialist discourses.

By Avon River

By Avon River remains a relatively obscure work, which has only just begun to benefit from the enormous recent increase of interest in the writings of H.D.[24] Moreover, while it offers many immediate pleasures, it is also a challenging text, since like many of H.D.'s works it is preoccupied with mystical and hermetic matters and the reader needs a certain amount of specialised knowledge in order to make sense of these. I begin, therefore, by sketching some of the intellectual and cultural contexts which shape its meanings.

By Avon River deploys the intertextual strategies which are central to H.D.'s literary production, as to that of most of her modernist peers – strategies which some critics have related to the experience of exile which was also common to many modernists:

> As cultural grafts, the expatriate moderns produced hybrid texts that might graft the Provençal lyric with the Japanese haiku, the Greek fragment with the French vers libre, the Japanese Noh drama with the Celtic saga. The flight from home freed the writer to explore the art of any time, any place, to re-fuse the shards of history into something new.[25]

Drawing particularly on classical Greek literature and legend and the European hermetic tradition, H.D.'s work engages with and re-creates many of the foundational myths of Western culture. Psychoanalytic theory both constitutes one such myth and provides H.D. with a language and a method whereby she can carry out her own process of revisionary myth-making. To quote Liz Yorke again,

> Like the projects of psychoanalysis, the work of reminiscence involves the unfixing of the stereotyped associations that cluster around the traditional thought-forms, the myths and stories of western patriarchal culture ... [R]eminiscence constitutes a struggle to reach further into the unconscious mind ... in order to find a new place of identification, a new position for the subject (*Impertinent Voices*, pp. 5, 91).

In *By Avon River* and elsewhere in H.D.'s canon, Shakespeare is fully implicated in this psychoanalytically-informed project of cultural revision. In Chapter 1 I touched on Shakespeare's importance for Freud, and sketched some of the ways in which his work and image have been generative for psychoanalytic discourse. In *Tribute to Freud*, composed in 1944, H.D. posits a profound sympathy between Freud and Shakespeare by quoting Matthew Arnold's celebrated sonnet on Shakespeare and commenting, 'I had not intended to include it in these notes, but perhaps my subconscious or unconscious mind recognised an intellectual family-likeness in "that victorious brow"'; to reinforce the point she adds that the name 'Sigmund' means 'victorious voice/speech/ utterance'.[26] The ease and pleasure of her appropriations of Shakespeare and Freud demonstrate that H.D. is neither alienated nor intimidated by the central documents of Western culture; in *By Avon River* and *Tribute to Freud* she confidently rewrites a powerful male precursor as an enabling source of intertextual material and revisionary methodology, in order to create a self-authorising female voice which acknowledges its relation to cultural tradition while asserting a difference from it.

By Avon River predates by several decades the current critical interest in literature and colonialism, and indeed it is not explicitly concerned with *The Tempest* as an intervention into colonial discourse at all. But it can be appropriated for a feminist exploration of *The Tempest*'s inscription within colonial discourse, because of its focus on the figure of Claribel, ambiguously placed in Shakespeare's play as the absent fulcrum of relations between European royalty and a distant, alien Africa, located 'ten leagues beyond man's life' – outside the boundaries of the known, civilised world. In the play, Claribel has accepted her marriage to an African king, if not willingly, at least without overt rebellion; yet it comes to be seen as a grievous error, the source of the Italian party's subsequent misfortunes. Peter Hume glosses the repetitive play made in *The Tempest* with the name of 'Widow Dido' by pointing out that Dido killed herself rather than be forced – like Claribel – to marry an African king.[27] *By Avon River*, in tracing Claribel's journey home from Africa and conflating it with the search for a home of the modern-day pilgrim to Shakespeare's grave, implies a future for Claribel which is not imaginable within the dramatic world of Shakespeare's play.

Leslie Fiedler assumes, in contrast, that Shakespeare's Claribel finds a future in Africa, with the reservation that the possibility of her new life there is entirely conditional on the fact of exile: 'to

succeed, the black–white marriage must be removed as far as possible from the world in which Shakespeare had previously
demonstrated its inevitable failure'.[28] Tracing the unhappy fate of
the union between black and white which first occurs in *Titus
Andronicus,* and is echoed in various ways in *The Merchant of
Venice, Antony and Cleopatra, Othello* and *Pericles,* Fiedler takes
a very positive view of the fact that it is finally achieved in this play
as the enabling precondition for all the other reconciliations. I
dissent from his account in that I both feel less enthusiastic about
Prospero's supposedly reconciliatory project, and would also
argue that just as that depends on the exclusion of Caliban and
Antonio, and the manipulation of Miranda, so also the exclusion
and manipulation of Claribel are fundamental to her 'enabling'
role. As H.D. puts it, 'Claribel was outside all of this, / *The Tempest*
came after they left her' (*By Avon River,* p. 6). This position 'outside' makes Claribel one manifestation of the figure of the exiled,
alienated woman who recurs in H.D.'s work, echoing her own
long experience of elective exile.

In 'Good Frend' [*sic*] H.D. repeatedly invokes Claribel as a kind
of present absence, silent and disembodied, yet somehow ubiquitous:

Read through again, *Dramatis Personae*;
She is not there at all, but Claribel,
Claribel, the birds shrill, Claribel,
Claribel echoes from this rainbow-shell
I stooped just now to gather from the sand;

Where? From an island somewhere …

(p. 6; ellipsis present in original)

The repetition of Claribel's name and the tightly woven pattern of
assonance make of the first stanza above a magical incantation, as
if Claribel were the genius of what is more often thought of as
Prospero's island. This identification with the natural world, itself
endowed with heavily symbolic resonances, is a recurrent feature
of the presentation of Claribel, whose name is made to rhyme
with asphodel, the flower of life, and who is associated with rosemary – the mystical rose of the sea, Ophelia's rose of memory.
Similarly, the symbolism of flowers, central to the esoteric tradition which *By Avon River* celebrates as the source and guiding

principle of Shakespeare's creativity, is an important structural element of the second part of the text, the essay 'The Guest', in which the wild flowers and apple-blossom of Warwickshire hold the key to the fragments of memory, desire and meditation which enable Shakespeare's final homecoming.[29]

The opening invocation of 'Good Frend', drenched with inter-textual echoes of Shakespeare, invites the reader to join with those semi-mythical figures who have also laid their symbolic flowers on the poet's grave, in solitary, triumphant or heart-broken homecoming:

> Come as you will, but I came home
> Driven by *The Tempest*; you may come,
>
> With banner or the beat of drum;
> You may come with laughing friends,
>
> Or tired, alone; you may come
> In triumph, many kings have come
>
> And queens and ladies with their lords,
> To lay their lilies in this place,
>
> Where others, known for wit and song,
> Have left their laurel; you may come,
>
> Remembering how your young love wept
> With Montague long ago and Capulet.

(p. 5)

It is significant that H.D. begins by recording these numerous Shakespearean pilgrimages and declaring her own participation in them, and only subsequently turns to an examination of the play's *dramatis personae* and to meditations on the historical voyage of the *Sea-Adventure*, Shakespeare's presumed source for *The Tempest*, and on the occasion of his play's first performance. The historical texts and contexts are already overwritten for the modern reader by the cultural mythology which has secured Shakespeare's survival, and which provides the occasion for the poem – the celebration of Shakespeare Day:

That was yesterday or day before yesterday;
Today (April 23, 1945, to be exact),
We stand together ...

(pp. 7–8)

The meaning of that date is emphasised by the dual dedication of *By Avon River*, 'For BRYHER Shakespeare Day April 23, 1945 & ROBERT HERRING St. George [sic] Day April 23, 1945'. The personal significance of this dedication has been explicated by Susan Stanford Friedman ('Remembering Shakespeare Differently', p. 144), and its public implications, within an English context, are also clear. But H.D. eschews the political, and presents the pilgrims' encounter with Shakespeare on this overdetermined date as a private, intimate experience, which, in its echo of the Song of Songs, has both religious and erotic overtones:

Tenderly, tenderly,
We stand with our flowers,
Our beloved is ours,
Our beloved is ours,
To-day? Yesterday?

(p. 9)

This association is developed and extended to embrace Claribel in Part II of 'Good Frend', entitled 'Rosemary':

And still the bells sway,
*My beloved is mine
    and I am his*;
And still the bells say,

The king's fair daughter
Marries Tunis; O spikenard,
Myrrh and myrtle-spray,
'Twas a sweet marriage.

(p. 11; italics present in original)

These lines echo the final fragment of the first section, 'The Tempest', and are further repeated as a kind of refrain later in this section. The troublesome marriage with the African king is here endowed with positive associations by being linked with the Song of Songs and with the plants celebrated in esoteric lore, which, as

[111]

the title indicates, are particularly important in this section of the poem.

'Rosemary' also offers the most fully developed exploration of Claribel's identity and function within H.D.'s text. Her very absence and silence are reconstructed as productive of language, evoking the speech and action of other women as she is defined, in a rhetorical move which is commonplace in H.D.'s poetry, by means of a series of negatives:

> I had no voice
> To chide the lark at dawn,
> Or argue with a Jew,
> Be merciful;
>
> I had no wit
> To banter with a clown,
> Or claim a kingdom
> Or denounce a throne;
>
> I had no hand
> To snatch a dagger,
> Or pluck wild-flowers,
> For a crown.

(p. 16)

Defining herself as absence and lack, Claribel simultaneously conjures up a vivid picture of her more fully realised Shakespearean sisters. Elsewhere H.D. offers a litany of names which represents the powerful presence in her own imagination of the many assertive, memorable female characters created by Shakespeare, including Rosalind, Juliet, Marina and Helena, and asks herself,

> Knowing these and others well,
> Seeing these whom I have loved,
>
> Hearing these – why did I choose
> The invisible, voiceless Claribel?

(p. 14)

She finds the answer when she allows Claribel to take on her own voice, to speak in her own poem:

I only threw a shadow
On his page,
Yet I was his,
He spoke my name;

He hesitated,
Raised his quill,
Which paused,
Waited a moment,

And then fell
Upon the unblotted line;
I was born,
Claribel.

(p. 15)

The reference to the 'unblotted line', evoking Ben Jonson's famous comment on the fluency of Shakespeare's writing, allows the textual birth of Claribel to stand as a representative image of Shakespearean creativity. H.D. does not fall into the sentimental trap of rescuing Claribel from the constraints of textuality; she is still no more than a shadow, a black mark on a white page, a name spoken and possessed by her male creator. Nevertheless, evanescent as she is, Claribel becomes for H.D. a key symbol of creativity and regeneration in Part III of 'Good Frend', 'Claribel's Way to God'. Here she ceases to be Shakespeare's creation and acquires an autonomous existence as she moves beyond the boundaries marked out for her in *The Tempest*, undertaking her own pilgrimage to the source of the female-centred esoteric tradition manifested in courtly love poetry and the worship of Sophia, the female incarnation of 'Wisdom, the Supernal Light' (p. 23) and 'Mary-of-the-Lily' (p. 25).

In 'The Guest' this esoteric tradition is presented still more emphatically as the source of Shakespeare's unique, historically transcendent genius and the organising principle of his entire dramatic and poetic output. The structuring conceit of 'Good Frend' – a woman writer's homecoming pilgrimage to Shakespeare's grave – is symmetrically matched by the ending of 'The Guest', which depicts Shakespeare's death as a home-coming enabled by the mediation of a creative female principle:

[113]

It was Judith, it was Juliet, it was Queen Eleanor. It was a plum-coloured sleeve and the shadow of a thin hand and the feel of the glass stem between his thumb and finger ... It was keeping back something. They had all, always kept back something. The metres ran on, recklessly or bound or ruled ... But something snapped. It was not the Venetian glass stem. He had come home because he loved Judith (p. 96).

H.D.'s answer to the historical silencing of Shakespeare's women, of whom Judith, I suggested in Chapter 1, has been the archetype, is to show that the female principle has always been at the heart of his writing. However, she avoids the danger implicit in such mysticism – of allowing women access to creativity only passively, as the male poet's Muse – by inscribing herself as writing subject into the structure of her text, and by writing beyond the plot of *The Tempest* to offer Claribel an alternative existence as subject of her own story. Shakespeare's Judith may remain regrettably silent, but the 'living tradition' (p. 30) of which Claribel is part enabled H.D. to make her own voice heard.

Snapshots of Caliban

Introducing *Snapshots of Caliban* to readers of her selected writings, *Because of India*, Suniti Namjoshi identifies it as part of a project to 'explore the bloodier aspects of gay liberation and women's liberation – things to do with who one loved, how and why it hurt, and what about the family' (p. 83). This reinflects an earlier version of the same statement which makes the poetic voicing of identity central: 'I thought I was tackling the bloodier aspects of women's liberation and gay liberation, but I think now that I may also have made some headway in taking the lesbian feminist perspective as central.'[30] Together, these two passages suggest that the writer's task is to transform the voice and point of view of poetry in ways which have ethical and political implications. Specifically, *Snapshots of Caliban* represents Namjoshi's attempt to address in poetic form a series of questions which have far-reaching ethical, epistemological and political implications:

for some time now I had been asking the question, what was my place in a world that often seemed absurd to me? All right, I was a lesbian, a lesbian feminist. But what was a lesbian? What was her relation to other people? And what about the problem of warring egos? Surely a cause, however just, had to be something more than the mere prevention of one set of egos from dominating another set of egos (*Because of India*, p. 83).

What, however, is the authority of such comments in relation to the interpretation of Namjoshi's poetry? Phrased as a series of tentative questions, this sketch of the concerns of *Snapshots of Caliban* resists the status of manifesto. The elliptical, ironic modes Namjoshi favours both resist assimilation to a facile polemical notion of what it means to write 'political poetry' and elude the anchoring of literary interpretation in extra-textual constructions of the author's identity. Yet in published articles on her own work, and on what it means to her to be a poet, Namjoshi insists on the cultural, historical and political specificity of her writing. To quote Craig Topping's recent analysis of her place among the burgeoning group of diasporic Indian writers who are inscribing new subjectivities and new voices in American literature,

> [her] use of revisionary fable and fragmented myth suggests a much wider range of imperialising discourses, including those of gender and sexuality ... The prevalent power of such naturalised discourses has previously outlawed and silenced the kinds of writing and history that Namjoshi's subversively comic writing strategies now evoke ... Truth, presence, and verifiably witnessed history are all called into question by [this] would-be discreet confessionalist. In that process, post-colonial literature is born.[31]

Why, then, does she choose *The Tempest* as the pre-text on which to found her exploration of the problem of warring egos, and how do her ironic, subversive and fragmentary strategies transform the meanings of Shakespeare's text?

On my first reading of the sequence – influenced, perhaps, by the work I had already done on Caliban-centred appropriations of *The Tempest* by post-colonial writers – I assumed that a single voice spoke in those sections of the text which were not marked as being by Prospero or Miranda; that it was to be identified with Caliban; and that this voice of resistance could be aligned with the authorial position *vis-à-vis* the text. On rereading, however, I came to feel that the question of who is speaking, and from what subject position, is actually far more elusive. One strand of feminist work on lyric poetry by women has suggested that the European lyric tradition actually makes it very difficult for the woman poet to claim a voice of her own, and Namjoshi often appears to concur with this view, extending it to emphasise the particular difficulties faced by the lesbian writer who seeks to locate her work in relation to that tradition:

> despite the richness of the poetic tradition, its whole universe was a rigidly heterosexual one, at the centre of which was a long continuity of male consciousness, which was itself patriarchal in its assumptions about all forms of order: the divine order, the meaning of history, the social order ... The real problem was not the lesbianism of the lesbian poet, but the male-centred heterosexualism of the lyric tradition.[32]

This emphasis on the limitations of the lyric tradition is problematised, in practice, by the many different poetic forms and voices which Namjoshi uses in her work. It is arguable, for instance, that *Snapshots of Caliban* is a descendant of Browning's 'Caliban upon Setebos' in its use of dramatised voices to re-imagine the relations between Shakespeare's characters.[33] The journey which Shakespeare's Prospero makes in order to be able both to renounce the magical source of his power over the island, and to acknowledge his own 'thing of darkness', is paralleled in Namjoshi's sequence by an even more fraught and ambivalent journey towards the acknowledgement of emotional responsibility, and an interdependence which does not have to be shot through with hostility, on the part of Caliban and Miranda as well as Prospero.

In the first poem of the sequence, an unidentified voice speaks:

> Not wrong to have wanted you,
>   but wrong
> should the desire, being thwarted,
>   turn to rage.
> And there is rage.
>   Cal, Cal, Caliban
> threshes her limbs. For this -
>   pardon.
> I and my creature
>   must seek for grace.

(p. 85)

This terse, elliptical stanza is typical of many poems in the sequence in that we cannot know whether the desire and rage are to be attributed to the speaker, to Caliban or to an unknown third person; neither is it clear whether pardon is being sought or granted. The echoes of Shakespeare's Caliban in the song and the declaration of apparent contrition are contradicted by the assertion of mastery implicit in the phrase 'I and my creature', which seems most appropriate to Prospero. These numerous undecidabilities exist in tension with the various possible interpretations of Shakespeare's *Tempest* which hover behind Namjoshi's text; yet the feminisation of Caliban marks a very clear departure both from the original and from prior re-creations of the play.

The final poem of the sequence, placed under the name of Prospero, makes this tangle of identity, acknowledgement and projection more explicit:

> I made them? Maiden and monster
> and then disdained them?
> Was there something in me
> that fed and sustained them?
> Are they mine or their own?
> I dare not claim them.

(p. 102)

The anonymity of the first poem, and the lack of linear narrative throughout the sequence mean that this shift towards acknowledgement of the other's existence in relation to the speaking self cannot be seen as development or progress. Prospero gets the last word, but in comparison with his Shakespearean counterpart he remains puzzled and powerless. If he 'dare not claim them', is that because he recognises that he has no right to do so, or because he is afraid to admit to his own responsibility and involvement with Miranda and Caliban? The use of questions which necessarily remain unanswered, and the intricately woven sound patterns, keep the snare of uncertainty as tight as it was in the first poem. Namjoshi's exploration of 'the problem of warring egos' does not offer any easy solutions.

Within the sequence, just five of the seventeen poems are attributed to named speakers. Amongst the others, two (XIV and XVI) are clearly voiced by Caliban, two (XI and XV) by Miranda, while the identity inscribed in the remaining poems is ambiguous.

My interpretation, based on intertextual resonances with Shakespeare's text and the thematic preoccupations of *Snapshots of Caliban*, is that it is Prospero who speaks in I, II, III, VI, XII and XIII, but clearly the deliberate ambiguity of these poems is what should be emphasised. The structure of the sequence thus enacts the painful and ambivalent entanglements between the speakers, the complexity of the negotiations in which they engage in their attempts to escape from the deadlock of 'warring egos', and the difficulty of locating and maintaining psychic boundaries between them, which are made explicit in the first and last poems. The central poem of the sequence, 'Prospero's Meditations', embodies this dynamic in one of Namjoshi's favourite forms, allegory:

> Two monsters are crawling out of my eyes
> and onto the sand, scrabbling and scuttling,
> climbing and sliding on top of one another,
> tipping over stones, doing themselves,
> and one another too, some damage perhaps.
> Of the two crabs, which is more dainty?
> Which one of the two least crab-like?
> Most graceful? Is there a lovelier sheen
> on one curved carapace, a subtler shine?
> Their function escapes me.
> > They have broken their claws.
> Oh my pretty playthings,
> > my shining instruments!

(p. 94)

I take the crabs to represent Caliban and Miranda, in the form of monstrous projections of aspects of the self which are unacceptable to Prospero and which have eluded his control and understanding ('Their function escapes me'). The relationship of difference within similarity which this seems to posit as existing between Caliban and Miranda is unusual in appropriations of *The Tempest*. More commonly, of course, Caliban is paired with Ariel, whose virtual omission from a sequence which explores the play's dynamics of power and desire is perhaps surprising.[34] The poem offers a very bleak picture of Prospero's sense of the relationships between himself, Caliban and Miranda, played out on a desolate psychic landscape. Although the first five lines heap up verbs which connote movement, they are all present participles,

evoking stasis, frantic but futile activity, rather than real movement. And the activity is clearly mutually destructive, with the fear
of 'some damage perhaps' becoming 'They have broken their
claws'; the significance of which for Prospero is that his 'pretty
playthings' are spoiled. Although the repeated questions in the
middle section of the poem seem to imply that one of the mon-
sters is – or should be – more dainty, graceful, subtle and less crab-
like than the other, nevertheless it is impossible for the reader to
distinguish between them, encapsulating the problem of differ-
entiating between different embodiments of rage, desire and ego-
tism which is the key theme of the sequence. As Namjoshi says in
her introduction,

> In *Snapshots of Caliban* I tried to create a female Caliban, with a
> strong ego and a healthy appetite, who just wanted what she
> wanted … [But] I found that though its manifestation differed,
> egoism itself was as central to the voices of Miranda and Prospero as
> it was to Caliban's (pp. 83–4).

Poem IV also exemplifies this point, representing a similar scenario to the one enacted in IX, in less metaphorical form:

> Outside his cell the children are playing.
> 'My sand-castle.' 'No, it's mine.'
> Caliban shouts, Miranda snivels,
> she kicks the castle. Caliban howls
> with bitter rage. Not very pretty,
> these little children. They start
> throwing sand. The sage emerges,
> his lips curled in quiet distaste.
> But the sun has come out. The children
> are happy. The sage withdraws
> to brood once again on the storms
> he will cause, the tempest he'll make.
>
> (p. 88)

Here again Prospero observes a contest for power between Caliban and Miranda, an egotistical struggle which is gently satirised
by being cast in the domestic, faintly comical form of a children's
fight over a sand-castle. Moreover, by juxtaposing this childish
fight with the sage's plans to create storms and tempests, and
emphasising the association by means of the internal rhyme on

[119]

'sage' and 'rage' (a key word in the sequence), the poem implies that they are not so very different from each other, extending the mockery to Prospero himself. At the same time, Prospero remains separate and apart – for eventually the antagonism between Caliban and Miranda will dissolve into complicitous laughter from which Prospero, uncomprehending, is excluded.

In contrast, the first three poems evoke an intense and dangerously intimate relationship between the unidentified speaker and Caliban, based on terrible mutual dependency and likeness:

> And so, we run across the sand:
> the little murderee
>   chased by monstrous me
> trying to save herself
>   and me from me.
>
> (II, p. 86)

The following poem recalls the dreams and circumscribed pleasures in the sights and sounds of the island enjoyed by Shakespeare's Caliban. Using commonplace words like 'strange' and 'brave' which resonate, in context, with their famous usage in Shakespeare's text, Namjoshi echoes her original without trying either to absorb or compete with it poetically. The tone of this segment is surprisingly tender and affectionate, suggesting an alternative to the tangle of antagonisms which underlies the sequence:

> Would I not speak,
>   and approaching her slowly
> try to make friends?
>   Indeed, as I watched the monster,
> would I not feel a monstrous grief?
>
> (p. 87)

Poem VI similarly dwells on this tension between a sense that Caliban has a right to her own identity – one which exceeds or contradicts the desires which others would project on to her – and fear of what acknowledging this autonomous identity might entail:

> ... I fear her dream. For there is something
> I dislike so thoroughly about Caliban:

    if she had her way, she would rule the island,
      and I will not have it.

(p. 91)

But the reader's acceptance of the speaker's point of view here has already been undermined by the previous segment. In this collection of fragmentary extracts from Caliban's journal the rape of which Shakespeare's Caliban is accused becomes 'one day when I said it to myself, "Miranda is nice", and told it to her, she didn't like it' (p. 89), and the fear that Caliban would rule the island if she could is expressed in her wistful claim, 'soon, very soon, I shall people this island (with nice people)' (p. 90).

In so far as Namjoshi's revision of *The Tempest* allows the desire for reconciliation to stand, it is Caliban and Miranda, marginal to the central plot of Shakespeare's play, who begin the communication which will make reconciliation a possibility when they confess their mutual hostility in the penultimate poem of the sequence (XVI). Miranda's contrition here is significant because it is the first moment in the sequence where she explicitly acknowledges her own identity and takes responsibility for her existence and desires, rather than projecting them on to Caliban and Prospero. The first segment in which she speaks, VIII, 'M's Journal', clearly indicates her sense of alienation and confusion:

    Shall I speak to Caliban? I should like to tell her
    how much I hate her.
      Caliban, this is a hate poem.
      You are squat and ugly.
      You are not the noble
        the beautiful other,
      You are part of me.
    But that's wrong, very wrong. Not what I intended to
    write at all. I shall cross it out.

(p. 93)

The typographical experimentation draws attention to the fault line which runs through Miranda's subjectivity, compelling her simultaneously to acknowledge and reject her involvement with Caliban: only the bald statement 'You are part of me' escapes being placed under erasure. It is significant that this self-division first comes to consciousness in writing, in the personal, even

solipsistic form of the journal, and as we have seen is only con-
fessed orally much later in the sequence, in XVI. The extent to
which Miranda derives this tenuous sense of self from her relations with others is further illustrated by poem XI:

> He talked of dukes,
>   palaces and peacocks,
> fabled fountains, many such things.
> He said I was a lady
>   – it was my birthright –
> fit for a king.
>   From his superior knowledge
> he made me a dream.
>   I listened
> and understood clearly
>   in myself I was nothing.

(p. 96)

Prospero speaks to his daughter of fabulous objects which mean
nothing to her; and over the course of the poem it becomes clear
that she herself is such an object, existing principally as a token to
be exchanged between her father and a future royal husband.
Prospero's power is emphasised by the ambiguity of 'he made me
a dream';[35] whether it means that he constructed a dream for
Miranda and implanted it in her unconscious, or that she herself
is the dream which he made, it testifies to his control over her self-
perception, extended in XV:

> Sometimes the airy substance of Miranda
> is beaten so fine that I am the sky,
> the air they breathe, the blueness of their sea.
> I am so pure, so snow-white, I can take
> any colour, fit any mould, be a bird
> or a bush, a thing or a dream.
> And then I know that it is my soul
> and not my body that is stretched so thin.

(p. 100)

It is communication with Caliban which finally enables Miranda
to escape this attenuated condition, when the implicit alliance
between them, excluding Prospero, crystallises in XVI, where they
apologise to each other for their mutual aggression:

We both started laughing. M. said she had not intended to kill me entirely, she had just wanted to make me sick. (I am learning irony.) I thanked her for it. She then explained why she was angry. P. overheard us, but we were not able to explain it to him (p. 101).

The hostility is dissolved and the incipient alliance between the two women which may enable them to evade Prospero's patriarchal control is secured in the beginnings of a communication which is not purely egotistical. The sign of this is the ironic laughter which echoes Namjoshi's preference for humorous, ironic modes in her other works. *Snapshots of Caliban* thus appears to enact the alliance between Caliban and Miranda, rejecting Prospero's colonial power, demanded by feminist critics like Lori Jerrell Leininger and Laura Donaldson. It is significant, though, that this unique appropriation of *The Tempest* by a black woman writer does not engage directly with issues of colonial history and power, but focuses instead on an exploration of the psychic dynamics which inform social structures of domination, of which Prospero's magic is seen to be only one, rather domestic, manifestation.

Indigo

Where H.D. revises *The Tempest* by giving a voice to the silent Claribel and Suniti Namjoshi re-creates the relationships between Caliban, Prospero and Miranda, Marina Warner's transformation of the Shakespearean text centres on Sycorax, Ariel and Miranda. Like Namjoshi, Warner has written of the genesis of her revision of *The Tempest* in the felt need to engage with a sense of the fissures and idiosyncrasies of her own experience and cultural location – more particularly, the fact of her descent from the English family who colonised St Kitt's (the novel's Enfant-Béate):

> My family's Creole past, gainsaid, erased, became the inspiration for *Indigo* … Because our family was involved in an enterprise that so resembles Prospero's theft, that foundation act of Empire, I felt compelled to examine the case, and imagine, in fiction, the life and culture of Sycorax, and of Ariel and Caliban … I wanted to hear their voices in the noises of the isle.[36]

So the third-person narrative point of view of *Indigo* shifts between Sycorax, Ariel and Miranda – the ostensible white British descendant of a Creole plantocracy, whose appearance is nevertheless marked by the sexual imperialism of her forefathers – positioning the experiences and perspectives of these diverse women as subversive and decentring of the Shakespearean narrative. *Indigo* does not presume to offer access to the 'authentic' experience of colonised native women; rather, it self-consciously represents a white author's textualisation of black women's voices. It seems important to me that white feminists should engage imaginatively with the discursive positioning – and indeed the lived experience – of the 'other woman', and such a creative engagement is part of the project of Warner's text. Moreover, in tracing the histories of colonialism, the novel shows that the use of genealogies anchored in physiology to establish taxonomies of racial identity is a flawed and confused project, albeit one which continues to structure social relations.

The novel is divided into four sections, with Miranda's story, narrated in the first and last sections, framing an account of the lives of Sycorax, Ariel and Caliban before and after the seizure of their island by Miranda's colonising ancestor. This structure averts the danger of a sentimental identification with the oppressed in favour of the foregrounding of Miranda's uneasy relationship with the categories of race, class and gender which served for so long to maintain her family's power. Moreover, Miranda's story is itself framed by the tales told by her nurse, Serafine, a native ('as far as anyone can be said to be native at all', p. 382) of that same Caribbean island, Enfant-Béate; tales in which 'everything risked changing shape' (p. 4), told by a woman who is older than Miranda's grandmother and was forcibly separated from her own family, but who nevertheless gives Miranda such mothering as she gets, and indeed ends the novel telling stories and offering maternal care to Miranda's 'real' mother, Astrid. As a descendant of the colonising Everard family who benefits from white privilege but is nevertheless 'kind of a high yellow' (p. 5), 'awfully swarthy' – a fact which, according to her grandfather, matters more for a girl than a chap (p. 237) – Miranda embodies the culmination of the histories set in motion by her ancestors, her racially ambiguous body bearing the marks of centuries of the economically-motivated sexual exploitation of black women by white men. Miranda's father, Kit, who also has 'a touch of the tar-brush' (p. 22), is not ashamed of his 'mixed blood', but resents his schoolboy nickname, 'Nigger': 'The words he knew from the islands themselves he would never let on to them, for they could turn local gradations to their own ends: musty, *métis*, quadroon, octoroon. The slavers had used charts like stockbreeders and tabulated blood degrees to the thirty-second drop' (p. 68). Later, the novel shows us his ancestor, also called Kit Everard, importing slaves from Africa to serve as 'studs' and 'brood mares for the plantation' (p. 177).

The novel's beginning, weaving together Miranda's twentieth-century childhood with Serafine's tales of the islands, places its re-creation of *The Tempest* on the cusp between past and future. The past it recounts begins in 1600, on the island of Liamuiga (later Enfant-Béate), when the first corpses washed overboard from a slave-ship arrive to disrupt the rhythms of Sycorax's life, with an ironic reversal of the encounter between Shakespeare's island woman and her first visitors: 'It was the beginning of a new world for her and her people, the start of a new time, and as yet Sycorax did not know it' (p. 82). The horrors and the wealth of the slave trade are both literalised in the lyrically described 'sea-changes' which the corpses have undergone, and which they voice in Sycorax's dreams:

> Another cried, 'Grit for oysters ...'
> Then another, 'Bonemeal for vines ...'
> And yet another, 'We'll make rich loam ...'
> 'From our carcasses, the melon and the gourd ...'
> 'From our flesh, mermaid's purses, dolphin garlands – Haha!' And
> another seemed to laugh too, and said, 'Blood roses for the coral,
> black dust for the sand ...' (p. 83)

Sycorax's occupation up to this moment has been the making of the indigo from which the novel takes its title, a process which offers a fitting metaphor for the transformations wrought by the novel upon *The Tempest* – a text which is itself already preoccupied with transformation – and upon the histories of colonialism with which it has come to be associated. In material terms, too, it is fitting because the raising of indigo as a cash crop and the production of dyed cloth played an important role in the slave economy of the Caribbean from the seventeenth century to the nineteenth, when production shifted to India.[37] Symbolically, it is an apt metaphor for the effects of colonial exploitation of natural resources and people, for the production of indigo demands the transformation of the landscape to provide dye baths and rinsing water, as well as carrying out a strange metamorphosis of the most thorough and intimate kind on the bodies of the people who produce it:

> Over a decade of dyeing, the indigo stained Sycorax blue ... A blueish bloom lay on her dark skin, blue-black as a damson when it's picked and fingers leave shiny marks on the maroon-purple skin underneath ... Her tongue, too, was blue, from tasting the grain of the indigo after she had ground it ... It was easy to mistake her grey eyes for blue as well (pp. 90–91).

The image of the damson associates Sycorax with the natural fertility of her island, while the artificial blueness of her eyes recalls Shakespeare's Sycorax, the 'blue-eyed hag' (I.ii.269). According to most editors of Shakespeare's text, blueness around the eyes is a sign of pregnancy; Warner's Sycorax, whose children have grown up and who is now too old to have any more, belatedly becomes a mother again by dark and indirect means, when she rescues Dulé – the Caliban figure – from his drowned mother's belly, an act which endows her with the dual role of wise woman and sorceress and thereby isolates her from her community.

At first, Sycorax attributes her powers to heal and transform only to her practical skills and her knowledge of plant lore; but gradually she internalises the community's view of her and comes to believe that the source of her power is magical. Stephen Orgel has shown that despite their overt differences, in Shakespeare's text Prospero and Sycorax are profoundly akin, different manifestations of the ambiguous potential of the magical power first wielded by Medea;[38] while Janet Adelman argues that the Shakespearean abjection of Sycorax's maternal body enables Prospero's appropriation of the generative power of that body.[39] Warner's Sycorax is the vivid embodiment of these tensions and ambiguities; and though she eventually succumbs to the assaults of the white men, her power, symbolised by the fetishised tree which stands in the churchyard, endures as long as that of Shakespeare's text, which it both subsumes and is contained by: 'The isle is full of noises, so they say, and Sycorax is the source of many ... The isle is full of noises' (pp. 77, 210).[40]

Sycorax acquires another child when she is asked to adopt Ariel, the abandoned Arawak girl:[41] like her 'a solitary, a dreamer, [who] doesn't fit in' (p. 97), Ariel will be her companion and help her with the dyeing, which is women's work. Later she is instructed in Sycorax's healing arts, and becomes her assistant in the performance of her magic, echoing the relationship between Prospero and his Ariel. Warner follows other appropriations of *The Tempest* in assigning to Caliban and Ariel different ethnic identities and a different relationship to the colonial power; but for Warner's Ariel, the decision to negotiate with the colonists is less a matter of political strategy than a function of her gender. In feminising Ariel, Warner literalises an aspect of Shakespeare's play, where the various guises Ariel adopts in order to carry out Prospero's bidding are predominantly feminine. The power dynamics of the relationship between Prospero and Ariel in the play are carried over into the relationship between Sycorax and Ariel in the novel, where the change of gender has the effect of recasting them as a daughter's struggle for autonomy from a too-powerful mother. As a result, Ariel's attempt at rebellion is presented as having a political charge which she neither knows nor controls, since it takes the form of her sexual relationship with Kit Everard, with whom she bears the island's first 'musty' child, and leads her inadvertently to betray Dulé/Caliban's planned uprising to Kit. Ariel spends the rest of her life in silent mourning for the disastrous consequences of her fumbled seduction of Kit; but since the narration of history is the prerogative of the victors, her tragedy is re-created as the tale of 'how the first Kit Everard won the love of an islander and how she saved him and his brave band of pioneers' (p. 224), one of the bedtime stories with a happy ending which Serafine will tell Miranda three centuries later.

In its narration of the inaugural moment of colonialism *Indigo* is less interested in the overt rebellion of the Caliban figure than in the fraught and painful negotiations with white male power which Sycorax and Ariel have to undertake. In the final section it explores the historical and political dimensions of the legacy of what Laura Donaldson called 'colonial Prosperity', of which both Caliban and Miranda, in their different ways, represent the victims. The novel's ultimate political preoccupation is with the question of whether some sort of reconciliation between the two of them is historically possible. In search of reconciliation, *Indigo* ends with what the text self-consciously identifies as a somewhat implausible romance, when the nineties Miranda, a commercial artist working for a 'Third World' development agency, meets again the black actor Shaka Ifetabe, formerly George Felix, who twenty years earlier had accused her of sexual colonialism, of being involved in anti-racist politics only because of her desire to 'get a bit of the other' (pp. 263–6).[42] Their second encounter occurs when Miranda walks into a rehearsal of *The Tempest*, in which he is playing Caliban, just in time to hear the stage Miranda's 'Abhorred slave' speech and Caliban's response to it, which prompts her to think 'Oh God, how I'd like to learn me a new language. Beyond cursing, beyond ranting' (p. 388). In this charged situation, her renewed desire for Shaka forces her to acknowledge the extent to which her own identity as a white woman is predicated on a fantasied dialectical relationship with blackness, as both self and other:

> You're trapped in the fantasy, that someone like him could melt you and take you down to the thing you've lost touch with – the longed-for, missing Primitive ... I am such a fucking racist ... even though I of all people shouldn't be. Self-hating, denying my links. But it felt like a fraud when I used to pretend to pass for black in those days. It wasn't any kind of answer ... (pp. 388–9).

Miranda's recognition of the political and historical stakes invested in her desire for Shaka – in her whole identity – is perhaps too glib to be aesthetically satisfying, although her self-conscious political correctness is fictionally motivated by the nature of her job, working as a photographer for a development organisation. As Marina Warner has said, speaking of her own hybrid heritage, 'It's too easy a solution to the problems of the past, to make a few realignments ... The history of denial in the past has forfeited someone like me the right to own in the present to the inheritance, much as I should like to' ('Between the Colonist and the Creole', p. 203). Miranda's awareness of the oppressive weight of history prompts her to dismiss as unrealistic the sudden surge of desire for Shaka Ifetabe which follows from her wish to learn a new language. As she tells herself,

> She wasn't living inside one of Shakespeare's sweet-tempered comedies, nor in one of his late plays with their magical reconcilia-

tions, their truces and appeasements and surcease of pain ... In her world, which was the real world of the end of the century, breakage and disconnection were the only possible outcome (p. 391).

Indigo's clear-eyed retelling of the narratives of shame which have both produced Miranda's fractured sense of identity and erected the very real barriers between her and her desires does not shrink from the painful realities of the post-colonial condition. In the end, though, *Indigo* is itself enough of a romance to allow the possibility of reconnection and healing to exist; and when Miranda and her Caliban – himself a native of Enfant-Béate, but a descendant of the slaves Miranda's family once owned there – eventually bear a daughter whom they name Serafine, the possibility of a different, more hopeful history in the future is tentatively held out.

In their re-creations of *The Tempest*, H.D., Suniti Namjoshi and Marina Warner all succeed in evoking the possibility of a future which is not already scripted by the narratives of shame which record the past. They do this by resisting *The Tempest*'s inscription as a wholly political text, turning away from the public realm which has constructed *The Tempest*'s significance as a document of English colonialism, and seeking refuge, variously, in mysticism; in a tentative lesbian renegotiation of the workings of desire and responsibility; and in the privatised sanctuary of a family which is no less bourgeois for being multi-racial. Yet I would argue that this elision of what Warner calls the 'large narratives' of the public domain does not represent a failure to engage with the politics of colonialism so much as a translation of the play's exploration of magic, power and desire into the subjective, feminised realm whose exclusion from Shakespeare's play is fully as political as its overt preoccupations with the exercise of public power. In making central what was excluded, then, these women's transformations of *The Tempest* enact a reimagining of its cultural significance which holds out the possibility of changing the political terms on which we make sense of the play.

Notes

1 *Indigo, or Mapping the Waters* (London, Chatto & Windus, 1992).
2 The poem is quoted from a memorial erected in 1648 to Sir Thomas

Warner, founding settler of St Kitt's and Marina Warner's ancestor: see her essay, 'Between the Colonist and the Creole: Family Bonds, Family Boundaries', in Shirley Chew and Anna Rutherford (eds), *Unbecoming Daughters of the Empire* (Hebden Bridge, Dangaroo, 1993), pp. 197–204.

3　London, Macmillan, 1949.

4　First published in *From the Bedside Book of Nightmares* (1984); reprinted in *Because of India: Selected Poems and Fables* (London, Onlywomen, 1989) – I refer to this edition.

5　A full bibliography is beyond the scope of this chapter, but see for example Paul Brown, '"This thing of darkness I acknowledge mine": *The Tempest* and the Discourse of Colonialism', in Jonathan Dollimore and Alan Sinfield (eds), *Political Shakespeare: New Essays in Cultural Materialism* (Manchester, Manchester University Press, 1985), pp. 48–71; Thomas Cartelli, 'Prospero in Africa: *The Tempest* as Colonial Text and Pretext', in Jean E. Howard and Marion O'Connor (eds), *Shakespeare Reproduced: The Text in History and Ideology* (London, Methuen, 1987), pp. 99–115; George Lamming, 'A Monster, a Child, a Slave', in *The Pleasures of Exile* (London, Allison and Busby, [1960] 1984), pp. 95–117; and Octave Mannoni, *Prospero and Caliban: The Psychology of Colonisation*, trans. Pamela Powesland (New York, Praeger, [1950] 1964). For a comprehensive survey, see Alden T. Vaughan and Virginia M. Vaughan, *Shakespeare's Caliban: A Cultural History* (Cambridge, Cambridge University Press, 1991).

6　'Caribbean and African Appropriations of *The Tempest*', *Critical Inquiry*, 13 (1987), 557–77 (577). Apart from *Indigo* I am not aware of any other appropriations of *The Tempest* with a central focus on colonial issues having been produced since Nixon's article was published, although there have undoubtedly been theatrical productions which explore colonialism. The most celebrated adaptations of the last few years – Peter Brook's production of *La Tempête* at the Théâtre des Bouffes du Nord (1990) and Peter Greenaway's film *Prospero's Books* (1991) – shared a turn away from 'political' approaches, as they are conventionally understood, and a focus on the power of Prospero's magic.

7　'Rewriting *The Tempest*', *World Literature Written in English*, 23 (1984), 75–88 (77). Brydon both extends and revises this analysis in a more recent article, 'Sister Letters: Miranda's Tempest in Canada', in Marianne Novy (ed.), *Cross-Cultural Performances: Differences in Women's Revisions of Shakespeare* (Urbana and Chicago, Ill., University of Illinois Press, 1993), pp. 165–84, offering an account of Suniti Namjoshi's *Snapshots of Caliban* which shares some common ground with my reading, although our conclusions differ substantially.

8 *Sister's Choice: Tradition and Change in American Women's Writing* (Oxford, Clarendon Press, 1991), pp. 27, 28. Showalter's preoccupations are very similar to mine, although we discuss different writers – she cites re-creations of *The Tempest* by Margaret Fuller, Harriet Beecher Stowe, Louisa May Alcott, Katherine Anne Porter, Sylvia Plath and Gloria Naylor – and, as I showed in Chapter 1, I disagree with her judgement that the rewriting of Shakespearean texts by black, 'Third World' or female authors is an essentially conservative and self-defeating strategy (p. 41).

9 'The Miranda Trap: Sexism and Racism in Shakespeare's *Tempest*', in Carolyn Ruth Swift Lenz, Gayle Greene and Carol Thomas Neely (eds), *The Woman's Part: Feminist Criticism of Shakespeare* (Urbana, Ill., University of Illinois Press, 1980), pp. 285–294 (p. 291). The impact of feminist and post-colonial thought on Shakespeare criticism is signalled by the inclusion of Leininger's essay in the most recent Signet edition of *The Tempest* (1987).

10 Theobald, for instance, felt that it would be 'in some sort an indecency in her to reply to what Caliban was last speaking of'; Capell concurred in wanting to exculpate Shakespeare from such an indecency, suggesting that the speech was attributed to Miranda by the players to break up the long period of silent inactivity which characterises the role in this scene. For these and other instances, see H. H. Furness (ed.), *A New Variorum Edition of Shakespeare, 'The Tempest'* (London, Lippincott's, 1892), p. 73. Modern editors usually assign the speech to Miranda, though this may have as much to do with changed notions about dramatic character and an increased preference for avoiding substantial emendation as with sexual politics.

11 *Decolonizing Feminisms: Race, Gender and Empire-Building* (Chapel Hill, NC, University of North Carolina Press, 1992).

12 On changes in the legal and discursive status of rape in the late sixteenth and early seventeenth centuries, see Lorraine Helms, '"The High Roman Fashion": Sacrifice, Suicide, and the Shakespearean Stage', *PMLA* 107 (1992), 554–65 (557–8); and Marion Wynne Davies, '"The Swallowing Womb": Consumed and Consuming Women in *Titus Andronicus*', in Valerie Wayne (ed.), *The Matter of Difference: Materialist Feminist Criticism of Shakespeare* (Hemel Hempstead, Harvester, 1991), pp. 129–51 (pp. 130–1).

13 In contrast, Ania Loomba argues powerfully for *The Tempest*'s complicity in upholding the myth of the black rapist as crucial to the exercise of colonial and patriarchal power, in *Gender, Race, Renais-*

sance Drama (Manchester, Manchester University Press, 1989), pp. 148–51.

14 For a variety of perspectives on the politics of the canon and its relation to higher education syllabuses, see the special feature in the *Times Higher Education Supplement*, 24 January 1992, 15–19.

15 SCEPCHE was the Standing Conference on English in Polytechnics and Colleges of Higher Education. The survey was carried out by Tim Cook of Kingston University for *PACE*, the SCEPCHE newsletter. I am very grateful to him for providing me with a copy of the survey report and samples of the press coverage.

16 Tim Cook, 'PACE Canon Survey Report', *PACE*, Spring 1992, 3–5 (5).

17 These opinions are attributed to one Arthur Pollard, whose ideological position is perhaps sufficiently indicated by the fact that he is Professor Emeritus of the University of Buckingham.

18 'Shakespeare and the Tyranny of Feminism', *Evening Standard*, 4 February 1993, 17.

19 For an indication of the extraordinary range and diversity of feminist criticism of Shakespeare see Philip C. Kolin (ed.), *Shakespeare and Feminist Criticism: An Annotated Bibliography and Commentary* (New York, Garland, 1991).

20 Peter Erickson, *Rewriting Shakespeare, Rewriting Ourselves* (Berkeley, Calif., University of California Press, 1991), pp. 111, 117.

21 *The Epistemology of the Closet* (London, Harvester, 1991), p. 50.

22 Liz Yorke, *Impertinent Voices: Subversive Strategies in Contemporary Women's Poetry* (London, Routledge, 1991), p. 1.

23 See my discussion of Derek Jarman's *Tempest*, Chapter 5 below.

24 Susan Stanford Friedman's article, 'Remembering Shakespeare Differently: H.D.'s *By Avon River*', in Marianne Novy (ed.), *Women's Revisions of Shakespeare* (Urbana, Ill., University of Illinois Press, 1989), pp. 143–64, represents the first substantial critical discussion of *By Avon River*. Raffaella Baccolini's unpublished Ph.D. thesis, 'Tradition, Identity, Desire: H.D.'s Revisionist Strategies' (University of Wisconsin, Madison, 1990) extends the process.

25 Susan Stanford Friedman, 'Exile in the American Grain: H.D.'s Diaspora', in Mary Lynn Broe and Angela Ingram (eds), *Women's Writing in Exile* (Chapel Hill, NC, University of North Carolina Press, 1989), pp. 87–112 (p. 89).

26 *Tribute to Freud* (Oxford, Carcanet, [1956] 1971), pp. 109–10.

27 *Colonial Encounters: Europe and the Native Caribbean, 1492–1797* (London, Methuen, 1986), p. 112.

28 *The Stranger in Shakespeare* (London, Croom Helm, 1973), p. 203.

29 'Of William Shakespeare, alone, can we visualize a chair drawn up before an open window, an apple-tree in blossom, a friend or two

and children' (p. 34); 'we are thinking of the Knotte Garden. How design it? ... Judith understood what he wanted with the garden' (pp. 35–6); 'the delicate fragrance of the flowers with the too-long green-white stems that he held toward Mary Arden' (p. 87); 'He held the flowers toward her. He had forgotten what she called them – not deadmen's-fingers anyway' (p. 92); 'he felt them, *things in heaven and earth* – and knew that the flowers would be different and the flowers would be the same' (p. 95). Flower imagery recurs in a very high proportion of the numerous Renaissance poems quoted in the essay.

30 'Rose Green Alone', in Betsy Warland (ed.), *InVersions: Writings by Dykes, Queers, and Lesbians* (Vancouver, Press Gang Publishers, 1991), pp. 45–55 (p. 49).

31 'South Asia/North America: New Dwellings and the Past', in Emmanuel S. Nelson (ed.), *Reworlding: The Literature of the Indian Diaspora* (New York, Greenwood Press, 1992), pp. 35–50 (p. 39).

32 Gillian Hanscombe and Suniti Namjoshi, '"Who wrongs you, Sappho?" – Developing Lesbian Sensibility in the Writing of Lyric Poetry', in Jane Aaron and Sylvia Walby (eds), *Out of the Margins: Women's Studies in the Nineties* (London, Falmer Press, 1991).

33 Robert Browning, 'Caliban upon Setebos' (1864), in *Robert Browning: Selected Poetry*, ed. Daniel Karlin (Harmondsworth, Penguin, 1989), pp. 188–94.

34 Ariel is mentioned in VII, but does not speak or act within the frame of the sequence. Pairings of Caliban and Ariel have included post-colonial approaches which cast Ariel as the 'good nigger' who chooses to align his interests with those of the colonial power, while Caliban represents rebellion against it; see Griffiths, '"This island's mine"'. Alternatively, one might think of the 1950s science-fiction film *Forbidden Planet*, which has Caliban as a lethal projection of the Prospero figure's id, Ariel as his super-ego.

35 Dreams are a significant recurring element in the sequence, as in Shakespeare's play: VII 'From Caliban's Notebook', declares 'They dreamed it. There was no storm, / no shipwreck, nobody came.' (p. 92); in VIII Miranda laments, 'All my pretty dreams smashed and broken', blaming Caliban (p. 93).

36 Warner, 'Between the Colonist and the Creole', p. 201.

37 Marsha Rowe, 'Shadow on Blue', in her *Sacred Space* (London, Serpent's Tail, 1991).

38 In the Introduction to his edition of the play, Orgel argues that Sycorax is based on Ovid's account of Medea in Book VII of the *Metamorphoses*, and points out that Prospero's valediction to his magic in V.i. uses the words of Ovid's Medea (William Shakespeare, *The*

Tempest, ed. Stephen Orgel (Oxford, Clarendon Press, 1987), pp. 19–20).

39 *Suffocating Mothers*, p. 237.

40 The Shakespearean phrase opens and closes the central section of the novel, which narrates the colonisation of the island.

41 Warner acknowledges Peter Hulme's *Colonial Encounters* as a source of inspiration, and her depiction of Ariel is clearly influenced by his account of Arawak culture.

42 On the usefulness of this colloquial phrase as a designation for the post-colonial entanglement of sexual and racial politics, see Suzanne Moore, 'Getting a Bit of the Other: The Pimps of Post-Modernism', in Rowena Chapman and Jonathan Rutherford (eds), *Male Order: Unwrapping Masculinity* (London, Lawrence and Wishart, 1988), pp. 165–92.

Chapter 4

'Strange worship': Oscar Wilde and the key to Shakespeare's *Sonnets*

Who was that young man of Shakespeare's day who, without being of noble birth or even of noble nature, was addressed by him in terms of such passionate adoration that we can but wonder at the strange worship, and are almost afraid to turn the key that unlocks the mystery of the poet's heart? Who was he whose physical beauty was such that it became the very corner-stone of Shakespeare's art; the very source of Shakespeare's inspiration; the very incarnation of Shakespeare's dreams?[1]

Oscar Wilde's tale *The Portrait of Mr. W.H.* constructs a narrative which claims to explicate the relationship between Shakespeare and the young man to whom the vast majority of his Sonnets are presumed to be addressed – the young man of whom Wilde speaks with wonder and fascination in this resonant passage. *The Portrait of Mr. W.H.* offers an account of this relationship which purports, in terms which recur insistently in connection with the *Sonnets*, to be 'the only perfect key to Shakespeare's *Sonnets*', a key which will 'unlock the secret of Shakespeare's heart' (*Works*, p. 1160). And just as Wilde suggests that the young man holds the 'key to the mystery of the poet's heart', so the questions of desire and identity raised here will provide the keys to my reading of Wilde's appropriation of Shakespeare. I mean, for instance, the assumption that the poet Shakespeare is to be identified with the persona who speaks in the *Sonnets* and that the poems have a biographical referent; the connection of homoerotic desire with differentiations of social class; the suggestion that a perilous secret lurks behind the door – within the closet, perhaps? – to which the *Sonnets* are the key; the notation of a delight which is simultaneously aesthetic and erotic in the beauty of the youthful male body; and the fact that words like 'adoration' and 'worship' had precisely sexual connotations in the late nineteenth-century sexual subculture of which Wilde was a member.[2] Desire between men generates the work of art, and the notion of the lovely young man as the inspiration of Shakespeare's art, the incarnation of Shakespeare's dreams, crystallises a particular conjunction of homoerotic desire, its object and its representation in a form it has held ever since. Alan Sinfield has recently argued convincingly that many of the features associated with Wilde's life and writing which we take to signal his homosexuality only in fact do so because it was he who brought them together in order to constitute the central terms of one of the most visible forms of modern homosexual identity.[3] I agree, and will argue in this chapter that Shakespeare was central to this act of self-fashioning, which has proved so much more durable and influential than Wilde could have foreseen.

Writing between men

In the first version of *The Picture of Dorian Gray*, published in *Lippincott's Monthly Magazine* in 1890, Basil Hallward, painter of that fatal picture, declares his love to Dorian with the words, 'It is quite true that I have worshipped you with far more romance of feeling than a man usually gives a friend. Somehow, I have never loved a woman.'[4] This passage was excised from the expanded version of the novel when it was published in book form in 1891, and it has been suggested that the motive for this was to protect Wilde from accusations that the story celebrated improper relations between men.[5] Yet even in the 1891 version, Basil still tells Dorian, 'I was dominated, soul, brain, and power by you … I worshipped you.'[6] Considerable interest in this passage was shown by the Marquess of Queensberry's defence in the libel case Wilde brought against him in 1895, the first of the three trials which brought about Wilde's downfall. Representing Queensberry, Edward Carson tried to entrap Wilde into admitting that Basil Hallward's words reflected his own feelings for young men. Wilde refused the snare – insisting as he did through all three trials that works of art find their origin in other aesthetic productions rather than the life of the artist, he declared that '[t]he whole idea was borrowed from Shakespeare, I regret to say – yes, from Shakespeare's *Sonnets*.'⁷ Invoking Shakespeare's name, Wilde distances Basil Hallward's scandalous desires from himself by tracing their genesis not to contemporary experience – although this could have furnished many models, as he undoubtedly knew – but to another literary work; one which was three hundred years old, and written by the most prestigious and authoritative figure in English literature. This attempt to cloak himself in Shakespearean respectability very nearly backfired, however, as Edward Carson retorted, 'I believe you have written an article to show that Shakespeare's *Sonnets* were suggestive of unnatural vice?' – 'On the contrary [responded Wilde] I have written an article to show that they are not. I objected to such a perversion being put upon Shakespeare' (*Trials of Oscar Wilde*, p. 129). Wilde's elegantly equivocal answer – which could be taken to mean either that Shakespeare's *Sonnets* are not guilty of representing love between men, or that there is nothing 'unnatural' and 'vicious' about such love – invokes precisely the biographical account of literary creativity that he had rejected a few moments earlier, in an attempt to disarm Carson's accusation by presenting himself as champion of the national bard's honour. The article mentioned here is, of course, *The Portrait of Mr. W.H.* While I am inclined to agree with Wilde that there is nothing 'unnatural' or 'vicious' about the text, contemporary readers certainly found it strongly suggestive of homoeroticism, and it undoubtedly does carry out an appropriation of Shakespeare and of the cultural authority invested in him which is designed to validate love between men as natural and beautiful. Throughout his career, indeed, Wilde invoked Shakespeare to legitimise the existence and representation of love between men. In *The Portrait of Mr. W.H.* he reinvents Shakespeare's *Sonnets* under the rubric of a theory which is based on a forgery, and which is constructed by means of a homoerotic textual exchange between three men, thus denying the possibility of anchoring the theory's production and meaning to a single, unified and authoritative figure.

At the beginning of *The Portrait of Mr. W.H.* Wilde defines 'Art' as being 'to a certain degree a mode of acting, an attempt to realise one's own personality on some imaginative plane out of reach of the trammelling accidents and limitations of real life' (Maine, p. 1089; *Works*, p. 1150). By detaching the question of the sexuality represented in the *Sonnets* from the possibility of extra-textual or historical ratification in the context of a theory which rests on speculation and forgery, Wilde is constructing an aesthetic response to the 'accidents and limitations of real life' which, at the period when he wrote the story, were already shaping the way he experienced his own sexuality. Within his writings, the complexity and subtlety of the relationship he sets up between acting and being plays a crucial and fruitful role; I discuss its significance in *The Portrait of Mr. W.H.* below. But the notion of acting came to have a dangerous reality for him, in that the legal battle between Wilde and Queensberry turned on the truth or otherwise of the latter's use of the phrase 'posing as a somdomite [*sic*]' to characterise Wilde's self-presentation. The sophistication of Wilde's distinctions between 'acting' and 'real life' – and thus implicitly between 'posing as a sodomite' and actually being one – was at odds with juridical discourse and the combative atmosphere of court, so that in the course of the three trials of 1895 the 'attempt to realise one's own personality' via a form of social performance became a trap, rather than a mode of escape or resistance. Yet the notion of performing an identity, even – or perhaps especially – a marginalised and stigmatised one has remained important in gay culture, functioning in Foucauldian terms as a reverse discourse which has enabled both gay men and lesbians to appropriate the social signifiers of oppression in order to demonstrate defiance and celebration.

Reading *The Portrait of Mr. W.H.* with the benefit of a century's hindsight, Wilde appears uncannily to anticipate these developments, inventing as he does an erotic politics based on camp, innuendo and secret cultural codes – all features which have been seen as characteristic of the modern gay subcultures which, according to one influential historical narrative, were being inaugurated in the 1890s.[8] Wilde's appropriation of Shakespeare is thus a founding moment of a particular version of gay identity which is constructed with reference to notions of performance, genius and the aesthetic. This act of appropriation is wilfully anachronistic: it seizes on the past precisely in so far as it can be made to illuminate or intervene in contemporary concerns. Wilde is not attempting to reconstruct the historical formation of male homosexuality in the Renaissance; rather, he uses Shakespeare's *Sonnets* to celebrate and sustain a self-conscious culture and discourse of male homosexuality in the late nineteenth century.

I want to propose that Wilde's appropriation of Shakespeare can helpfully be analysed as a historically displaced version of the processes of writing between men described by Wayne Koestenbaum in his *Double Talk: The Erotics of Male Literary Collaboration*.[9] Taking Freud's collaborations with Breuer and Fliess as his starting-point, Koestenbaum argues that this activity is inflected by both homoerotic and homosocial dynamics: 'By collaborating with Breuer, Freud sought to fuse male bonding and scientific labour, and to appropriate the power of female reproduction' (p. 18). Koestenbaum's analysis dovetails neatly with Eve Kosofsky Sedgwick's influential account of 'male homosocial desire', which delineates a kind of bonding between men whose erotic interests are presumed to be heterosexual. The integrity of the realm of homosocial desire is maintained by the continued exclusion and oppression of gay men and all women in the interests of facilitating the exchange of power between men and thus maintaining the patriarchal, homophobic status quo.[10] Within this formulation, the distinction between homosocial and homoerotic desire is crucial. The concept of the homosocial proposed by Sedgwick places women as mediators of men's desire for each other. Where the prescribed homo*social* desire to exchange symbolic and material power among men is mapped on to prohibited homo*erotic* desire, the figure of the woman who mediates these exchanges comes to embody the dangers represented by femininity and homosexuality – coded as an effeminate dereliction of the duties of masculinity – both of which have to be repressed in order for these patriarchal transactions to be secured.

Discussing the homosocial context of Shakespearean sexual politics, Stephen Greenblatt has commented that

> Male writers in the Renaissance regard gender as an enduring sign of distinction, both in the sense of privilege and in the sense of significant differentiation. A male in Renaissance society had symbolic and material advantages no woman could hope to attain, and he had them by virtue of separating himself … from women. All other significant differential indexes of individual existence (social class, religion, language, nation) could at least in imagination be stripped away, only to reveal the underlying and immutable natural fact of sexual difference.[11]

It is by no means self-evident that gender had a more fundamental status than all other discourses of difference in the Renaissance. And Greenblatt overlooks the possibility that if gender is indeed to be privileged, it may be because there is a circular relation between sexual difference and social power – since their difference from women was a material source of their power, Renaissance men clearly had a vested interest in maintaining sexual difference as a master discourse. Moreover, this analysis fails to consider that men in twentieth-century society also gain considerable advantages by separating themselves from women and aligning themselves with other men, provided this male bonding is not perceived as sexual. Patriarchy, homophobia and the homosocial exchange of power are thus revealed as mutually interdependent, and the oppressions of gay men and all women as congruent – though by no means identical or coextensive.

The handful of critical discussions of *The Portrait of Mr. W.H.* which have been published in the last few years have mostly been by men and have appeared in contexts which imply or assert the writer's affiliation with gay male identities and politics.[12] My position as a woman and feminist intervening in this exclusively masculine discourse may thus appear to be uncomfortably analogous to that of the women whose function, in the concept of the homosocial which I discuss below, is to facilitate the exchange of cultural capital between men. I do want to stress that my concern here is with discursive positioning, and not with a version of identity politics which would claim that only gay men are entitled to write about male homosexuality, etc. The range of texts discussed throughout this book should make it sufficiently clear that this is not my position. However, I hope to turn this apparently anomalous position to advantage, in that my discussion of Wilde's appropriation of Shakespeare is tacitly informed by a sense of the importance of the intersection of the history and politics of male homosexuality with feminist concerns in relation to sexuality – male and female, gay/lesbian and straight. In terms of Wilde's *fin-de-siècle* milieu, important recent work has explored, for example, the relation of early male homosexual identities to the emergence of the figure of the New Woman (in Wilde's time, as in Shakespeare's, the masculine woman and effeminate man are almost invariably mentioned in the same breath), and the sexual purity campaigns.[13] My focus on the literary relations between

Wilde and Shakespeare and their cultural repercussions does not allow for a thorough exploration of the discourses of male homosexuality which were emerging in late nineteenth-century England, and which crystallised so influentially around the figure of Oscar Wilde; an account which aspired to be definitive would need to interpret these in the total context of the period's sexual politics. What I want to do is to weave together feminist and gay concerns by reading Wilde's appropriation of Shakespeare for the points which reveal their imbrication or the uneasiness of their relation. Because readings of texts as canonical and culturally prestigious as Shakespeare's and Wilde's have their own politics as they circulate in the academy and the world, it seems to me vital that they should not be abandoned by feminist readers, but that we should actively seek to disrupt the circuit of homosocial exchange, at the same time as aligning feminism with antihomophobic critique.

Relevant here is the debate which has raged in recent years about the sexual and institutional politics of the uneasy relationship between the new historicist critique of which Greenblatt's 'Fiction and Friction' is a celebrated example, and the issues prioritised by its academic contemporary, feminist criticism of Renaissance literature.[14] At the end of the 1980s something approaching a consensus existed amongst feminist Renaissance scholars concerning the marginalisation and displacement of women in the work of some of the most prominent new historicists.[15] Within new historicism, a sense that gender and sexuality do constitute crucial sites for the regulation of subjectivity and the exercise of power sometimes appeared to coexist with a queasiness about the material realities of a culture which is both heterosexist and patriarchal, and a desire to maintain a certain distance from the political commitments of the feminist and lesbian/gay movements, which represent primary stigmatised others of this culture. A fruitful way of unpicking these tensions might be via the Bakhtinian conceptual framework elaborated by Peter Stallybrass and Allon White in *The Politics and Poetics of Transgression*, where they speak of 'the political imperative to eliminate the debasing low which conflicts with a desire for [the] Other'.[16] If new historicism's desired Other has often been the absolute patriarchal power whose aura has traditionally endowed the elite cultural productions of the Renaissance with such glamour, then women have come to embody the 'debasing low' which needs to be eliminated from accounts of the Renaissance, lest they should disrupt the Self/Other dyad of powerful male critic/powerful male cultural icon, by introducing an unruly and disruptive third term. This is perhaps one source of the recent fascination in Renaissance scholarship with androgyny, hermaphroditism and cross-dressing: the critic constructs a figure which is both/neither the Same and the Other to be the object of desire. The fetishisation of the doubled figure who, as in Feste's song, is both 'high' and 'low' (*Twelfth Night*, II.iii.39-40), opens up a space where the critic can take pleasure in the erotics of power without becoming locked into a subject position which would also implicate him in this politically charged dialectic of high and low.

Just such a fetishised doubled figure – the effeminate youth Willie Hughes – is central to Wilde's appropriation of Shakespeare in *The Portrait of Mr. W.H.*, where he serves as the feminised, excluded third term which mediates the relationship between the culturally more powerful and prestigious figures of Wilde himself and Shakespeare. Wilde concurs with Greenblatt in perceiving the Renaissance as an 'essentially male culture' (*Works*, p. 1182), with the difference that for him, this culture 'found its fullest and most perfect expression' in gender ambiguity: in the performance of female roles on the stage by young boys. The myth of Willie Hughes facilitates the creation of a homosocial bond between Wilde and Shakespeare – a bond which is then used to valorise love between men. This is achieved in part by means of the appropriation of metaphors of female reproductive capacity in the service of a narcissistic reproduction of the self. This project is also enjoined in the *Sonnets*, and is crucial to the early development of Freud's theories of subjectivity, which were beginning to be formulated at the time Wilde was writing of Shakespeare, and are central to the most committed modern account of Shakespeare's Sonnets as a homoerotic text, Joseph Pequigney's *Such is My Love*. Like Wilde, Pequigney appropriates the *Sonnets* as a historically distant anticipation of contemporary erotic identities, noting 'a remarkable coincidence between Freud's theories of inversion and the bisexual psychology adumbrated in the *Sonnets* ... [S]o well does [Freud's] account accord with the one presented in Shakespeare that the sequence could usefully be considered a proof-text for the psychoanalyst'.[17] While the place of male homosexuality in Freudian theory is intensely controversial, Freud often represented his own intellectual bonds with other men in highly sexualised metaphors; he described himself as having been fertilised by his mentor Charcot, and spoke with pleasurable anticipation of the annual meetings with Fliess which he called 'congresses' (Koestenbaum, p. 36). The erotic investments of Freud's bonds with men thus came to be cathected in the labour of constructing psychoanalysis, a system which was to be of exceptional importance in the interpretation and regulation of modern male homosexuality. In particular, the Freudian concept of narcissism is curiously entwined with the sexual mythology of Shakespeare's time, the structure of desire depicted in the *Sonnets*, Wilde's representation of love between men and the very form of Wilde's appropriation of Shakespeare.

The figure of Narcissus is repeatedly reinflected in those works by Wilde which appropriate Shakespeare to underwrite a myth of homoerotic desire. And the structure of desire embedded in the myth was, of course, associated with homoeroticism long before Freud endowed it with a virtually canonical role in the psychoanalytic formation of homosexual identity;[18] gay poet and critic Gregory Woods has suggested that 'the myth is homosexual, even if male homosexuality (contrary to Freud) only partially and intermittently meets the conditions of the myth'.[19] In noting the cultural longevity of the association of narcissism with homoeroticism, I do not intend to endorse the pathologising role which the concept of narcissism has frequently played in the psychoanalytic regulation of homosexual lives.[20] My preoccupation is rather with the way Wilde rewrites one of the key tropes of Classical and Renaissance representations of sexuality – a trope which represents erotic desire as being grounded in likeness – as a figure for a relation which embodies cultural and erotic generosity within the play of likeness and difference.

Narcissism and literary history

When Narcissus died the pool of his pleasure changed from a cup of sweet waters into a cup of salt tears, and the Oreads came weeping through the woodland that they might sing to the pool and give it comfort.

And when they saw that the pool had changed from a cup of sweet waters into a cup of salt tears, they loosened the green tresses of their hair and cried to the pool and said, 'We do not wonder that you should mourn in this manner for Narcissus, so beautiful was he.'

'But was Narcissus beautiful?' said the pool.

'Who should know that better than you?' answered the Oreads. 'Us did he ever pass by, but you he sought for, and would lie on your banks and look down at you, and in the mirror of your waters he would mirror his own beauty.'

And the pool answered, 'But I loved Narcissus because, as he lay on my banks and looked down at me, in the mirror of his eyes I saw ever my own beauty mirrored.'[21]

Wilde's narcissistic fable, entitled 'The Disciple', can be construed as an elegant allegory of the forms of desire and identification which are invested in his appropriation of Shakespeare. The pool, I suggest, represents Wilde himself, while Shakespeare, of course, is Narcissus, whose generally acknowledged pre-eminence is significant to the mirroring subjectivity of the pool only as a reflection of its own existence. In returning the reflection of Narcissus back to him as the object of his desire, the pool facilitates the deadly satisfaction of that desire at the same time as gratifying its own wish to recognise the reflection of itself in another. The play of difference and identification destabilises the binary relation between subject and other, self and reflection.

The contexts, as well as the content, of Wilde's narcissistic fable, place it within a cultural and textual economy of homosexual exchange. In *The Portrait of Mr. W.H.* Wilde locates Shakespeare's *Sonnets* within a similar economy. Misrepresenting the historical contexts of patronage and manuscript circulation in which the *Sonnets* were originally produced, Wilde states that they were 'for private circulation only among a few, a very few friends' (Maine, p. 1103; *Works*, p. 1167). The *Sonnets* are reconstructed in the image of the homosexual coterie publications with which Wilde himself was involved – magazines such as *The Spirit Lamp* and *The Chameleon*, and the collectively written work of homosexual pornography, *Teleny*. Wilde's narcissistic fable was first published in 1893 in *The Spirit Lamp*, which was edited by his lover Lord Alfred Douglas and acted as the focus of an aesthetically inclined homosexual coterie with which both men were closely involved, and within which the fable had apparently been in circulation for some time before it was published. A self-dramatising private performance of it is related by André Gide in his tribute to Wilde, where he describes a dinner party at a restaurant in Paris in 1891, at which he met Wilde for the first time. Wilde holds forth hypnotically and interminably throughout the meal, and as the select party is leaving the restaurant, he draws Gide aside, telling him that because he appears to 'listen with his eyes', he will be accorded a privileged position as auditor and spectator of Wilde. The Irishman then tells his version of the myth of Narcissus, and Gide concludes his recounting of the incident by noting a remark by Wilde which underscores the significance of the anecdote: 'Puis Wilde, se rengorgeant avec un bizarre éclat de rire, ajoutait: – "Cela s'appelle *Le Disciple*".'[22] Gide's attentiveness to Wilde is rewarded by the latter's engineering of this incident which epitomises the narcissistic and homoerotic pleasures of literary discipleship, even as it places Gide in the role of Wilde's disciple.

Wilde's gesture is essentially a generous one, in that the construction of the tale suggests that neither is Narcissus subjugated to the pool, nor vice versa. The mutually satisfying relationship between the two offers an image of literary discipleship which is not hierarchical, but reciprocal. This is consistent with Wilde's theory of criticism as being always a kind of appropriation, which is itself a work of creation and which tells us as much about the critic as about the work or artist criticised:

> The critic will indeed be an interpreter, but he will not be an interpreter in the sense of one who simply repeats in another form a message that has been put into his lips to say ... [B]y curious inversion, it is only by intensifying his own personality that the critic can interpret the personality and work of others, and the more strongly this personality enters into the interpretation, the more real the interpretation becomes, the more satisfying, the more convincing, and the more true.[23]

The Portrait of Mr. W.H. enacts this process, constituting both a work of art and a work of criticism, and thereby substantiating Wilde's claim that literature is inextricable from interpretation. This process of making interpretations of works of literature and literary history under a homoerotic rubric is extended in the lovingly detailed study of the important but ambivalent relationship between Wilde and Gide as homosexual artists which plays a crucial role in Jonathan Dollimore's recent *Sexual Dissidence*. Here, Wilde's appropriation is in turn appropriated for the construction of a narrative which makes aestheticised conversations between writers a key element in the construction of a particular account of modern gay identity.[24]

At the beginning of a recent book which seeks to historicise the ways in which early modern culture could represent men's desire for each other, Bruce Smith warns that the reader should,

> heed Ovid's tale of Narcissus ... [and] delight in what we find not so much because it reflects our own self-image as because it invites us to look at that image in new ways. We should come away, like the Elizabethan voyagers, possessed of a wider world in which the imagination can play.[25]

The admonitory use of the figure of Narcissus at the beginning of a book on homosexuality is clearly highly overdetermined. Implicitly addressing a gay male readership, Smith assumes that 'people read literature of the past to enhance their lives in the present', an assumption which is often an important motivating factor in work on the history of sexuality. However, he is anxious that the emotional and political desires which often attach to this approach to literary history should not generate a sort of anachronistic narcissism, whereby the past is returned to the reader only as an image of his or her own present. This anxiety is at the heart of one of the key issues for the nascent project of gay (and lesbian) history/historiography: the difficulty of identifying exactly what constitutes its object of study, and its relationship to the past.

To schematise, there have been two main lines of enquiry: the social-constructionist approach, closely associated with the work of Michel Foucault,[26] which dates the invention of the modern homosexual from the late nineteenth century, and is chary about the extent to which twentieth-century categories are appropriate for talking about earlier manifestations of same-sex desires and practices at all; and the approach hinted at in the title of the essay collection *Hidden from History*, which suggests that a continuous but subterranean current of gay and lesbian history is waiting to be discovered by the contemporary gay-affirmative historian.[27] While it is clearly anachronistic to map the constructions and characteristics of modern gay identity back on to a period earlier than about 1870, nevertheless that does not mean that it is impossible to find or reconstruct any sort of categories for talking about homoerotic desires and identities prior to that time. In other words, to say that the modern form of homosexual identity did not exist before the word 'homosexual' was coined in 1869 is not necessarily to say that same-sex relationships or sexual practices had no cultural meaning before that time. The evident impossibility and undesirability of projecting back on to the past the categories which are at play in the late twentieth-century West for making sense of sexual identity does not mean that the past was totally devoid of such categories, although the understanding of both sexuality and identity involved in constructing them is more than likely to be very different from our own. Bruce Smith's book is just one example of many recent attempts to find out what sort of languages were available in the past for talking about same-sex desires.[28] Whereas I see the present discussion of Wilde's use of Shakespeare as a further contribution to this project, I am not going to suggest that this is also what was at stake for Wilde himself. On the contrary, I contend that the dynamic of narcissistic anachronism against which Bruce Smith warns us is exactly what is at play in Wilde's appropriation of Shakespeare. What, then, was the nature of this appropriation?

'The only perfect key to Shakespeare's *Sonnets*'

Flatteringly, Shakespeare, the outstanding figure of English literature, was invoked by many of Wilde's early reviewers, both as a direct influence on his poetry and as the gold standard against which the talent of the ambitious young writer was to be measured.[29] But this association could also be put into play to satirise what hostile critics perceived as Wilde's aesthetic posturing and self-aggrandisement. A *Punch* cartoon of 1892, satirising the opening of *Lady Windermere's Fan*, shows Wilde leaning langorously on a pile of fashionable French novels, smoking a cigarette and manipulating a group of young aesthetes like puppets, while a bust of Shakespeare – presumably displaced from his pedestal by the novels – reels in horror on the floor. The caption mockingly identifies the caricatured figure as 'Shakespeare Sheridan Oscar Puff, Esq.', stigmatising Wilde's self-promoting decadent affectations by contrasting him unfavourably with the glories of the dramatic past.[30] Apparently unabashed by such satire, in both his writings and the social self-presentation which formed almost as substantial a part of his *œuvre* Wilde liked to weave a net of allusions which implied a special kinship between himself and Shakespeare. He once told Lady Archibald Campbell – a society figure and contributor to the magazine *The Woman's World*, which Wilde edited – that he thought he looked like Shakespeare, and that he intended to have a bronze medallion made, juxtaposing his own profile with Shakespeare's.[31] According to his biographer Richard Ellmann, Wilde felt there was a certain kinship between himself and Shakespeare, in so far as they were both married men and the fathers of two children when their lives were transformed by love for a teenage boy. In Wilde's case, the adolescent object of his affections, Robert Ross, was his first male lover, who figures as a 'muse' not unlike Willie Hughes.

Ross was seventeen when the encounter took place – the same age, according to *The Portrait of Mr. W.H.*, as Willie Hughes, the addressee of the *Sonnets* and the object of Shakespeare's affections – and Wilde told him 'the story is half yours, and but for you it would not have been written' (Ellmann, p. 281). The background to this assertion is Wilde's claim that he and Ross worked out their theory of the *Sonnets* over a cheap dinner in a Soho cafe. Just as the sonnet theory within the text of *The Portrait of Mr W.H.* is generated between men, in a subcultural setting which privileges friendship, aestheticism and intimate social gatherings, so Wilde traces the origin of the theory to a similar dynamic in his own life. As Neil Bartlett writes, in the course of his own appropriation of Wilde to interpret and underwrite his experience as a gay man, 'the two men [Wilde and Ross] are conjuring a whole tradition, a heady mixture of eroticism and erudition which made literary history into the justification and ennoblement of the love which was the basis of their own culture, the worship of beautiful boys' (*Who Was That Man?*, p. 194). Within *The Portrait of Mr W.H.* the anonymous narrator also identifies with Shakespeare, sharing his erotic fascination with Willie Hughes to the extent of imagining, in one passage, that he actually is Shakespeare watching the object of his desire on stage – and given the fiction's inter-

est in gender ambiguity, the fact that the plays singled out for special attention all involve female characters disguising themselves
as young men is clearly not irrelevant: 'I saw *As You Like It* and
Cymbeline and *Twelfth Night* and in each play there was some
one whose life was bound up into mine, who realised for me
every dream, and gave shape to every fancy' (*Works*, p. 1195).
Relinquishing this fantasy of complete identification, the narrator
nevertheless insists that the Willie Hughes theory of the *Sonnets*
offers him a mirror in which he finds his own desires reflected, a
narrative which recounts 'the whole story of my soul's romance'
(*ibid.*). This moment of recognition that we must look 'in art for
the legend of our days' (p. 1196) – that a fiction of the past may
be the key to making sense of a present which is itself constantly
in process of creation as a work of art, a theory, a forgery – crystallises the entire structure of Wilde's appropriation of Shakespeare.

During his trials, Wilde repeatedly invoked Shakespeare to
affirm the noble, pure and aesthetic nature of his love for Lord
Alfred Douglas ('Bosie'). A key piece of evidence against him was
a love letter he had written to Douglas in thanks for sending him
one of his poems:

My Own Boy,
Your sonnet is quite lovely, and it is a marvel that those red rose-leaf
lips of yours should have been made no less for music of song than
for madness of kisses. Your slim gilt soul walks between passion and
poetry. I know Hyacinthus, whom Apollo loved so madly, was you in
Greek days (*The Trials of Oscar Wilde*, p. 112).

At the trials, this letter was repeatedly used as evidence that there
was an erotic or sexual relationship between Wilde and Douglas;
a charge which Wilde repudiated by arguing that the letter was no
mere personal communication but a work of art, and as such
exempt from the norms of bourgeois moral judgement. He sup-
ported this claim by reference to Shakespeare, insisting under
cross-examination: 'I think it is a beautiful letter. It is a poem. I
was not writing an ordinary letter. You might as well cross-exam-
ine me as to whether *King Lear* or a sonnet of Shakespeare was
proper' (*ibid.*, p. 133). At best, this is dangerously disingenuous,
since Wilde must have known full well that arguments about the
propriety of Shakespeare's *Sonnets* had been raging for a century

by this time. He is trying to counter bourgeois morality as embedded in the legal system in terms of his own oppositional code, and inevitably the attempt is doomed to failure, because what he uses as a defence – the irrelevance to art of accepted canons of normality – is precisely the kind of notion that made so many people want to attack him in the first place.

Midway through the second trial, Wilde responded to the repeated accusations that he practised in his life and represented in his art a love between men which was unnatural and shameful, with a speech which is a classic example of the strategy of justifying gay love by pointing to the great and good homosexuals of the past – summoning up a kind of multi-cultural version of what Quentin Crisp once memorably called the 'stately homos of England':

> 'The love that dare not speak its name' in this century is such a great affection of an elder for a younger man as there was between David and Jonathan, such as Plato made the very basis of his philosophy, and such as you find in the sonnets of Michelangelo and Shakespeare. It is that deep, spiritual affection that is as pure as it is perfect. It dictates and pervades great works of art like those of Shakespeare and Michelangelo, and those two letters of mine, such as they are. It is in this century misunderstood ... It is beautiful, it is fine, it is the noblest form of affection. There is nothing unnatural about it. It is intellectual, and it repeatedly exists between an elder and a younger man (*Trials*, p. 236).

Wilde places his relationship with Bosie as the latest manifestation of an ancient and dignified tradition in which an older man acts as a mentor figure, initiating a younger man into all that is finest about the culture to which he will belong. Significantly, he does not actually deny that it contains any physical or sensual element – such a denial would serve only to draw attention to this possibility – but stresses instead its spiritual and intellectual qualities, just as, in the expanded version of *The Portrait of Mr. W.H.*, he characterises the love between Shakespeare and his boy actor as idealised to the point of mysticism, the embodied 'soul ... of neo-Platonism', comparing it there too to Michelangelo's love for Tommaso Cavalieri (*Works*, pp. 1174–5). In court, this impassioned speech drew applause from many of his listeners; yet as Neil Bartlett has demonstrated, it is not, as one might expect, a spontaneous plea for tolerance, but reworks unconnected passages from *The Picture of Dorian Gray* (*Who Was That Man*, pp. 203-4); it also incorporates material from *The Portrait of Mr. W.H.*[32] Appropriately enough, in Wilde's case Life imitates Art.

In *De Profundis*, the great letter of self-justification written to Bosie from Reading Jail, Wilde reiterates the claim that the incriminating letter was a Shakespearean work of art, while placing it in a context of exclusively masculine but ostensibly desexualised literary exchange between himself and Douglas:

> You send me a very nice poem, of the undergraduate school of verse, for my approval: I reply by a letter of fantastic literary conceits ... The letter is like a passage from one of Shakespeare's sonnets, transposed to a minor key ... It was, let me say frankly, the sort of letter I would, in a happy if wilful moment, have written to any graceful young man of either University who had sent me a poem of his own making, certain that he would have sufficient wit or culture to interpret rightly its fantastic phrases.[33]

Bosie is criticised, not for his bad faith in failing to support Wilde through his ordeal, but for being a bad reader: for failing to interpret correctly the encodements of the nascent homosexual culture. The terms of the rebuke are themselves indicative of the defining characteristics of this culture, which is aesthetically elitist and socially exclusive.

Wilde goes on to enumerate the numerous, increasingly damaging ways in which his Shakespearean letter was misread. His trial and conviction for gross indecency – an event of unique importance in the history of male homosexuality – was structured by a contest for the right to interpret an intimate letter which came to bear the full weight of English cultural authority instantiated by the figure of Shakespeare. To quote Bartlett again,

> What Wilde and the court were contesting was not the evidence, but who had the right to *interpret* that evidence. It is no accident that the line *the Love that dare not speak its name* haunted the trial, and has stayed with us ever since. It is not the love itself which was on trial, since even the law, even our parents acknowledge that some men do have sex with other men. What was on trial was the right to speak (invent and articulate) the name of that love. The question

was, and is, who speaks, and when, and for whom, and why (*Who Was That Man?* p. 149).

If Bartlett is right to assert that what was really on trial in Wilde's three encounters with the English legal system was the right to articulate the name and existence of love between men and the question of who had the right to give voice to this love, then *The Portrait of Mr. W.H.* can be seen as Wilde's principal literary attempt to make Shakespeare speak for the interests of men who loved men.

The 'Willie Hughes' theory of Shakespeare's *Sonnets*, which Wilde playfully offers and withholds in the story, was not in fact his invention. It was first proposed by Thomas Tyrwhitt in 1766, and achieved a certain degree of legitimisation when Edmond Malone endorsed it in his 1790 edition of the *Sonnets*. Like Wilde, Tyrwhitt correlated the initials 'W.H.' in the dedication with the wordplay of sonnet 20 ('A man in hue all hues in his controlling') to arrive at this conclusion. Moreover, for both Tyrwhitt and Malone, as in *The Portrait of Mr. W.H.*, the Willie Hughes theory is bound up with the assumptions that the first 126 sonnets are uniformly addressed to one man, and that they are autobiographical. Although such conjectures had been by no means self-evident before Malone produced his edition, by the time James Boswell came to revise it in 1821 he could note that 'it seems to be generally admitted that the poet speaks in his own person'.[34] The swift assimilation of this understanding of the *Sonnets* into the general culture is signalled by Wordsworth's declaration, in terms which, as we have seen, Wilde was later to endow with a homoerotic inflection, that 'with this key / Shakespeare unlocked his heart'.[35] The possibility that this identification could lead to worrying speculation about Shakespeare's private life was also articulated – and firmly refuted – by Malone: 'Such addresses to men, however indelicate, were customary in our author's time, and neither imparted criminality, nor were esteemed indecorous' (*Plays and Poems*, p. 191).

By Wilde's time, the assumption that Shakespeare's Sonnets were autobiographical was firmly entrenched, though the Willie Hughes theory remained contentious. Wilde floated this theory twice, in the two different versions of *The Portrait of Mr. W.H.* In the second version the sonnet theory itself and the associated reflections on love between men are developed at much greater length, and in ways which substantially alter the significance of Wilde's representation of literary homoeroticism. Both texts, however, share the same narrative frame, which is itself a crucial element of the construction of the theory and of Wilde's appropriation of Shakespeare for gay culture. I do not believe that *The Portrait of Mr. W.H.* is offered as a serious contribution to Shakespearean scholarship – indeed, it could plausibly be seen as a satire on the crazed ingenuity which some scholars have brought to the study of Shakespeare.[36] But as Wilde said, 'to be suggestive for fiction is to be of more importance than a fact',[37] and his fictional use of the *Sonnets* is by no means dependent on the facts with which literary scholarship is traditionally concerned. In an essay on Shakespeare's dramatic use of historical information he asserts that 'the aesthetic value of Shakespeare's plays does not, in the slightest degree, depend on their facts, but on their Truth, and Truth is independent of facts always, inventing or selecting them at pleasure'.[38] Wilde himself was, of course, equally independent of facts throughout his career, and he made a variety of contradictory claims for the truth value of the Willie Hughes theory. This being so, the presentation of the theory in a fictionalised context may well be as significant as its content; so at this point I will briefly summarise the framing narrative.

The tale is recounted by an anonymous narrator, to whom one Erskine tells the story of his dead friend, Cyril Graham, who 'had a strange theory about a certain work of art, believed in his theory, and committed a forgery to prove it' (Maine, p. 1089; *Works*, p. 1150). Cyril believed that, working purely from internal evidence, he had found 'the true secret of Shakespeare's *Sonnets*' (Maine, p. 1092; *Works*, p. 1153): that they are addressed to a boy actor of Shakespeare's company, called Willie Hughes. Erskine is sceptical, and Cyril grows quite desperate when his demand for independent evidence that Willie Hughes actually existed proves hard to satisfy. However, when Cyril suddenly presents Erskine with the portrait of Mr W.H. – found clamped to the side of an Elizabethan chest which he had fortuitously bought at a farmhouse in Warwickshire – his friend is convinced and delighted, and together they prepare an edition of Shakespeare's *Sonnets* to which the portrait will be the frontispiece. Inevitably, Erskine discovers that the portrait is a forgery, and accuses Cyril of dishonesty and of failing to believe in his own theory. They quarrel, and Cyril kills himself in order to prove his faith in the theory. He leaves Erskine the portrait and a suicide note, charging him with the responsibility of giving the theory to the world; believing it to be invalidated by the lack of evidence, Erskine declines to do so.

The narrator, enthralled by this tale of deceit and desire, quickly comes to believe that the theory is 'the only perfect key to Shakespeare's *Sonnets* that has ever been made' (Maine, p. 1099; *Works*, p. 1160), and against Erskine's advice devotes himself to researching it. After three weeks of solitary communing with Shakespeare and Willie Hughes he writes an impassioned letter to persuade Erskine that they must do justice to Cyril Graham's memory by giving his theory to the world. Curiously, as soon as this is done he loses all faith and interest in the whole business. Erskine, however, is by now fully convinced of the truth of the theory, and the narrator's defection sparks off a second quarrel, after which they have no further contact for two years. Then the narrator suddenly receives a letter from Erskine, postmarked Cannes, declaring that he too is going to sacrifice his life for the sake of the Willie Hughes theory. The narrator is distraught: 'To die for one's theological beliefs is the worst use a man can make of his life, but to die for a literary theory! It seemed impossible' (Maine, p. 1111; *Works*, p. 1200). He hastens off to Cannes where he discovers that the late Erskine had in fact known for months that he was dying of consumption, and that he has bequeathed the narrator the portrait of Mr. W.H. The narrator concludes by reflecting that 'there is really a great deal to be said for the Willie Hughes theory of Shakespeare's *Sonnets*' (Maine, p.1112; *Works*, p.1201).

Lord Alfred Douglas, Wilde's companion during the period in the early 1890s when he was revising and expanding *The Portrait of Mr. W.H.*, concurred with this judgement and became fully convinced of the literal truth of the theory, devoting considerable amounts of time in later life to preparing a book which we might see as the edition which Erskine and Cyril failed to publish. In it Douglas criticises Wilde for spoiling a perfectly good theory by wrapping it up in a 'very foolish and unconvincing story'.[39] Douglas sees the *Sonnets* as a homosocial narrative, but not a homosexual one; in his autobiography he declares firmly, 'though I believe it is the fashion nowadays to accuse Shakespeare of having had the same vices as Wilde, this merely shows the ignorance and baseness and stupidity of those who make such accusations'.[40] Rather missing the point of his ex-lover's story, Douglas in his last years became as obsessed as Cyril Graham with the search for documentary evidence of Willie Hughes's existence. Almost incredibly, he found something very much like it, with the discovery in the archives of Canterbury Cathedral of a reference to one Will Hewes, apprentice to shoemaker John Marlowe – Christopher Marlowe's father.[41] It hardly takes an overheated imagination to construct a scenario in which the playwright notices the comely youth and whisks him off to find fame and fortune as a boy player in the theatres of Shakespeare's London – rather as attractive young working-class men could find a niche for themselves in the homosexual subculture in which Douglas and Wilde lived three centuries later.

Regenia Gagnier, one of the best recent critics of Wilde, has noted that according to his contemporary biographers, Frank Harris and Robert Sherard, the critical response to Wilde's Shakespearean narrative was unequivocal: '*Mr. W.H.* confirmed Wilde's homosexuality for many suspicious readers while it simultaneously affirmed the Cause for homosexual coteries.'[42] And yet within the story, the possibility that Shakespeare actually indulged in a specifically homo*sexual* relationship is repeatedly denied. Wilde thus detaches many of the symbolic attributes associated with the representation of homoeroticism from the homosexual practices which were invoked in his own conviction for 'gross indecency'. In doing so, he enacts a specifically literary version of the shift from act to identity which many historians have seen as central to a major transformation in the cultural understanding of sexuality in this period. This is demonstrated within the context of the trial by the terms of the prosecutor's interest in *The Portrait of Mr. W.H.*, in the comment I quoted earlier, 'I believe you have written an article to show that Shakespeare's *Sonnets* were suggestive of unnatural vice' (*Trials*, p. 130). 'Suggestive' is a key word here, both because of its importance in relation to the theory that Wilde was caught up in a major shift in the cultural conception of homosexuality, which substituted a mode of self-presentation, a form of identity evoked by the conjunction of a range of cultural signifiers, for particular bodily acts,[43] and also because of its continuing importance as a strategy in gay culture and discourse. In my reading of the story, I will try to show what it is about the 'suggestiveness' of *The Portrait of Mr. W.H.* and the discourses of sexuality with which it intersects that makes its appropriation of Shakespeare so intelligible and significant as a specifically homosexual one, and indicate how this particular appropriation inaugurates a strategy for representing and legitimising gay desire which has had long-lasting consequences.

What, then, were the contexts which made *The Portrait of Mr. W.H.* so prone to interpretation as a gay text? Several critics have emphasised the significance of the fact that the period from 1889 to 1893 when Wilde was writing the two versions of the story coincides with both the controversial publication and revision of the two versions of *The Picture of Dorian Gray*, and a series of homosexual scandals involving prominent men.[44] Throughout his career, Wilde persistently recycled a limited set of materials; *The Portrait of Mr. W.H.* and *The Picture of Dorian Gray* were roughly contemporary with each other in composition and publication, and have a great deal in common, besides the superficial similarity of the structuring motif, reflected in the titles, of a mysterious portrait of a beautiful young man.[45] For example, the profound structural resemblance, with the narrative being triangulated between three men who are differentiated by age, and whose affection is inflected by a certain mutual rivalry, also echoes the overlapping erotic triangles of Shakespeare's *Sonnets*. Thematically, both are preoccupied with the complex relations between eroticism and aestheticism. More generally, an account of the critical reception of *The Picture of Dorian Gray* can help to clarify how it is that these works which firmly resist the imputation to their characters of homosexual practices are so readily interpreted as emblematic of a certain homosexual identity or sensibility.

As Ed Cohen points out, discussing *The Picture of Dorian Gray*, it is necessary 'to consider how a text that (re)presents no sexualised relations between men has been so consistently (if not universally) understood to depict erotic intimacies between its male characters'.[46] Reviewers repeatedly castigated the novel for being unmanly, effeminate, insincere, vicious and flamboyant – all of which were beginning to function, by the 1890s, as code words with homosexual connotations. A particularly magnificent example of this genre of review is worth quoting at some length:

It is a tale spawned from the leprous literature of the French Decadents – a poisonous book, the atmosphere of which is heavy with
the mephitic odours of moral and spiritual putrefaction – a gloating
study of the mental and physical corruption of a fresh, fair and
golden youth, which might be horrible and fascinating but for its
effeminate frivolity, its studied insincerity, its theatrical cynicism, its
tawdry mysticism, its flippant philosophising, and the contaminat-
ing trail of garish vulgarity which is over all Mr. Wilde's elaborate
Wardour Street aestheticism and obtrusively cheap scholarship
(quoted in Gagnier, *Idylls of the Marketplace*, p. 43).

The reference to the 'French Decadents' is part of a widespread
tendency among hostile reviewers to stress Wilde's unEnglishness
– which often seems to be virtually synonymous with unmanli-
ness – and the passage, evoking as it does dishonesty, triviality,
effeminacy and bad taste, clearly implies that he is 'not quite one
of us' in a number of other ways. The emphasis on cheapness and
vulgarity has obvious connotations in terms of class, and hostility
was frequently provoked by Wilde's elimination or mockery of the
bourgeoisie in his plays. This is significant because of the way
homosexuality is inflected with class in his life and writing. The
difference in age and class position between Wilde and the young
men with whom he associated became one of the most incriminating factors at his trials; during his own libel action against
Queensberry he was cross-examined on his relationships with
working-class young men at great length and with considerable
hostility on the part of Edward Carson (*Trials of Oscar Wilde*, pp.
142–52). To some extent this pattern in Wilde's life also reflects
the composition – and perhaps even more the representation – of
the homosexual subculture of 1890s London. In the words of the
Scots Observer's reviewer: 'Mr. Wilde has brains, and art, and
style; but if he can write for none but outlawed noblemen and
perverted telegraph-boys, the sooner he takes to tailoring (or
some other decent trade) the better for his own reputation and
the public morals' (Gagnier, p. 43). Tailoring has been a cliché of
effeminate homosexuality since at least the sixteenth century.[47]
More immediately significant here is the reference to 'outlawed
noblemen and perverted telegraph-boys', invoking the notorious
Cleveland Street scandal of 1889, in which a homosexual brothel
which included among its clients many powerful and aristocratic

men was closed down amid a blaze of outraged publicity. Many of the working-class men – telegraph-boys – who manned it were sentenced to hard labour, while Charles Hammond, the 'madam', escaped to America, and one of the more prominent clients, Lord Arthur Somerset, went into permanent exile on the Continent.[48]

The Cleveland Street affair was the first highly publicised prosecution under the Labouchère Amendment to section 11 of the 1885 Criminal Justice Act, under which Wilde was convicted six years later. Thus his works were being interpreted in the light of highly publicised court cases involving homosexuality long before his own trial fixed the association of homosexuality, criminality and aestheticism in the cultural imagination. And it may be that this nexus of associations had further damaging implications for his encounter with the legal system, since H. Montgomery Hyde has argued that the desire to protect men in high places from public homosexual scandal may have played a significant role in Wilde's eventual criminal prosecution and conviction. Bosie's older brother Viscount Drumlanrig had supposedly accidentally shot himself while cleaning his gun in 1893; it has been suggested, however, that he was trying to avoid the scandal which would have undoubtedly surrounded threatened revelations concerning the nature of his relationship with Lord Rosebery, then Prime Minister. It has been argued that in the Wilde case political pressure was applied to ensure a conviction, for fear that Queensberry, if thwarted, would reveal that homosexuality was rampant at the very centre of English public life.[49]

The use of Shakespeare, the national bard who occupies a position at the centre of English culture, to create a highly public discourse of aestheticised male homoeroticism is thus a very astute – if somewhat risky – intervention into a conspiracy of silence surrounding the presence of male homosexuality at politically and culturally central locations. Draining love between men of sexual content, Wilde reinscribes the 'suggestion of unnatural vice', which aroused 'an equal mixture of disgust and indignation' in Shakespeare's eighteenth-century editor George Steevens,[50] and made Henry Hallam lament 'it is impossible not to wish Shakespeare had never written [the *Sonnets*]',[51] as a legitimate instance of an innocently pederastic practice which centred on an older man's initiation of a physically, intellectually and spiritually beautiful boy into a shared aesthetic and cultural heritage stretching back to the Greeks. The cultural and political contexts of the late 1880s and early 1890s made it possible to construct texts and acts which were not in themselves revelatory of homosexual activity as encodements of a homoerotic sensibility. In *The Portrait of Mr. W.H.* Wilde deploys this code himself in order to make Shakespeare the prestigious embodiment of this sensibility.

Unlocking the secret of Shakespeare's heart

I want now to look more closely at how this appropriation of Shakespeare is carried out in *The Portrait of Mr. W.H.*, by means of the representation of the beautiful effeminate youth as the object of desire. Early in the text, the narrator describes the portrait of Mr. W.H.:

> He seemed about seventeen years of age, and was of quite extraordinary personal beauty, though evidently somewhat effeminate. Indeed, had it not been for the dress and the closely cropped hair, one would have said that the face, with its dreamy wistful eyes and its delicate scarlet lips, was the face of a girl (Maine, pp. 1089–90; *Works*, pp. 1150–1).

In this description Willie Hughes remains curiously anonymous, interchangeable with any one of a number of other beautiful youths; this verbal portrait could equally well depict Cyril Graham, Dorian Gray or even Lord Alfred Douglas. Later, Wilde tacitly underlines this identification as he constructs a palimpsest of the *Sonnets* which re-creates Willie Hughes in the image of his own object of desire, weaving footnoted references to nine of the sonnets into the fabric of his text. Given the similarity of the image of Willie Hughes evoked here to the terms in which Wilde described Douglas, the latter's search for the real Willie Hews takes on a somewhat uncanny aspect:

> I could almost fancy that I saw him standing in the shadow of my room, so well had Shakespeare drawn him, with his golden hair, his tender flower-like grace, his dreamy deep-sunken eyes, his delicate mobile limbs, and his white lily hands ... Yes; who else but he could have been the master–mistress of Shakespeare's passion ... the delicate minion of pleasure, the rose of the whole world ... the lovely boy whom it was sweet music to hear, and whose beauty was the

very raiment of Shakespeare's heart, as it was the keystone of his dramatic power?[52]

The last phrase is particularly important. I spoke earlier of the significance of the theatrical as constitutive of identity, in terms both of Wilde's own thinking about it and of the accusation of 'posing as a somdomite [*sic*]' which initiated the disastrous sequence of trials. The relationship between Shakespeare as playwright and Willie Hughes as actor is the keystone of Wilde's theory, where it is imaged as a homoerotic 'marriage of true minds', of which the great female roles in Shakespeare's plays are the offspring – the children of a narcissistically doubled male motherhood. Sonnet 53 is central to this account: the narrator sees it as Shakespeare's compliment to Willie Hughes 'on the versatility of his acting, on his wide range of parts, a range extending, as we know, from Rosalind to Juliet, and from Beatrice to Ophelia' (Maine, p. 1100; *Works*, p. 1163). This tribute is significant in that it points to the ambivalent attraction of the boy actor, who is eroticised by performance – by being what he is not. His desirability lies not in the conflation of the boy actor's male body with the female role, but in the gap between them; the gap which must be filled by the actor's skill and the playwright's creative imagination: 'Shakespeare invites us to notice how the truth of acting, the truth of visible presentation on the stage, adds to the wonder of poetry, giving life to its loveliness, and actual reality to its ideal form' (Maine, p. 1101; *Works*, p. 1163). Whereas many critics since Malone have tended to see the *Sonnets* as offering privileged access to the truth of Shakespeare's subjectivity, Wilde inverts this, arguing that the performance or posing demanded by drama is more truthful.

Wilde's protagonist confesses that he finds the early sonnets with their exhortations to procreate puzzling: 'The boy-player of Rosalind had nothing to gain from marriage, or from the passions of real life' (Maine, p. 1102; *Works*, p. 1164). He suggests that acting offered Willie Hughes a kind of self-sufficient, narcissistic erotic pleasure which is superior by virtue of its artificiality to the real-life demand to invest in an other erotic object – by implication, a woman. The breeding sonnets are explained by identifying Willie Hughes as the 'only begetter' referred to in the dedication of the *Sonnets*, and asserting that 'the marriage that Shakespeare

proposes for Willie Hughes is the "marriage with his Muse" ...
[T]he children he begs him to beget are no children of flesh and
blood, but more immortal children of undying fame' (Maine, p.
1102; *Works*, p. 1165). In a unique reformulation of the homosocial triangle sketched by Eve Kosofsky Sedgwick, the feminine
intermediary which facilitates the consummation of desire
between men takes the form of Shakespeare's muse; this disembodied feminine figure enables the poet and the actor to unite in
male motherhood. Another palimpsest of the *Sonnets* culminates
with the narrator's voice merging with Shakespeare's, in asserting
to Willie Hughes: 'My thoughts, also, are my "children". They are
of your begetting, and my brain is: "the womb wherein they
grew"' (*Works*, p. 1167). In this '"marriage of true minds"' (*ibid.*),
women are written out of the scenario of heterosexuality, their
function to be only the disembodied, inert medium through
which male bonding passes. At the same time, homoeroticism
entails the deconstruction of the binary oppositions of gender, as
Shakespeare's brain becomes the womb which gives birth to the
children he fathers on the effeminate Willie Hughes.[53]

Effeminacy is repeatedly associated with acting in Wilde's
works, echoing an anxiety which dates back at least to Shakespeare's time. The fear that performance necessarily entails effeminisation runs through many of the anti-theatrical tracts published
between about 1580 and the closing of the theatres in 1642, and
in such works this process of theatrical effeminisation is often
assumed to culminate in the sin of sodomy.[54] Wilde appropriates
and inverts this discourse, ascribing positive value to theatrical
effeminacy. In *The Portrait of Mr. W.H.* the narrator makes an
explicit connection between the association of effeminacy with
the theatre – particularly in Shakespeare's theatre, where female
roles were played by boys – and the content of the *Sonnets*:

> Along with most students of Shakespeare, I had found myself com-
> pelled to set the *Sonnets* apart as things quite alien to Shakespeare's
> development as a dramatist ... But now that I began to realise the
> truth of Cyril Graham's theory, I saw that the moods and passions
> they mirrored were absolutely essential to Shakespeare's perfection
> as an artist writing for the Elizabethan stage, and that it was in the
> curious theatric conditions of that stage that the poems themselves
> had their origin (*Works*, p. 1162).

The narrator's comprehension of the homoerotic basis of Shakespeare's poetry and theatre is facilitated by the intermediary of Cyril Graham, himself an effeminate youth whose main interests are poetry and acting: '"at Eton he was always dressing up and reciting Shakespeare"' (Maine, p. 1091; *Works*, p. 1152). At Cambridge, Cyril triumphs as Rosalind:

> It was a marvellous performance. In fact, Cyril Graham was the only perfect Rosalind I have ever seen. It would be impossible to describe to you the beauty, the delicacy, the refinement of the whole thing. It made an immense sensation ... [E]ven when I read the play now I can't help thinking of Cyril. It might have been written for him (Maine, p. 1092; *Works*, p. 1153).

Cyril Graham's preference for lounging at home, working on a homoerotic theory of Shakespeare's *Sonnets* when he should be preparing to enter the Diplomatic Service, represents a dereliction of public, masculine responsibilities in favour of a feminised domestic space. This space transgresses the norms of Victorian domestic politics because it excludes women – as does Dorian Gray's home; as does the relationship between Shakespeare and Willie Hughes. The femininity which is inextricable from Victorian domesticity thus becomes embodied in an effeminate youth who is the object of homoerotic desire. This gives an interesting reinflection to Gwendolen's remark in *The Importance of Being Earnest*, that 'once a man begins to neglect his domestic duties he becomes painfully effeminate, does he not? And I don't like that. It makes men so very attractive.'[55] It is worth asking why Gwendolen dislikes effeminacy: because it reveals a distressing contrast with the conventional, assertive masculinity she is supposed to admire, or because it makes a man attractive to other men? Whatever the precise significance of her complaint, its effect is implicitly to deride the Victorian sexual politics which placed the most desirable image of masculinity at the heart of the domestic space, as respectable paterfamilias and support of dependent femininity, at the same time as problematising the woman's restricted role in this Manichaean scheme. To quote Rita Felski,

> the feminised male deconstructs conventional oppositions between the 'modern' bourgeois man and the 'natural' domestic woman; he is male, yet disassociated from masculine rationality, utility, and

progress; feminine yet profoundly unnatural. Whether hailed as subversive or condemned as pathological, his femininity signifies an unsettling of automatized perceptions of gender.[56]

By the last decades of the century, however, the ostensibly respectable version of masculinity was being hotly contested, as the social purity movements exposed the proliferation of prostitution and the sexual double standard, arguing that the heart of the Victorian home was hollowed out by a male sexuality, represented as bestial and excessive, which needed to be restrained in the interests of women.[57] Via this discourse, heterosexual masculinity has a submerged but profound connection with the kind of closeted male homosexuality, hidden and denied in the interests of maintaining the appearance of powerful homosocial bonds and a publicly irreproachable, conventionally masculine identity, which I discussed earlier in relation to *Dorian Gray* and the homosexual scandals in high places which recurred in the decade preceding Wilde's trial. The most obvious manifestation of this connection is the 1885 Criminal Law Amendment Act, which contained the Labouchère Amendment prohibiting 'acts of gross indecency' between men, under which Wilde was convicted. This Act's main concern – riding on the momentum feminism and the social purity movements had gained from the repeal of the Contagious Diseases Acts – was to regulate male heterosexuality by raising the age of consent for girls and extending stricter control over brothels, so that the relation of the Labouchère Amendment to the Act as a whole is difficult to clarify.[58] It was no less effective for that in controlling male homosexuality, as phenomena as varied as the Wilde trials, the 1961 film *Victim* and the autobiographical accounts of homosexual life in twentieth-century Britain given by 'ordinary' gay men in recent works of oral history all testify.[59]

This conjunction of attempts to regulate male hetero- and homosexuality exposes a complex network of connections between class, gender and sexuality. Campaigns around social purity were motivated in part by a desire to protect working-class prostitute women from the marauding sexuality of middle- and upper-class men; but they also aimed to protect the middle-class woman and her home from contagion by the infection her husband brought back from the streets. Similarly, homosexuality was sometimes seen by male radicals in terms of the corruption of 'poor but honest' young working-class men by members of an effcte and decadent aristocracy. The radical paper *The North London Press* responded to the Cleveland Street affair with a satirical poem which depicted Somerset as 'My Lord Gomorrah', sitting in France gloating over his escape while 'the wretched, vulgar tools / Of his faederastian [*sic*] joys, / … lay in prison, poor scapegoat fools; / Raw, cash-corrupted boys.'[60] The relationships between masculinity, effeminacy, homosexuality and class in this period are extremely complex. On the one hand, there is the example of effeminate working-class men like Frederick Park and Ernest Boulton, who from about 1870 lived as queens called Fanny and Stella, Stella being the consort of MP Lord Arthur Clinton; while on the other, for a middle-class socialist like Edward Carpenter, working-class virility represented both a sexual ideal and a way of putting into sexual practice his democratic beliefs. Outside an avowedly socialist context, however, this could be reinflected as the posh queen/rough trade model which was used to discredit Wilde in court.

Wilde's appropriation of Shakespeare similarly involves a complex negotiation between constructions of gender, sexuality and class. Eschewing the discourse of same-sex love posited on egalitarian manliness which was simultaneously being constructed elsewhere in the culture, for example by the writer Edward Carpenter, Wilde appropriated a cluster of notions associated with aestheticism, dandyism and the upper class in order to establish effeminacy as a recognisable, if controversial, signifier of a certain kind of homosexual identity.[61] Across the corpus of his work, he rewrote masculine effeminacy in contradictory and inconsistent ways. He adheres to a venerable tradition in placing the effeminate youth always as the object of a more conventionally virile man's desire, never as the subject of desire for another himself (with the exception of Dorian Gray's love for Sibyl Vane, the significance of which I shall consider in more detail below). Wilde repeatedly flirts with the popular conception of pederastic homosexuality as the successor to the classical Greek practice of man–boy love as a kind of mentor–disciple relationship, in which a virile, powerful adult male inducts into adult masculinity a sexual partner who is his equal in class terms, but inferior by virtue of his youth and the residual effeminacy associated with it.

James M. Saslow has argued that although this structure had remained important and prestigious in representations of love between men in the Renaissance – in the revival of the classical images of Hercules and Hylas, Apollo and Hyacinthus, and so on – in terms of actual sexual relationships, it bore a very negative inflection:

> The Renaissance conflation of effeminacy, hermaphroditism and homosexuality pivots around the disapproval of passivity in men – specifically, taking a passive or receptive role sexually … Any male who seems deficient in masculine power and aggression is liable to the scornful suspicion that he might therefore also act a passive role in sodomy with another man.[62]

But Wilde also rewrites effeminacy as active and creative, not passive, in ways which are related to the kind of appropriation of female reproductive power I mentioned earlier as a part of the homoerotics of literary collaboration – examples of this process might be Cyril Graham's generation of the sonnet theory and the shared male motherhood of Willie Hughes and Shakespeare in their creation of the plays' female roles. The effeminate youth thus becomes a sort of phallic mother, a better woman than a real woman. As Eve Kosofsky Sedgwick neatly puts it, in the *Sonnets* 'the fair youth, "woman's face" and all, is presented as exaggeratedly phallic – unitary, straightforward, unreflective, pink, and dense' (*Between Men*, p. 44). Similarly, Joseph Pequigney argues that the figure described in Shakespeare's sonnet 20 represents a woman with a penis, and suggests that the psychic and erotic significance of such a figure is analogous to the boy actors' performance of female roles on Shakespeare's stage.

The 1893 version of *The Portrait of Mr. W.H.* contains an extended rhapsody on the real-life peers of Willie Hughes, including one Dicky Robinson, who was 'known for his exquisite taste in costume, as well as for his love of woman's apparel' (*Works*, p. 1179), and 'Kynaston, of whom Betterton said that "it has been disputed among the judicious, whether any woman could have more sensibly touched the passions"' (*ibid.*). The 'exquisite', 'subtle … fascinating … ambiguity of the sexes' (p. 1180) which constitutes, for the narrator, one of the great pleasures of Shakespearean drama, is traced to the Elizabethan theatre's exclusion of female performers, and is seen as vital in preventing 'that over-realistic identification of the actor with his *rôle*' (*ibid.*) which flaws modern drama. If the beauty of Willie Hughes 'seemed to combine the charm of both sexes, and to have wedded, as the *Sonnets* tell us, the grace of Adonis and the loveliness of Helen' (p. 1178), this charming ambiguity is, it seems, most compelling when performed by a boy. The narrator rejoices in the differentiation between performer and role maintained by the boy actor, by means of which the masquerade of femininity produces a new type of object, far more appealing than a 'real' woman: 'the players of these parts were lads and young men, whose passionate purity, quick mobile fancy, and healthy freedom from sentimentality can hardly fail to have suggested a new and delightful type of girlhood or of womanhood' (*ibid.*). Similarly, in *The Picture of Dorian Gray*, Sybil Vane becomes the object of Dorian's affections while she is functioning as the belated reincarnation of the Shakespearean boy actor, playing the roles originally created by Willie Hughes. She is delightful as long as she is performing; but as soon as she falls in (heterosexual) love and begins to identify with the Shakespearean role, she loses her ability to act and is reduced to 'play[ing] Juliet like a wooden doll' (p. 73). Real emotion makes her performance 'false ... stagy ... absurdly artificial' (p. 72); it was artifice – a ghostly echo of the artifice of gender that made the 'new ... type of girlhood' embodied by the boy actors so delightful – that made it convincing. If life, in Wilde's appropriation of Shakespeare for homoerotic culture, imitates art, it is because artifice in this context is the very condition of desire. The narrator of *The Portrait of Mr. W.H.*, as I noted above, concludes by remarking that 'there is a good deal to be said for the Willie Hughes theory of Shakespeare's *Sonnets*'. But this approval should not be taken to indicate that he believes the theory to be true. The point of the theory lies precisely in its juxtaposition of its flaunted status as forgery with strenuous efforts both to prove that it is true and to act as if it is. Modern gay identity is no less real and powerful a force in the lives which are made legible by it for being a construct – a historical fiction, one might say. The refusal of the discourse of truth in Wilde's appropriation of Shakespeare is a very canny strategy, answering neatly to the over-determined conditions in which, in the 1890s as in the 1990s, homoerotic desire can be lived and represented.

Critical perversities and perverse appropriations

Wilde's homoerotic appropriation of Shakespeare depends, then, on an emphasis on Shakespeare as a practising playwright, to the extent that even the *Sonnets* are re-created as exemplary of the aesthetic and erotic investments of Shakespeare's theatrical practice. In contrast, the twentieth century has seized on the question of Shakespeare's sexual identity within the context of the burgeoning discipline of academic literary criticism; and while the possibility that something which we could more or less helpfully call homoerotic desire is represented in some of the plays has achieved a measure of general acceptance, the idea that the *Sonnets*, read as autobiographical documents, inscribe Shakespeare's own homoeroticism remains troublesomely central to the debate. Anxieties about the nature of Shakespearean sexuality are, of course, a function of the continuing social proscription of homosexuality; but their special intensity in Shakespeare's case appears to be a matter less of his ascribed sexual identity than of his unique cultural status. According to Simon Shepherd,

> Discussion of homosexuality in Shakspeer [*sic*] seems to be motivated not by an interest in Renaissance sexuality but by Shakespaire's [*sic*] national status. Criticism's task is to discover a fitting sexuality for the National Bard. The task is specifically taken up by and shaped by *literary* criticism, for the literature is what is to be protected. The literature belongs to the nation.[63]

Conversely, commentary on Shakespeare has become constitutive of what counts as literary criticism; in the words of gay critic Gregory Bredbeck, 'the history of commentary on Shakespeare's sonnets is also the history of how to read humanistically'.[64] The critical tradition which replaces religion with literary criticism as the secular humanist arbiter of morality finds its key figure in Shakespeare; and since in the area of sexual morality this tradition is almost invariably committed to the maintenance of heterosexuality, the notion that Shakespeare might have been anything other than a morally unimpeachable family man is inevitably disconcerting. Thus James Winny, a critic writing at the time when the modern gay liberation movement was emerging as a cultural and political phenomenon, warned against biographical interpretations of the *Sonnets* on the grounds that

> If the *Sonnets* had the literal truth claimed for them, it would be difficult to resist the inference that Shakespeare was a homosexual and an adulterer ... Readers who heard Shakespeare speaking in every word of the *Sonnets* seem to have been too enraptured by the experience to recognise the moral implications of the attachments which they describe.[65]

The seductive pleasure of communing directly with the authentically Shakespearean voice presumed to speak in the *Sonnets* has the regrettable side-effect of endangering the reader's moral judgement. Winny defends Shakespeare from the 'outrageous and indefensible slander' – namely, the imputation of homosexuality – to which a biographical reading of the *Sonnets* may give rise, by arguing that this approach is critically inept and theoretically invalid; yet he has recourse to biographical detail – the fact that Shakespeare was married and a father – in order to oppose an interpretation of the *Sonnets* which might locate their representation of homoeroticism in Shakespeare's own sexual identity. Winny is thus cornered into arguing 'that the *Sonnets* are neither autobiographical nor fictional, and that in another sense they are both these things' – a position which, he is forced to admit, 'will seem perverse' (p. 22).

Winny's discomfort is common to many critics of the *Sonnets*, caught between a post-Romantic analysis which locates the subject's self-present interiority as knowable in and through the language of his poetry, and thus seems to offer a desirable privileged access to Shakespeare's own feelings; and a post-Freudian analysis which locates the 'truth' of Shakespeare's feelings precisely in the silences and repressions of his text. As Simon Shepherd points out, liberal humanist critical discourse cannot deploy the historical and political strategies necessary to make sense of these contradictions, nor can it make sense of the question mark placed over Shakespeare's sexual identity by this uncomfortable conjunction of discourses, except in terms of its own scandalised sense of propriety ('Shakespeare's private drawer', pp. 98, 100). Hence Winny's anxiety that his complicity with the revelation of Shakespeare's perversity will make him too appear perverse is reinflected in a certain perversity in the construction of his book on the *Sonnets*. Although its title is *The Master–Mistress*, Winny expends considerable amounts of energy in evading the subject of sexual ambiguity, and does not get round to discussing sonnet 20, from which his title is drawn, until the book is three-quarters over. The book flaunts perversity in order to repudiate it. The introduction is devoted to the history of biographical speculations about Shakespeare's sexuality, which Winny resists by arguing that the true meaning of the *Sonnets* can be assessed only in terms of 'Shakespeare's imaginative field, whose nature and significance have not yet been explained' (p. 22) – replacing one anxiety-producing enigma with another, more comfortable one, specially constructed for the purpose. The question of homosexuality can be evaded, but not entirely repressed; once the key of biographical speculation has been turned, the closet door will not stay shut. Yet Oscar Wilde's appropriation of Shakespeare, at once defiantly political and sexually enigmatic, seems to suggest that in the end what is actually in the closet is neither here nor there. Perhaps the question that really needs to be asked is not 'Was Shakespeare gay?', but rather, 'Why do we care whether Shakespeare was gay – what does Shakespeare's sexual identity matter to us?' A recent Channel 4 documentary, 'Shakespeare: or, What You Will', presented by out gay actor Simon Callow, drew on historical evidence, social construction theory, the ruminations of literary critics and the insights of performers and directors to offer tentative answers to both these questions before concluding, as did Wilde, that the ultimate significance of Shakespeare's sexuality is thoroughly, if indirectly, political. Closing the programme, Callow's final words suggest that it is precisely the elusiveness and indeterminacy of Shakespearean sexualities which make it useful and important to enlist Shakespeare as an ally in the struggle against sexual and social intolerance: 'As more and more polarisation occurs, as people tend to take up more and more extreme positions, the fact that Shakespeare offered us a world in which all kinds of things coexist is something we should constantly acknowledge and affirm.' Callow is here appropriating Shakespeare for a modern ideology of sexual liberalism; to argue that sexual identities were not constructed as exclusive and monolithic in the Renaissance is by no means to suggest that this produced tolerance of diversity. The liberal inclusiveness which Callow claims to find in Shakespeare presupposes that a range of stigmatised categories did exist in the early modern period, whereas the constructionist argument which the programme had earlier invoked problematises the notion that such categories are historically continuous, suggesting therefore that the understanding of sexual identity on which liberalism depends did not in fact exist in Shakespeare's time. But as his reference to our own difficult times implies, what is at stake in Callow's claim is not principally historical truth, but political effectiveness. In my final chapter, I will explore some of the ways in which Shakespeare has already been pressed into service in the cultural and sexual politics of the last decade, focusing on the films, writing and activism of Derek Jarman.

Notes

1 This passage is a quotation from Oscar Wilde's fiction *The Portrait of Mr. W.H.* There are two versions of the story: the first was published in *Blackwood's Magazine* in 1889; the second, revised and expanded version was completed in 1893, but not published until 1921. Despite the flurry of critical attention the story has enjoyed in recent years, there is still no satisfactory modern edition of the later version. The 1889 version is reprinted in Oscar Wilde, *The Works of Oscar Wilde*, ed. G. F. Maine (London, Collins, 1948), pp. 1089–112, which I cite as Maine; the 1893 version is in the volume I use to refer to other texts by Wilde, the revised edition of *The Complete Works of Oscar Wilde* (London, Collins, 1966), cited throughout as *Works*. The passage quoted here can be found in Maine, p. 1094, and *Works*, p. 1155.

2 Numerous examples of the vocabulary of late nineteenth-century homoeroticism, particularly as it focused on the idealisation of beautiful boys, can be found in Timothy d'Arch Smith, *Love in Earnest: Some Notes on the Lives and Writings of English 'Uranian' Poets from 1889 to 1930* (London, Routledge & Kegan Paul, 1970) and Brian Reade, *Sexual Heretics: Male Homosexuality in English Literature from 1850 to 1900* (London, Routledge & Kegan Paul, 1970).

3 *The Wilde Century* (London, Cassell, 1994).

4 Oscar Wilde, *The Picture of Dorian Gray*, ed. Donald L. Lawler (New York, Norton Critical Edition, 1988), 1890 version, pp. 173–281 (p. 232). This edition includes both the 1890 and 1891 versions of the novel and is the only currently available edition of *Dorian Gray* to reprint the 1890 version. According to Lawler, Wilde originally wrote 'than a man should ever give a friend', and the change to the milder 'usually gives a friend' was made in the typescript by the editor of *Lippincott's Monthly Magazine*, John Marshall Stoddart.

5 Neil Bartlett, *Who Was That Man? A Present for Mr. Oscar Wilde* (London, Serpent's Tail, 1988), p. 112.

6 *The Picture of Dorian Gray*, *Works* pp. 17–167 (p. 93).

7 H. Montgomery Hyde (ed.), *The Trials of Oscar Wilde* (London, William Hodge and Co., 1948), p. 129.

8 Works which both participate in the construction of this narrative and meditate on its cultural and political significance include Bartlett, *Who Was That Man?* and Sinfield, *The Wilde Century*.

9 London, Routledge, 1989.

10 *Between Men: English Literature and Male Homosocial Desire* (New York, Columbia University Press, 1985).

11 'Fiction and Friction', in his *Shakespearean Negotiations* (Oxford, Clarendon Press, 1988), pp. 66–93 (p. 76).

12 See especially William A. Cohen, 'Willie and Wilde: Reading *The Portrait of Mr. W.H.*', *South Atlantic Quarterly*, 88 (1989), 219–45; Claude J. Summers, '"In Such Surrender There May Be Gain": Oscar Wilde and the Beginnings of Gay Fiction', in his *Gay Fictions, Wilde to Stonewall: Studies in a Male Homosexual Literary Tradition* (New York, Continuum, 1990), pp. 29–61; and Lawrence Danson, 'Oscar Wilde, W.H., and the Unspoken Name of Love', *English Literary History*, 58 (1991), 979–1000.

13 The most important contemporary works which brought together these concerns under the umbrella of sexual pathology were Havelock Ellis and John Addington Symonds, *Sexual Inversion* (London, Wilson & Macmillan, 1897) and Richard Krafft-Ebing, *Psychopathia Sexualis* (London, F. J. Rebman, 1893). For an outstanding recent feminist study of late nineteenth-century sexual politics, see Judith R. Walkowitz, *City of Dreadful Delight: Narratives of Sexual Danger in Late-Victorian London* (Chicago, Ill., University of Chicago Press, 1992).

14 Although it is necessarily an over-simplification, I think it is useful to maintain a distinction between North American new historicism, as practised (in Renaissance studies) by Greenblatt, Louis Adrian Montrose and Leonard Tennenhouse, for example, and British cultural materialism, often metonymically represented by the collection edited by Jonathan Dollimore and Alan Sinfield, *Political Shakespeare: New Essays in Cultural Materialism* (Manchester, Manchester University Press, 1985; revised second edition 1994).

15 For an overview of these debates and the academic/political situation in which they were produced, see Ann Thompson, 'Are There any Women in *King Lear*?', in Valerie Wayne (ed.), *The Matter of Difference: Materialist Feminist Criticism of Shakespeare* (Hemel Hempstead, Harvester, 1991), pp. 117–28. It would be fair to say that

the feminist critique of the sexual politics of both new historicist and some cultural materialist work applies primarily to books and essays published in the 1980s; recent work in this field does tend to be more attentive to sexual politics. For some examples of such work see below, n. 28.

16 London, Methuen, 1985, p. 29.

17 *Such is My Love: A Study of Shakespeare's Sonnets* (Chicago, Ill., University of Chicago Press, 1985), p. 81.

18 Freud's most direct statements on the association of homosexuality and narcissism are to be found in 'Psycho-Analytic Notes on an Auto-biographical Account of a Case of Paranoia (Dementia Paranoides)', (1911), Pelican Freud Library vol. 9 (Harmondsworth, Penguin, 1979), pp. 129–209; 'On Narcissism' (1914), Pelican Freud Library vol. 11 (Harmondsworth, Penguin, 1984), pp. 59–92; and *Introductory Lectures on Psychoanalysis*, Lecture 26 'The Libido Theory and Narcissism', (1916–17), Pelican Freud Library vol. 1 (Harmondsworth, Penguin, 1973).

19 *Articulate Flesh: Male Homo-eroticism and Modern Poetry* (New Haven, Conn., Yale University Press, 1987), p. 19.

20 For two very different but mutually illuminating accounts of the role played by psychoanalysis in the construction and regulation of male homosexuality, and its possible usefulness for gay theory, see Kenneth Lewes, *The Psychoanalytic Theory of Male Homosexuality* (New York, Simon and Schuster, 1988), and John Fletcher, 'Freud and his Uses: Psychoanalysis and Gay Theory', in Simon Shepherd and Mick Wallis (eds), *Coming on Strong: Gay Politics and Culture* (London, Unwin Hyman, 1989), pp. 90–118.

21 'The Disciple', *Poems in Prose, Works*, pp. 843–50 (p. 844).

22 'Then Wilde, puffing out a bizarre burst of laughter, added, "That is called *The Disciple*"' [my translation] (*Prétextes* (Paris, Mercure de France, 1929), pp. 270–1).

23 'The Critic as Artist', *Works*, pp. 948–98 (p. 972)

24 Jonathan Dollimore, *Sexual Dissidence: Augustine to Wilde, Freud to Foucault* (Oxford, Clarendon Press, 1991).

25 *Homosexual Desire in Shakespeare's England: A Cultural Poetics* (Chicago, Ill., University of Chicago Press, 1991), p. 29.

26 Foucault's *History of Sexuality*, vol.1, *An Introduction* (London, Allen Lane, 1979) is the theoretical *locus classicus* of this approach. The best-known and most prolific historian of the social construction of male homosexuality in Britain is Jeffrey Weeks: see for example *Coming Out: Homosexual Politics in Britain from the Nineteenth Century to the Present* (London, Quartet, 1977; revised and updated 1990), and *Against Nature: Essays on History, Sexual-*

ity and Identity (London, Rivers Oram Press, 1991).

27 Martin Duberman, Martha Vicinus and George Chauncey (eds), *Hidden from History: Reclaiming the Gay and Lesbian Past* (Harmondsworth, Penguin, 1991). The problematic relationship of the gay historical enterprise to feminist history is clearly signalled by the book's presumably unwitting borrowing of its title from Sheila Rowbotham, *Hidden from History: Three Hundred Years of Women's Oppression and the Fight Against It* (London, Pluto, 1973).

28 Similar recent projects which focus on the Renaissance include, on male homosexuality, Alan Bray, 'Homosexuality and the Signs of Male Friendship in Elizabethan England', *History Workshop Journal*, 29 (1990), 1–19; Gregory W. Bredbeck, *Sodomy and Interpretation: From Marlowe to Milton* (Ithaca, NY, Cornell University Press, 1991); Jonathan Goldberg, *Sodometries: Renaissance Texts, Modern Sexualities* (Stanford, Calif., Stanford University Press, 1992), and as editor, *Queering the Renaissance* (Durham, NC, Duke University Press, 1994). Less work has been done around the question of Renaissance lesbian sexualities/identities: the best-known study in the field is still Judith C. Brown, *Immodest Acts: The Life of a Lesbian Nun in Renaissance Italy* (Oxford, Oxford University Press, 1986). For more recent work which benefits from the growth in lesbian and gay studies, see Elaine Hobby, 'Katherine Philips: Seventeenth-Century Lesbian Poet' in Elaine Hobby and Chris White (eds), *What Lesbians do in Books* (London, Women's Press, 1991), pp. 183–204 and Valerie Traub, 'The (In)Significance of "Lesbian" Desire in Early Modern England', in Susan Zimmerman (ed.), *Erotic Politics: The Dynamics of Desire in the Renaissance Theatre* (London, Routledge, 1992), pp. 150–69. Emma Donoghue's *Passions Between Women* (London, Scarlet Press, 1994) covers the period from 1660 to 1800 but raises questions which are relevant to the earlier period too.

29 Karl Beckson (ed.), *Oscar Wilde: The Critical Heritage* (London, Routledge & Kegan Paul, 1970), pp. 11, 29, 32, 35, 316–17, 407.

30 My attention was drawn to the existence of this cartoon by Joseph Bristow's paper '"The Future Belongs to the Dandy": Oscar Wilde and a Different Class of Man', given at Liverpool University, February 1993, and I am very grateful to him for providing me with a copy of the picture. The cartoon was drawn by Bernard Partridge and first published in *Punch*, 5 March 1892 – for an account of its original contexts, see Joel H. Kaplan, 'A Puppet's Power: George Alexander, Clement Scott, and the Replotting of *Lady Windermere's Fan*', *Theatre Notebook*, 46 (1992), 59–73.

31 Richard Ellmann, *Oscar Wilde* (London, Hamish Hamilton, 1987), p.

281.

32 See *The Picture of Dorian Gray*, *Works*, pp. 41, 97; the relevant material in *The Portrait of Mr. W.H.* is part of a long passage added to the 1893 version, pp. 43–7.

33 *De Profundis ... 'Epistola: in Carcere et Vinculis'*, ed. Vyvyan Holland (London, Methuen, 1949).

34 For Malone and Tyrwhitt, see *The Plays and Poems of William Shakespeare*, ed. Edmond Malone, 10 vols (London, J. Rivington & Sons, 1790), X, p. 191. Boswell is quoted in Margreta de Grazia, *Shakespeare Verbatim: The Reproduction of Authenticity and the 1790 Apparatus* (Oxford, Clarendon Press, 1991), p. 154. The various arguments which have identified Willie Hughes as both 'Mr. W.H.' and the addressee of the *Sonnets* are examined and refuted in the Variorum *Sonnets*, ed. Hyder Edward Rollins, 2 vols (Philadelphia, PA, J. B. Lippincott, 1944), pp. 180–5.

35 William Wordsworth, 'Scorn not the Sonnet', *Poems*, ed. John O. Hayden, 2 vols (Harmondsworth, Penguin, 1977), II, p. 635.

36 See for instance Samuel Butler, *Shakespeare's Sonnets Reconsidered* (London, 1899).

37 'Pen, Pencil and Poison', *Works*, pp. 932–47 (p. 947).

38 'The Truth of Masks', *Works*, pp. 999–1017 (p. 1009).

39 *The True History of Shakespeare's Sonnets* (London, Martin Secker, 1933), p. 34.

40 *The Autobiography of Lord Alfred Douglas* (London, Martin Secker, 1929), pp. 61–2.

41 Rupert Croft–Cooke, *Bosie: The Story of Lord Alfred Douglas* (London, W. H. Allen, 1963), p. 337.

42 *Idylls of the Marketplace: Oscar Wilde and the Victorian Public* (Aldershot, Scolar Press, 1987), p. 20.

43 This notion has become a commonplace of gay history; for a detailed account which focuses on the constitutive role played by Wilde's trials in this process, see Ed Cohen, *Talk on the Wilde Side: Towards a Genealogy of the Discourse on Male Homosexuality* (London, Routledge, 1993).

44 The best account can be found in Gagnier, *Idylls of the Marketplace*; see also Claude J. Summers, '"In Such Surrender There May Be Gain"'.

45 On Wilde's incessant and blatant use of materials which establish intertextual relationships within his own *œuvre* and with the works of other writers, see Ian Small, *Conditions for Criticism* (Oxford, Clarendon Press, 1991), pp. 113–16.

46 *Talk on the Wilde Side*, p. 251. For an extended consideration of this question, see Cohen's article 'Writing Gone Wilde: Homoerotic

Desire in the Closet of Representation', *PMLA*, 102 (1987), 801–13.

47 Simon Shepherd, 'What's so Funny about Ladies' Tailors? A Survey of some Male (Homo)sexual Types in the Renaissance', *Textual Practice*, 6 (1992), 17–30.

48 At the time, Somerset was Assistant Equerry to Prince Albert Victor, oldest son of the Prince of Wales and second in line to the throne, and it has been suggested that royal intervention actually made the affair less of a scandal than it might have been (Bartlett, p. 246).

49 See for example H. Montgomery Hyde's Introduction to *The Trials of Oscar Wilde*, pp. 9–101 (p. 79). There is no conclusive evidence about the precise nature of Drumlanrig's involvement with Rosebery, but the argument put forward by Hyde and cited here has taken on the status of common knowledge; see Gagnier, *Idylls of the Marketplace*, p. 206, and Sinfield, *The Wilde Century*, p. 73. The pretence in *The Portrait of Mr. W.H.* that Cyril Graham also accidentally shot himself while cleaning his gun seems rather uncanny in this context.

50 Quoted in Pequigney, *Such is My Love*, p. 30.

51 Hallam made the comment in his *Introduction to the Literature of Europe*; it is quoted in Alfred Tennyson, *The Poems of Tennyson*, ed. Christopher Ricks (London, Longman, 1969), p. 861.

52 Maine, pp. 1104–5; *Works*, p. 1169. The sonnets referred to are (in order of citation) 20, 126, 109, 8, 22; I have omitted references to 26, 1, 2 and 95. The term 'minion' has long had homoerotic connotations.

53 For an account of Renaissance literary collaboration which sees it as a form of homoerotic sexual/textual reproduction, see Jeff Masten, 'My Two Dads: Collaboration and the Reproduction of Beaumont and Fletcher' in Goldberg (ed.), *Queering the Renaissance* (1994), pp. 280–309.

54 See Lisa Jardine, '"As boys and women are for the most part cattle of this colour": Female Roles and Elizabethan Eroticism', Chapter 1 of her *Still Harping on Daughters: Women and Drama in the Age of Shakespeare* (Brighton, Harvester, 1983), and Laura Levine, 'Men in Women's Clothing: Anti-theatricality and Effeminization', *Criticism*, 28 (1986), 121–44.

55 *The Importance of Being Earnest*, *Works*, pp. 321–69 (p. 351).

56 'The counter-discourse of the feminine in three texts by Wilde, Huysmans, and Sacher-Masoch', *PMLA*, 106 (1991), 1094–1105, quoted in Sinfield, *Wilde Century*, p. 74.

57 See Frank Mort, *Dangerous Sexualities: Medico-moral Politics in England since 1830* (London, Routledge & Kegan Paul, 1987), and Judith Walkowitz, *City of Dreadful Delight*.

58 Wilde's friend and biographer Frank Harris suggested that Labouchère was trying to discredit the whole Act by means of this amendment, a view with which F. B. Smith has recently concurred in 'Labouchère's Amendment to the Criminal Law Amendment Bill', *Historical Studies*, 17 (1976), 165–73. In contrast, Ed Cohen, in *Talk on the Wilde Side* (p. 92) and Jeffrey Weeks, in *Coming Out* (p. 16) both see the Amendment as consistent with the Act's overall onslaught on predatory male sexuality. Cohen goes on to offer a detailed account of the crucial significance for Wilde's trials, and thus for the construction of modern homosexuality, of the 1885 Act's shift from a focus on the act of sodomy as a sexual crime to the much vaguer – more 'suggestive', perhaps? – notion of '"acts of gross indecency" [which] had no particular specificity save for the genital similarity of the sexual actors', in Chapter 4 of his book, 'Legislating the Norm: From "Sodomy" to "Gross Indecency"', pp. 103–25 (p. 119).

59 *Victim*, which was directed by Basil Dearden and starred Dirk Bogarde, dramatised the popular description of the 1885 Act as the 'Blackmailer's Charter'. On the Act's effect on the lives of ordinary gay men, see for example Hall Carpenter Archives/Gay Men's Oral History Group, *Walking After Midnight: Gay Men's Life Stories* (London, Routledge, 1989); and Kevin Porter and Jeffrey Weeks (eds), *Between the Acts: Lives of Homosexual Men from 1885 to 1967* (London, Routledge, 1990).

60 Quoted in Richard Dellamora, *Masculine Desire: The Sexual Politics of Victorian Aestheticism* (Chapel Hill, NC, University of North Carolina Press, 1990), p. 11.

61 See Sinfield, *The Wilde Century*.

62 *Ganymede in the Renaissance: Homosexuality in Art and Society* (New Haven, Conn., Yale University Press, 1986), pp. 80, 82.

63 'Shakespeare's Private Drawer: Shakespeare and Homosexuality', in Graham Holderness (ed.), *The Shakespeare Myth* (Manchester, Manchester University Press, 1988), pp. 96–110 (p. 97).

64 *Sodomy and Interpretation*, p. 167.

65 James Winny, *The Master–Mistress* (London, Chatto & Windus, 1968), p. 8.

Chapter 5

'The past is our mirror':[1]
Marlowe, Shakespeare, Jarman

On the night of the Lesbian and Gay Pride March in June 1989, Derek Jarman went for a walk on Hampstead Heath and found himself in the midst of an appropriately seasonal Shakespearean scenario: a group of students taking advantage of the full moon to shoot a film version of *A Midsummer Night's Dream*. Jarman's description of this unlikely event in his autobiographical work *Modern Nature*[2] contrasts it with the nocturnal activities which Hampstead Heath more commonly witnesses, juxtaposing the amateur director's attempts to exert control over the rather inept proceedings with the Heath's reputation as the incarnation of modern London's 'green world', the location of precisely the sexual pursuits and confusions of identity which also characterise that Shakespearean wood near Athens:

> Further down the path a group of lads had built a large bonfire round which they sat in silence, adrift in the night ... Back 'on set' Puck was leaping about putting his magic flower on some fallen tree-trunks, on which a young woman with slicked back hair draped herself in an outfit by Yohji or Katherine from Sloane Street.

The innately, effortlessly carnivalesque nature of the Heath's homosexual subculture is contrasted with the designer decadence of the film – though, ironically, Jarman's description of the young woman taking part in the shoot is itself dependent on the reader's familiarity with particular icons of 'designer culture'. The contrast between the two elements of the scene, heavily loaded as it is in favour of the young gay men whom Jarman depicts as resisting the pleasures of commoditised culture, participates in the book's continual reworking of the nature/culture dichotomy.

[177]

As its title implies, Jarman's project here is to invent, discover or record 'modern nature'. This phrase is first used in *Modern Nature* as a description of the garden at his home in Kent, the creation of which provides the book with its focus, and which is closely connected with the making of the film *The Garden* during the period covered by these journals. But it is also central to the book's other key preoccupation, with the politics of sexual identity. Both the state regulation of homosexuality in Britain and individual homophobia are frequently justified with reference to the claim that homosexuality is unnatural, even *against* nature; and it is part of the purpose of *Modern Nature* – as of all Jarman's cultural work, as film-maker, activist, painter and writer – to argue that modern homosexuality is in fact its own nature.

Layering fantasy, desire and the immediacy of the sexual act, Jarman concludes the anecdote in a mood of playful inversion:

> Further on a group of young men were making love under the trees. Others walking home were stopped by scouts and pushed back in the bushes, before they stumbled across the set. I wished I had my own camera. The film of this film would have made the finest *Midsummer Night's Dream* that had ever been recorded – and to think they missed all those *real* fairies (p. 103).

The sophistication of a meta-cinematic meditation on Shakespeare's meta-theatrical play collapses into wryly affectionate bathos with the invocation of one of gay culture's most well-worn jokes. Clearly it would not be fruitful to guess, from these offhand comments, at what kind of film Jarman might have made of *A Midsummer Night's Dream*, nor to set out a point-by-point account of the resemblances between Shakespeare's play and this midsummer night on Hampstead Heath – although some sense of what Jarman's vision of the play might have been can be gathered from his comments in response to an Italian offer to stage or film it, eschewing camp in favour of emotional intensity: 'No-one has made a successful adaptation of the play; both Lindsay Kemp and Reinhardt went for bust in glitter and glamorous faeries – at the expense of *ossessione*, the love compulsion in the play' p. 134). But the vivid tableau which Jarman's words conjure up does provide an apt image of some of the aesthetic and political uses to which Shakespeare is put in his work.

The description of the young gay men whose magical, sexualised territory the Heath becomes at night sitting quietly in the darkness while the film students usurp their space to make an inane film of a play about magic and sex, clearly marks the extent to which the gay community and what Jarman calls 'Heterosoc' (i.e. heterosexual/heterosexist society) are thoroughly dichotomised and alienated from each other. The gay men are associated with 'nature', the film crew (to whom heterosexuality is tacitly imputed, though of course this can only be a matter of conjecture and rhetoric on Jarman's part) with flamboyant artifice, in an inversion of the usual stereotypes. Yet if Hampstead Heath is what passes for the green world of 'nature' in London, it is nevertheless thoroughly artificial, a man-made landscape which has to be strenuously maintained in order to satisfy urban fantasies of the natural; a fact which both exposes the extent to which the category of 'nature' is socially contingent and undermines the nature/artifice dichotomy which Jarman is playing with here, and which has for so long been beloved of certain kinds of Shakespeare criticism. In *At Your Own Risk* Jarman laments the decision to clear areas of shrub and undergrowth from Hampstead Heath in an attempt to prevent them being used for cruising, and declares 'Nature abhors Heterosoc … Nature is Queer.'³ A similar reconstruction of the category of the 'natural' is enacted by his wry description of the gay men who cruise the Heath at night as 'the *real* fairies'. The use of this phrase also exemplifies the tactic, long enshrined in camp and recently reasserted by the 'new queer politics', of appropriating terms which are meant to carry a homophobic, derogatory charge, and using them as a defiant badge of identity. Finally, the film which Jarman longs to make of this nighttime scene, juxtaposing the creation of another film of *A Midsummer Night's Dream* with sex between men, would be thoroughly typical of the films he has already made, which repeatedly stage a collision between prestigious cultural artefacts and explicit gay sex.

I wrote the first draft of this chapter in the summer of 1993, at a time when it was becoming clear that Jarman's courageous and honourable fight with AIDS could not last much longer. Returning to his work now, almost a year after his death in February 1994, what strikes me most forcibly about *Modern Nature*'s appropriation of *A Midsummer Night's Dream* is its reluctance to acknowledge its own status as elegy – for Jarman himself, and for

the fragile nocturnal carnival he celebrates here. This elegiac quality is in part a matter of the way that Jarman's illness and death
took on the aspect of cultural events, as well as being so powerfully incorporated into the artworks of the last years of his life. But
the note of elegy is also one which is frequently struck in Jarman's
films and writing. Elegy memorialises love and loss, grief and
desire, at the intersection of the private and public; it asserts the
continuing emotional and aesthetic resonance of what belongs to
the past, at the same time as acknowledging the pain of the fact
that the past can never quite be returned to us. The key achievement of Jarman's career was, it seems to me, to appropriate the
richest and most prestigious resources of the cultural past and to
make of them a highly politicised and intensely pleasurable intervention in the present. As I argued in Chapter 4, Oscar Wilde's
appropriation of Shakespeare both drew on the playwright's cultural authority in order to legitimise gay identity and presented an
image of that sexual identity which was closely associated with the
production and consumption of the artefacts of high culture. This
strategic use of Shakespeare had the effect of foregrounding certain issues about the relationship between the identity of the
artist and the significance of his work; issues which, in the late
twentieth century, remain central to sexual and cultural politics.
The work of Derek Jarman directly addressed these intertwined
questions about sexuality, art and identity. Embracing writing,
painting and the making of gardens as well as the films for which
he is best known, it was produced in a constant negotiation both
with the frequently harsh realities of life for gay men in modern
Britain and with a cultural past which enshrines many of the
values Jarman perceived as being under assault in contemporary
society.

As my title suggests, Jarman, like Wilde, engaged in a narcissistic and deliberately anachronistic appropriation of the culture of
the past, in the service of legitimising contemporary gay participation in the making and interpretation of culture. Discussing his
decision to make a film based on Christopher Marlowe's *Edward
II*, Jarman insisted that his appropriation was not merely anachronistic, however, because he saw the present as the culmination of
the past, and modern gay identity as the accretion of long centuries of desire and oppression: 'we are the sum of those past
experiences'.[4] Moreover, he resisted charges that his films repre-

sent a shocking break with cultural tradition, consistently claiming that his work, and the values and issues it addresses, are consonant with the central traditions of English art and history – a view endorsed by the *Daily Telegraph*'s film critic, Hugo Davenport, who notes that 'for all his reputation as a radical, his work has always been pervaded by a strong sense of ancestral Englishness, of the irreplaceability of a shared past. "My art has always been Tory art", he says. "Politically I'm not a Tory; culturally I am."'[5]

In this chapter I shall consider the significance of what may, in the light of some commonplace modern assumptions about the politics of sexuality, culture and history, appear to be a certain tension between, on the one hand, the value Jarman places on cultural continuity and the continuing emotional and artistic resonance of the elite cultural traditions of the past; and on the other, his commitment both to avant-garde work in various media and to a radical sexual politics which rejects many of the values usually labelled 'traditional'. For me, Jarman's work is important precisely because it refuses to abdicate the resources of art and history to the representatives of conservatism and reaction, insisting instead that the most apparently dispossessed and marginalised members of a society have a right of access to its central treasures – and that, moreover, these treasures may turn out to belong, in symbolically important ways, to the dispossessed.

Reclaiming the queer past

In his search for the cultural traces of a queer past, Jarman has long found a key source of inspiration in Shakespeare. His version of *The Tempest*, released in 1980, represented the fulfilment of a long-held ambition to direct a film based on that play, while *The Angelic Conversation* (1985) takes the form of a visual meditation on Shakespeare's *Sonnets*. Moreover, Shakespeare's life and works provide frequent points of reference in Jarman's autobiographical writings. Across all forms and media, Jarman's appropriations of Shakespeare reveal an idiosyncratic mixture of elements, combining an irreverent attitude towards the poetic and dramatic texts; surprisingly conventional assumptions about the artist as self-originating transcendent genius; and the repeated assertion that the love represented in the *Sonnets*, 'the greatest love poetry in the world', in which Jarman claims to hear the authentic voice of Shakespeare's own desires, is homosexual love.[6] However, Jarman's primary interest lies not in proving that Shakespeare was homosexual, but in re-creating, within the terms of his own aesthetic, a range of texts drawn from an international homosexual 'great tradition' which includes Caravaggio, Marlowe and Britten as well as Shakespeare.

Having declared that works of art bring him little pleasure unless they are based on their creator's life,[7] Jarman does not engage directly with the vexed question of Shakespeare's own sexual identity, choosing to focus on the traces of homosexual desire which he finds inscribed in the poems, rather than on the lived experience often presumed to have generated them. In contrast, his creative use of Christopher Marlowe's *Edward II* is much more closely bound up with the modern gay community's tendency to claim Marlowe, however anachronistically, as the first major 'gay' figure in English literature, and to search for moments in his life and writings which appear to prefigure recognisably gay formations of desire and identity. The different positioning of Shakespeare and Marlowe in relation both to cultural authority and sexual politics is inflected in Jarman's films of *The Tempest* and *Edward II*; but I want to argue that the differences between these films are as much a function of the changing social and political circumstances of their production as of the two playwrights' divergent cultural status. Before turning to the films themselves, therefore, I want to sketch the context of sexual politics in which they were made and can be read.

On 5 April 1993, at the Cadogan Hotel – where Oscar Wilde had been arrested exactly ninety-eight years earlier – the lesbian and gay rights organisation, Stonewall, held a press conference to launch its international legal challenge to the continuing policing of gay men's lives under the terms of the 1967 Sexual Offences Act. This measure had effectively repealed the Labouchère Amendment, under which Wilde was convicted, without entirely decriminalising private, consensual sexual activities between men.[8] Representing Stonewall, the Shakespearean actor and gay activist Ian McKellen celebrated gay men's contribution to culture while critiquing their continued legal stigmatisation by pointing out that both *An Ideal Husband* and *The Importance of Being Earnest*, which were being performed in the West End when

Wilde was arrested, were also enjoying successful revivals in the spring of 1993.[9] As Stonewall's political strategy demonstrates, Oscar Wilde and the particular version of male homosexual identity with which he is associated continue to represent the most widely accessible and publicly intelligible form of gay identity currently available in Britain; and this legitimacy remains bound up with Wilde's cultural prestige as both a canonical literary figure and a commercially successful West End dramatist.

The Stonewall group is perceived by some activists to be the most cautious and 'establishment' of the groups currently campaigning for lesbian and gay rights. The decision to launch a major campaign at the Cadogan Hotel with an invocation of the shade of Oscar Wilde may therefore be taken to suggest that Wilde too is now enough of an establishment figure to enhance their cause. It is worth asking how Wilde – so thoroughly stigmatised and humiliated in the 1890s – came to achieve this degree of relative cultural acceptability by the 1990s. In the previous chapter I argued that he appropriated the cultural prestige and authority associated with Shakespeare in order to construct and legitimise an aestheticised version of male homosexual identity. I believe that the transformation of Wilde's status which allowed Stonewall to reinscribe the scene of his arrest as the site of their legal challenge is largely a function of this identification of homosexuality with (high) culture. I am specifically concerned here with the increased respectability of representations of or by gay men which are allowed the status of 'art' – although even these often remain controversial, of course, in ways which are bound up with larger social anxieties about art, as the critical response to Derek Jarman's films demonstrates.

Alan Sinfield has argued that in Britain the construction of a certain notion of 'high culture' precisely in terms of effeminate homosexuality continues to provide an important set of terms for regulating the uneasy relations between sexuality, class and access to artistic production and cultural power.[10] He suggests that these associations were effectively institutionalised in the post-war period, when welfare capitalism identified elite culture as one of the social benefits – like economic security, adequate housing and health care – which had traditionally been enjoyed by the upper class and should now be made available to everyone. The 'high' culture which had previously identified a distinctive class was thus reconstructed as a hegemonic national culture. Obviously, the idea that access to a national cultural heritage was desirable for all members of the population who could be educated to appreciate it did not originate with welfare capitalism; a substantial body of work produced in the last decade has traced the institutionalisation – some might say imposition – over the course of more than a century of a national literary heritage in which Shakespeare has been the key figure.[11] In much of this work the elite culture which is to be propagated through institutions such as the BBC and the state education system is portrayed as bullishly assertive, nationalistic, masculine and heterosexual. What is distinctive about Sinfield's account is that he nuances this rather reductive scenario with reference to an alternative construction of elite culture as the preoccupation of an effeminate and self-regarding leisure class; an association which gives rise to the popular stereotype, uniting philistinism and homophobia, of the artistic 'queen'. There is a curious irony in this stereotype, however, since as I noted in Chapter 5, many middle- and upper-class homosexual writers and artists have deliberately sought to transgress class barriers, seeking out working-class men for companionship, sex and love.

Derek Jarman came from an upper-class army family, and as a young artist and stage designer working in London in the 1960s belonged to the bohemian, aesthetic milieu which in some circles subsumed gay subculture for middle- and upper-class men. But his commitment to a radical gay politics in which allegiance to a shared sexual identity cuts across class distinctions and his personal relationships with working-class men both find expression in his films' frequent engagement with questions of class. Both *Jubilee* and *The Last of England* depict the dispossession of an underclass, offering an apocalyptic vision which eschews the realist critique of those contemporary British film-makers, such as Ken Loach and Mike Leigh, who are more often associated with the exploration of class issues, preferring to use inventive cinematic imagery to comment vividly on social injustice. Conversely, while *Caravaggio* dwells on the relations between poverty, violence and art, its Italian Renaissance setting distances it from any reflection on the place of class in English culture. However, Jarman's own class background has repeatedly aroused negative reactions which are projected on to his films and used to query his artistic commitment to a radical engagement with any forms of oppression other than that which he experienced as a gay man. Adopting the pose of the plain (heterosexual) man, the *New Statesman*'s columnist Sean French dismissed Jarman's political activity by declaring that 'his rebelliousness is itself an aspect of the confidence of his class', before complaining that he 'makes his own films with an aristocratic disdain for such matters as technical competence, plausibility, narrative interest and so on'.[12] This is, of course, a classic way of smearing both the art and politics of the avant-garde at one stroke, though in this case such *ad hominem* arguments are perhaps invited by Jarman's deliberate erosion of the boundaries between his art and his life; he has defined art as 'the attrition between private and public worlds'.[13] French's sweeping criticism fails to do justice, however, to Jarman's consistent critique of the class from which he came, and the attempt to find alternatives to this kind of stratification within the gay community, which inform all his work.

Curiously, another critic, Catherine Bennett, has attributed precisely the same aesthetic 'failings' in Jarman's work not to his upper-class origins, but to his homosexuality:

> His films have habitually looked fragmented ... structured by linked images conveying little more than a haze of homosexual absorption and an acute eye for light and colour. Indifferent, for the most part, to the demands of narrative or the courtesies of communication, Jarman's films have always been separatist, magnifying his own gay sensibility to the point that he became a saint in his own world, exclusive, or simply uninteresting, to many outside. Jarman's art is a peacock's tail, quite inseparable from Jarman.[14]

The peacock's tail is, of course, a way of coding homosexual 'flamboyance', and the notion that homosexual artists are incapable of anything other than a narcissistic display of the deviant self is a cliché of homophobic discourse. It is true that Jarman's deliberate reliance on associative juxtapositions of visual and aural imagery and his use of non-narrative cinematic forms contrast sharply with the particular pleasures offered by mainstream realist film, which evidently provides the criteria of excellence used by Bennett and French. The point is that this aesthetic of disruption and openness is accompanied by an explicit hermeneutic, which Jarman was almost always at pains to explain to interviewers – including Catherine Bennett, in the encounter which formed the basis of the article from which I quote here. He repeatedly emphasised that his artistic goal was to make the meaning of his films as open to diverse interpretation as possible, creating emotive and evocative images which will resonate with the different experiences and preconceptions viewers bring to them. The implicit corollary of this hermeneutic is therefore that critics like Bennett and Sean French may be revealing more about their own attitudes to class and sexuality than about Jarman's films. His emphasis on the active role of the spectator in constructing the meaning of a film is consonant with the strand of lesbian and gay film theory which stresses the activity and mobility of the queer spectator, who has often proved able to appropriate the most heterosexist of Hollywood narratives as sources of illicit or oppositional pleasures and desires.[15] This dynamic is reversed in Jarman's films, where it is the gay viewer who is addressed, and heterosexual spectators who are unused to adopting a fluid viewing identity are forced to come to terms with the marginalisation of their taken-for-granted pleasures. The outraged sense of exclusion which both Bennett and French reveal in their critiques of Jarman's films thus springs from their sense of an entitlement to be addressed by the aesthetic and narrative structures of cinema, betraying an unquestioning assumption of the cultural centrality of heterosexuality.[16] Challenging this assumption is one of the crucial tasks of Jarman's cultural work.

The entanglement of questions of class and sexuality in these negative responses to Jarman's work chimes with the larger argument I have been making about the imbrication of class issues in the construction of modern homosexuality. Jarman's most sustained and straightforward engagement with class issues as well as questions of state politics is to be found in one of his more recent films, *Edward II*. This growing politicisation may be traceable to the conjunction of the diagnosis of his own HIV+ status with the increased political activity of the gay community in various campaigns against homophobia/heterosexism and for lesbian and gay rights – Jarman was closely associated, for example, with the controversial direct action group Outrage. As with the case of Oscar Wilde, art – in this instance, Derek Jarman's films – constituted both a symptomatic instance of what was at issue in these struggles over the politics of sexuality, and a site of cultural con-testation. In particular, the campaigns against Clause – later Sec-tion – 28 of the 1988 Local Government Act may well prove to have been as crucial for the construction of gay identities and communities in the late twentieth century as the trial of Oscar Wilde was a hundred years earlier.

Section 28 sought to prevent local authorities from using their financial resources to 'promote homosexuality', and as such it was part of Thatcherism's onslaughts on both the autonomy of local government and the lifestyles of people who choose to live outside the nuclear family. In an important feminist assessment of the impact of Section 28 and the lesbian and gay community's response to it, Jackie Stacey identifies three strategies which were deployed in the campaigns against the measure, drawing respec-tively on the discourses of biological essentialism, artistic individ-ualism and radical libertarianism: she calls them the 'born that way' argument, the 'Oscar Wilde' argument, and the libertarian argument.[17] Of these, it was the 'Oscar Wilde' argument, advanced by the well-organised and relatively well-funded Arts Lobby, which achieved most visibility and legitimacy. This argument was primarily a response to the part of Clause 28 which sought to pre-vent local authorities from using any part of their funding to pro-mote homosexuality. It was feared that this aspect of the Clause would lead to censorship of libraries and publicly funded theatres and arts centres, and the restriction of public access to great works of gay art and literature – Marlowe's *Edward II* and Shake-speare's *Sonnets* were frequently cited as being in danger, along with the works of Oscar Wilde and David Hockney, among others. It is significant that Shakespeare himself is secured from the taint of a stigmatised sexual identity, entering the debate via the repre-sentations of sexuality in a particular text, whereas 'Oscar Wilde' tends to function in this context as a cultural figure with an inde-pendent existence as a metonym for a particular form of gay iden-tity. Works by lesbians were rarely mentioned in the campaign, although a number of lesbian performers, artists and writers were associated with the Arts Lobby.

In contrast to the generally philistine tenor of Thatcher's reign, this aspect of Section 28 appears to attribute extraordinary power to works of art, implying that representations of homosexuality have an inherently proselytising quality, 'promoting' the invidious attractions of 'pretended family relationships' to hapless hetero-sexuals. The understanding of sexuality as fluid and subject to change which is entailed by this fear of heterosexuals succumbing to homosexual persuasion is, of course, in contradiction with the belief in the nuclear family as a natural social formation, which is also enshrined in the Section. Interestingly, this question of the malleability of sexual identity was rarely addressed in the campaigns against the measure. Where the interests of gay readers and spectators were invoked, it was in terms of their need to recognise themselves and thereby find affirmation in works of art. In this account, the power of art lies not in its ability to change sexual orientation, as the supporters of Section 28 seemed to fear, but in its capacity to confirm and reinforce an already existing but oppressed and stigmatised sexual identity. This essentialist under-standing of the relation between sexuality and art extended to the question of the right of artists to produce representations of homosexuality. The central plank of the argument was a demand for freedom of artistic expression, which is crucially seen in this context as self-expression: homosexual identity and its cultural representation are construed as being inextricably interwoven.

By demonstrating the widespread presence of homosexuality at the heart of British culture, the 'Oscar Wilde' argument seeks to prove that homosexuality is neither contemptible nor easily sup-pressible; Mrs Thatcher and her Local Government Bill, it sug-gests, are but poor opposition for the massed ranks of Plato, Michelangelo, Shakespeare *et al.* Moreover, if men such as these – the acknowledged elite of Western culture – were homosexual, then it hardly seems appropriate to construe homosexuality as a disease, handicap or failing; it has even been implied that the reverse is true, and that the association of gay men with high cul-ture is due to their innate artistry and sensitivity. Jackie Stacey acknowledges the strategic effectiveness of this approach, noting that it

> highlighted the number of [gay] contributors to British culture who were already valued within conventional establishments, such as the theatre or literature, and who were thus difficult to dismiss and discredit. Since many of these 'masters' were a fundamental com-ponent of British cultural education, their exclusion from publicly funded bodies such as schools, museums and art galleries became

increasingly unrealistic as more and more of them were associated with homosexuality ('Promoting Normality', p. 294).

However, from a feminist point of view Stacey finds this argument problematic because it implicitly suggests that if a work conforms adequately to the aesthetic criteria of the dominant culture, the deviancy of its producer can be excused. Hence, perhaps, the relative invisibility of lesbian artistic production in this campaign, since lesbian work has often challenged the bourgeois, patriarchal notions of universality and excellence which the 'Oscar Wilde argument' tends to uphold by emphasising self-expression rather than sexual oppression. In their comprehensive account of the campaigns around Clause 28, Sue Sanders and Gill Spraggs note that the arts lobby was criticised by some campaigners against the clause, who feel that the disproportionate attention given in the media to supposedly 'elitist' concerns, such as access to plays and books, distorted public understanding of the implications of the clause and distracted attention from the fears of less powerful groups, such as lesbian mothers whose families were stigmatised as 'pretended'.[18]

More recently, the strategy of invoking the glories of the homosexual contribution to high culture in the past in order to defend the rights of lesbians and gay men in the present has been used in response to research undertaken as part of the international Human Genome Project, which appears to have identified a shared genetic component in homosexual men. Procedurally, the research appears to be seriously flawed,[19] but that did not deter either the *Daily Mail* from running a headline declaring 'Abortion hope after "gay genes" finding',[20] or the former Chief Rabbi, Lord Jakobovits, from advocating genetic engineering to eliminate homosexuality.[21] By far the most common positive response to these attacks on gay rights has been to emphasise how much culture would be deprived if gay men were genetically engineered out of existence, as in this *Independent* editorial:

> Leaving aside the Hitlerian eugenic attitudes implied, only a glance is required at the list of homosexual geniuses down the ages – from Michelangelo to Britten, Bacon, and Nureyev – to show the catastrophic loss that would inflict ... The contribution of lesbians and gay men to making society more civilised can hardly be overestimated.[22]

As in the campaign against Clause 28, the focus shifts from sexual oppression to artistic expression, and symbolic cultural capital – which, despite the writer's courteous nod towards lesbians, has mainly been amassed by gay men – becomes the crucial site of resistance.

Similar responses have been evoked by the apparently genocidal threat posed to the gay community by AIDS. In Larry Kramer's *The Normal Heart*, the first 'AIDS play' to attract a large mixed audience on Broadway and in the West End, the protagonist, Ned Weeks, shifts the centre of gay identity away from sexual preference and on to cultural achievement, declaring 'I belong to a culture that includes Proust, Henry James, Tchaikovsky, Cole Porter, Plato ... The only way we'll have real pride is when we demand recognition of a culture that isn't just sexual.'[23] If I point out that of the eighteen men I have omitted from Kramer's list of the great and the good only one – James Baldwin – is of anything other than white European heritage, it is not to fault Kramer for being less than impeccably politically correct, but to expose the inherent limitations of this strategy, which centrally demands the insertion of homosexual identity and cultural production into the dominant culture. Ned Weeks's moving celebration of gay men's cultural heritage works to achieve this by demonstrating that to a large extent the dominant culture is *already* gay men's culture. Politically, this clearly has certain advantages for those who wish to underline the acceptability and respectability of homosexuality. But it remains to ask, what about the numerous 'invisible men' – not to mention the invisible women – who do not make it on to Kramer's list? The political strategy of celebrating the cultural achievements of gay men does differentiate the white gay movement from the movements for liberation of black people and women, to which in many ways it is indebted. For it clearly shows that, whereas black people and women have sought to highlight their exclusion from cultural privilege and authority, gay men have always had access to those things – have, indeed, played a central role in defining and maintaining them.

Discussing recent challenges to the conventional canon of Western literature, Eve Sedgwick explores the significance of a question which has often been deployed by the keepers of the canon against those who either seek entry to it, or wish to displace its boundaries: 'Has there been, ask the defenders of a monocultural curriculum, not intending to stay for an answer, has there ever yet been a Socrates of the Orient, an African-American Proust, a female Shakespeare?'[24] Sedgwick concedes that, as I demonstrated in Chapter 1, this has also been a question which feminists, among others, have found it productive to ask themselves, at the same time as challenging the assumptions about artistic excellence which it enshrines. By way of demonstrating the gulf between the feminist and the gay male critical projects, though, she goes on to pose another set of questions, analogous to the first but very revealing in their difference:

> Has there ever been a gay Shakespeare?
> Has there ever been a gay Socrates?
> Has there ever been a gay Proust?
> Does the Pope wear a dress? If these questions startle, it is not least as tautologies. A short answer, though a very incomplete one, might be that not only have there been a gay Socrates, Shakespeare, and Proust, but that their names are Socrates, Shakespeare, Proust; and, beyond that, legion (*Epistemology of the Closet*, p. 52).

There is, of course, a deliberately polemical over-simplification in Sedgwick's claim, since she has done as much as anyone to nuance the categories available to us for making sense of sexual identity, forcing a recognition that it can only be partly meaningful to yoke together within the anachronistic category 'gay' the different historical moments and discursive regimes of sexuality which are here exemplified by Socrates, Shakespeare and Proust. Nevertheless, her witty and startling assertion makes an important point about the congruence of male homosexuality with the cultural values and institutions which other dispossessed groups have sought to challenge. Naming men's love and desire for each other and locating it in the cultural landscape of the past need not entail changing the contours of that landscape very much, if Sedgwick is right to argue that male homosexuality lies concealed in plain sight at its heart. Bruce Smith has made a similar point, noting that the Renaissance texts in which he finds homosexual desire inscribed were popular, privileged works in their own time, and have remained canonical ever since, so that homosexualities are not, he argues, hidden *from* history, but hidden *in* it.[25]

My argument is not that the strategy of defending gay men's lives with reference to the homosexual contribution to high culture is always unacceptable, but rather that its undoubted use-fulness in some contexts has to be weighed against the disadvantages inherent in its erasure of the political categories of race, class and gender. Reading across Jarman's work in various media reveals internal tensions around this strategy: between, for example, his apparently comfortable use of it in the choice of various gay icons of high culture as the subject-matter for several of his films, and his participation in the elitist, incestuous gay world centring around the arts in 1960s London which is conjured up in his autobiographical writing, on the one hand; and on the other, his engagement with radical, grass-roots, anti-establishment politics, such as his involvement with the direct-action group Outrage, or his criticism of Ian McKellen for accepting a knighthood from the party that imposed Section 28.[26] This last matter reveals the complexities of gay cultural politics particularly acutely, since McKellen, having finally come out of his glass closet, had earlier campaigned energetically against Clause 28, taking his one-man show 'Acting Shakespeare' on tour to raise funds and awareness around lesbian and gay issues. The controversy over the knighthood gave the straight, mainstream media the opportunity to portray the gay community as riven by personal and political animosity, enabling the press to gloss over Jarman's key point, which was that while he would have been happy for McKellen to accept his knighthood in recognition of his services to the theatre, he objected to the assumption that knighting an out gay man signalled a major shift in governmental attitudes to homosexuality.

It is undoubtedly true that there are significant divisions within the politically-concerned gay community about both aims and strategy. At the risk of appearing to endorse a naive liberal pluralism, however, I would like to suggest that this need not be seen only in terms of animosity and conflict, but also as an appropriate diversity and hybridity in a world where 'social upheaval has been accompanied by the fragmentation of old political constituencies and allegiances ... [and] the rise of new sources of collective identity and attachment'.[27] Ian McKellen's generous tribute to Jarman on the latter's death, remarking that 'his artistry, politics and private life were indivisible and their impact will survive him',[28] shows that the political, the sexual and the aesthetic, while inextricably connected, are not coextensive. It is therefore essential to remain flexible and responsive, artistically and politically. Thus there is clearly a historical factor at work in Jarman's cultural politics, in that the range of issues with which he was involved, and the strategies he used, kept pace with larger changes in focus over the quarter-century since the Stonewall riots inaugurated the gay liberation movement, from his triumph as Alternative Miss World in 1975 to his eventual iconic status as the best-known 'out' HIV+ man in Britain.

Throughout that period Jarman made independently-produced, low-budget feature films which share the project of 'reclaiming the Queer Past' ('A Footnote to My Past', *Dancing Ledge*, p. 7), and which construct a contemporary gay cultural politics by means of a dialogue with the history of gay cultural production. These films include *Sebastiane* (1976), which is based on the last days of St Sebastian, long established as a gay icon, and which not only invokes the high camp/high church/high culture nexus beloved of some gay men, but takes it to the lengths of being entirely scripted in Latin, which throughout most of European history has functioned as the principal language of the homosocial realm;[29] *The Angelic Conversation* (1985), a mystical and homoerotic meditation on a handful of Shakespeare's *Sonnets*; *Caravaggio* (1987), with its portrait of the artist as bisexual; and a filmed performance of Benjamin Britten's *War Requiem* (1989), the text of which is based on Wilfred Owen's poems. The two films I intend to discuss in some detail here are *The Tempest*, which – despite early plans to present Antonio and Sebastian as 'hysterical Queens' and to bring out the 'homosexual overtones' of Trinculo's 'misery acquaints a man with strange bedfellows'[30] – does not propose a homosexual aesthetic with reference either to Shakespeare as author, nor in any very direct way to any of the characters, but has nevertheless been judged by most of its critics to be an extremely queer film; and *Edward II*, in which Jarman brings the two sides of his work together explicitly and self-consciously, making the king's enemies at court into a satire on all that is most loathsome about Thatcher's Britain, and juxtaposing Marlowe's poetry with tender gay sex scenes and an attack by riot police on extras drawn from the lesbian and gay activist group Outrage.

This synthesis of political and aesthetic preoccupations can be read as participating in a wider movement in marginal and oppositional culture/politics which seeks the dissolution of any separation between cultural production and political activity, accomplished, in the words of black gay critic Kobena Mercer, by

> entering into the ambivalent and over-determined spaces where race, class, gender, sexuality, and ethnicity intersect in the social construction and lived experiences of individual and collective subjectivities ... The cultural production of images has become an area of permanent contestation and is no longer seen as peripheral to politics.[31]

This is consonant with Jarman's own emphasis on the homogeneity of his political and artistic work, across a variety of media and issues, exemplified by the collages he produced in the early 1990s, which juxtaposed the hospital paraphernalia used to treat his AIDS-related illnesses with scraps of celluloid salvaged from out-takes from his films:

> I don't see gaps between things. It's all a continuum, so that ideas that are floating around can be expressed in various ways, either in film or in paint, or written, and it seems to me that divisions have been forced upon us to a certain extent by capital and various other historical imperatives.[32]

A number of commentators have placed Jarman's films, particularly *Edward II*, under the rubric of the 'New Queer Cinema', one version of this collapsing together of art and politics. Jarman has been identified as the 'grand old man' of this cinematic movement, which includes the release in the last couple of years of such revisionary films as Tom Kalin's *Swoon*, a reinvestigation of the murder case which inspired Hitchcock's *Rope*, and which, in the words of the director, puts the 'homo' back into 'homicide'; *The Hours and Times*, which imagines a weekend of frustrated desire between John Lennon and the Beatles' homosexual manager Brian Epstein, and takes its title from Shakespeare's sonnet 57; and Gus Van Sant's *My Own Private Idaho*, discussed in Chapter 1. One commentator defines what is common to all these films thus:

> Call it 'Homo Pomo': there are traces in all of them of appropriation and pastiche, irony, as well as a reworking of history with social constructionism very much in mind ... [T]hese works are irreverent,

energetic, alternately minimalist and excessive. Above all, they're
full of pleasure.[33]

In what follows, I illustrate some of the ways in which this post-
modern aesthetic combines with a passionate commitment to
radical sexual politics and an equally deeply-felt love of the English cultural past in the autobiographical and cinematic works in
which Jarman celebrates and problematises the multiple cultural
traditions which intersect in his work and life. Shakespeare and
Marlowe emerge from this *mélange* less as tokens of institutionalised cultural authority than as fertile, pleasurable resources
from a queer past which has much to offer to the beleaguered present.

The Tempest: 'A continually changing mirror'[34]

Jarman began making notes and sketches for a possible version of
The Tempest as early as 1974; in one of these notebooks, written
in Rome in 1976, he describes Shakespeare's play as 'a continu-
ally changing mirror in which we can see ourselves reflected'. I
find this an intriguing statement – of course all mirrors change
when new things to be reflected are presented to them, but
Jarman here seems to suggest that as a mirror, *The Tempest* itself
has a protean quality. It is as if the changeability of the mirror/the
play is what makes our reflection visible to us. This labile, protean
quality is appropriate to the many revisions and transformations
Shakespeare's play has undergone over the last four centuries, as
well as to the magic of the film itself and the flexible viewing
strategies which are called for by its mixture of elements. A total-
ising account of the film's narrative and visual construction would
not, therefore, be desirable, or perhaps even achievable; I have
chosen to focus here on the film's engagement with questions of
cultural power and difference.

Jarman has written of the hopes and desires which motivated
the making of *The Tempest* in his first volume of autobiography,
Dancing Ledge, and has discussed the film extensively in interviews. Statements of authorial intention always need to be han-
dled with care, of course; Jarman was a charming and loquacious
but distinctly playful interviewee, and though his comments in
interviews are often extremely revealing, they do need to be inter-

preted with caution. In particular, his remarks about his intentions as scriptwriter and director are always undercut by his insistence that as far as possible, he tries to keep his films open to the play of diverse interpretations; he was drawn to *The Tempest*, he said, precisely because of the openness of Shakespeare's play: 'No one can actually pinpoint the meaning. It floats – is it about forgiveness, is it about coming of age, is it about magic? All those elements are in it but not actually resolved.'³⁵ A key aspect of the putative openness of *The Tempest* is Jarman's hope that the film would be accessible to people who would not normally consider watching Shakespeare.³⁶ To draw in such an audience, he could capitalise on the cult following of films like *Sebastiane* and *Jubilee*; while following the scandal which attended those works, a film of what is often perceived as one of Shakespeare's best-loved and most innocuous plays must have appeared to offer Jarman the opportunity to redeem his somewhat *louche* reputation. But while *The Tempest* did prove to be one of the most popular and critically acclaimed of his films, there was little about it which would allay the anxieties of viewers shocked by his earlier work. In this respect, Jarman's adherence to the traditional practices of the low-budget avant-garde were crucial, particularly in so far as he frequently drew his performers from among his social circle, or from fringe and avant-garde workers in other media; certain actors, notably Karl Johnson, Tilda Swinton and Nigel Terry, have appeared in several of his films. Apart from this group, it is rare for the performers to be known primarily as film actors. They bring to their roles both their own following and particular qualities which are associated with their other work; Toyah Wilcox, who played Miranda, is a singer who in the late 1970s was closely identified with the punk movement, while the film's Caliban, Jack Birkett, is a dancer and mime artiste who had worked with the Lindsay Kemp company and also had his own drag act. Casting decisions of this kind may well have helped to draw in people who would not normally think of themselves as Shakespeareans, but must also have exacerbated the anxieties of a more conservative potential audience.

Making a connection between the self-conscious cinematic art of Jarman's *Tempest* – what some critics have identified as its campness – and the 'characteristically Elizabethan [*sic*] reflexivity' of Shakespeare's play, Mark Nash argues that 'Jarman is not concerned so much with representation as presentation ... He doesn't really offer an interpretation so much as a personal appropriation, a staging of elements.'[37] This analysis certainly accords with Jarman's assertion, 'I didn't want to impose an intellectual conception on the play ... I wanted to bring the thing alive' (quoted in Sutton, *Time Out*). However, he only arrived at this position at the end of a process, extending over six years, which explored the possibility of bringing some very distinctive intellectual and aesthetic concepts to bear on *The Tempest*.

The earliest notes for a possible film of *The Tempest* can be found in a notebook dating from the autumn of 1974, which would make the entire thing a psychodrama enacted within the mind of a Prospero maddened by delusions of power and obsessive attention to cabalistic studies (BFI archive, item 12). Characters such as Ariel and Miranda are to be little more than puppets voiced by Prospero; yet the spectator will also be distanced from Prospero by the device of setting the courtiers' scenes on a balcony overlooking the room in which he is confined as in a madhouse. This is very much a Renaissance *Tempest* – Prospero's own appearance is to be based on a Titian painting, while his bedlam is a decrepit room in a Venetian palazzo, adorned only with Giorgione's mysterious painting *The Tempest* (*c*. 1508) and a mosaic floor inlaid with magical symbols. Returning to the subject two years later, Jarman made Prospero's psyche less all-inclusive, so that only Ariel and Caliban remained as projections of his ego, but still saw the film centrally as an exploration of Prospero's dangerous fantasies of magic as a means to power: 'he is unable to see his exploitation of Caliban and Ariel and however he resolves his own tragedy the maxim that all power corrupts remains essentially true' (BFI archive, item 13).

Although these early plans to make Prospero the controlling consciousness of the entire film were eventually modified, he remains central to *The Tempest*. Oddly enough, Jarman himself has been identified with the protagonist of the only Shakespeare play he filmed; in an article entitled 'Prospero with a Day-Glo Banner', the journalist Tristan Davies asserts that 'sitting in his shack surrounded by pebbles, plants and other exotica [Jarman] could almost have been the model for Peter Greenaway's Prospero ... [he] sits, Prospero-like, sniffing flowers as if grasping at a memory of happier times'.[38] Ironically, the role of Prospero in

Greenaway's *Prospero's Books* was played by John Gielgud, who had been tentatively linked with those early incarnations of Jarman's project which anticipated Greenaway's version to the extent that the entire action was to be contained within Prospero's mind. In most ways, however, Greenaway's deeply reactionary film is the antithesis of Jarman's *Tempest*. Greenaway's Prospero is a patriarch *par excellence*, and the film stages his renunciation of his power only as a pretext for the conspicuous display and consumption of cultural capital. The desire to identify Jarman with Prospero is intriguing, given that Prospero as maker of theatrical magic has often been conflated with Shakespeare. The magus is a figure whose involvement with power and illusion stands in an oblique, often troubling relation to the cultural mainstream, a role which seems appropriate to Jarman's idiosyncratic combination of cultural centrality and oppositionality. In one way, his canonisation in 1991 by the Sisters of Perpetual Indulgence could be seen as endorsing his magus-like status – it was primarily a camp political gesture, of course, but there is also something in it which is a tribute to Jarman's otherness, the integrity and independence of the vision which manifests itself in his work.[39] Certainly, Jarman's *Tempest* emerges from the conjunction of magic and power, in that it is crucially concerned with the use of cinematic magic to stimulate the spectator's engagement with its exploration of power.

As a Renaissance magus, Jarman's Prospero recalls the presence of the Elizabethan scholar and magician Dr John Dee in the 1977 film *Jubilee*, which contrasts England in the Silver Jubilee year of Elizabeth II with the reign of Elizabeth I.[40] At the end of *Jubilee*, which represents a desolate and apocalyptic present, 'our heroines flee from the dying cities … to a dream England of the past: the England of stately homes' (*Dancing Ledge*, p. 173). In *The Tempest*, the devastated urban landscape of the earlier film is transposed to the 'endless corridors and lost rooms' (*ibid.*) of the decaying Tudor mansion, Stoneleigh Abbey – though it would be a mistake to read the use of this location as a quest for accurate period detail, since the film was shot in the deserted Georgian wing of the house. Jarman has said that this choice of setting was primarily motivated by the desire to avoid the temptation of filmic literalism and the consequent clash between language and setting which he sees as bedevilling other Shakespeare films:

> For *The Tempest* we needed an island of the mind, that opened mys-
> teriously like Chinese boxes: an abstract landscape so that the deli-
> cate description in the poetry, full of sound and sweet airs, would
> not be destroyed by any Martini lagoon. The budget was only
> £150,000. Britain was the magic isle. I sailed as far away from trop-
> ical realism as possible (*Dancing Ledge*, p. 186).

Stoneleigh Abbey fulfils this role admirably; at the same time, particularly with the ending of *Jubilee* in mind, it is hard to resist
seeing the choice of location as a comment on, or sardonic and
critical contribution to, the tradition of the stately home as microcosm of the national culture. Despite the critiques offered of Prospero's abuse of power in Jarman's earlier notebooks, the film
ultimately appears unable to challenge Prospero's omnipotent
rule over his tiny, shabby realm; nevertheless, this claustrophobic
little society seems to be at as much of a dead-end as the England
depicted in *Jubilee*. Colin MacCabe argues that the disorientation
of represented space which the film's setting enacts is crucial to
its subversive fracturing of representational space; it is impossible
to make sense of how the various rooms of the house are located
in relation to each other, or of the spatial relation between the
interior and exterior scenes.[41] Since the film is set 'not on an
island, but in a ruined aristocratic house, an imperial monument'
(*Dancing Ledge*, p.186), this disorientation has the effect of
revealing the fault lines in the cultural formation of which that
house is a microcosm. Conversely, the outdoor scenes – filmed
among the dunes of Bamburgh in Northumberland – drain away
all sense of place. Saturated in the same misty blue as the found
footage of the storm at sea which opens the film, the scenes on
the beach take place in a perilous, impermanent utopia – a non-
place in which the rules and hierarchies which shape the social
world to which the stately home belongs are put in question, and
all things are executed by whims and contraries.

Looking back at *Jubilee* in 1984, Jarman noted that its apocalyptic contrast between past and present turned out to be
prophetic: 'Dr Dee's vision came true – the streets burned in Brix-
ton and Toxteth' (*ibid.*). This use of a metaphorical device which
juxtaposes the decay and violence of contemporary urban life
with the glories of a period conventionally identified as England's
golden age is consistent with Jarman's strategy of using an

idealised fantasy of the past to critique the all too real failings of the present, as critic David Hirst notes, drawing on an interview with the film-maker:

> Jarman sees the significance of magic as deeply political. Shakespeare, strongly influenced by Dee, was, he feels, making a statement about the superiority of Renaissance values ... over the reactionary attitude which dominated the new century when James I came to the throne ... [Jarman's] film is a stand against the puritanism and conservatism which have developed here in the last decade.[42]

Magic is both the subject and method of Jarman's version of *The Tempest*: 'Film is the wedding of light and matter – an alchemical conjunction' *(Dancing Ledge*, p. 188).[43] Though his library was perhaps not as large as Prospero's, Jarman possessed a substantial collection of books on magic, and the details of magical practices represented in the film are all drawn from his own research into the Elizabethan esoteric tradition. Heathcote Williams was cast as Prospero because he shared the film's interest in the occult to the extent of being skilled in practical magic himself; Jarman describes him as being identified with the role of benevolent magus, rather than performing it *(Dancing Ledge*, p. 183).

However, this very positive account of Prospero's role seems to be at odds with the more questioning attitude to his power which was signalled in Jarman's earlier thinking about the film, and I am reluctant to endorse it. Arguably, the highly pleasurable experience of watching the film uses cinematic magic to reconcile the viewer to the dispositions made by Prospero. But the claim made for the benign nature of Prospero's magic is undercut by the plethora of recent critical accounts which have argued that in this play, magic *is* power.[44] Extending this assumption in a Foucauldian reading of the play which makes the deployment of power its central theme, Colin MacCabe argues that in *The Tempest* 'Prospero's reign is one of terror', and his relationship with Ariel, 'with its barely suppressed sexual undertones' is an allegory for the workings of Walsingham's secret service, for which Marlowe was forced to spy:

> Jarman's homosexuality is what leads him to concentrate on the repression at the heart of the English state, from which all the other

repressions follow. The complete containment of sexuality within sanctified heterosexual marriage, the rigorous policing of desire and excess, the focusing on male sexuality and the denial of female sexuality: these are the fundamental themes of *The Tempest* ('Throne of Blood', 13).

The idea that, in Jarman's words, 'the whole of the modern British state is founded on the repression of homosexuality'[45] was to become crucial to his interpretation of Marlowe's *Edward II*. As far as *The Tempest* is concerned MacCabe's gloom-ridden account is salutary in so far as it questions the idealisation of Prospero's stealthy power by proxy. Given the numerous critiques which have challenged the perception of Prospero as an entirely benign figure in recent years, it has become hard to accept him as the incarnation of benevolent omnipotence without also seeing the scope for the abuse of power. For example, from a feminist point of view the extreme infantilisation of Toyah Wilcox's Miranda could be interpreted as a disturbing picture of a daughter who is entirely subjugated to her father. Reviewing the film on its first release, Mike Sutton praised Wilcox's 'thoughtful' and 'wilful' performance, but also had reservations about the film's sexual politics:

> Shakespeare's last plays may be about regeneration, but primarily they involve the regeneration of the masculine, patriarchal order … Jarman's energy during shooting seems to have been concentrated on injecting life into the rather thin, symbolic characters of the original, rather than modifying the play's patriarchal premise.[46]

Conversely, Jack Birkett's performance as Caliban is so delightful that it is hard to square with the fairly conventional interpretation of him, offered by the film, as a 'baddy' – albeit a rather ineffectual one. Hence Prospero's maltreatment of Caliban appears unnecessarily vindictive, and given the traces of racial difference which distinguish Williams and Birkett, it is difficult not to find overtones of a master–slave dynamic in their relationship. Birkett's performance, which Mike Sutton nicely describes as 'a heady concoction of menace, petulance and camp' (*ibid.*) was largely his own creation; it was part of Jarman's policy of openness to allow his performers considerable creative input, which sometimes makes for an intriguing clash of acting styles. In this context, however, I find this quest for openness problematic, since it evokes resonances with the recent debates about *The Tempest*'s status as a colonial text which the film has difficulty accommodating. Early plans for the film had included a black, beautiful, sympathetic Caliban, wearing a mother-of-pearl necklace to symbolise the loveliness of the world he had shared with Sycorax, and a green and red costume associating him with the elements of earth and fire (BFI archive, item 13). In the end, though, Jarman explicitly eschewed the interest in colonialism which has loomed so large in reproductions of *The Tempest* in recent decades, telling one interviewer, 'it was very possible to make Caliban black, but I rejected it because I thought it would load the whole film in one way, make it more specific than general' (Sutton, 33). Jarman's phrasing here reproduces a racist paradigm which sets whiteness up as neutral and universal, blackness as a 'marked', deviant condition. Yet as Richard Dyer has convincingly argued,[47] this pretence at neutrality is essential to the processes by which whiteness reproduces itself as the invisible, ubiquitous dominant term; true neutrality is not achieved by denying the relations of power which differentiate white and black. Moreover, Birkett's distinctive appearance, not easily assimilable to racial discourse's binary categories 'white' and 'black', troubles the very association of skin colour with racial identity on which Jarman is relying here.

The tensions which I find around the representation of Caliban in Jarman's *Tempest* are exacerbated by the screen image of Sycorax. In Chapter 4 I noted that revisionary interpretations of the significance of Prospero's magic have drawn attention to similarities between Prospero himself and Sycorax. One of Jarman's innovations is to present Sycorax on screen, in a scene which provoked objections from many of the film's critics. A close-up on Sycorax's face shows an exotic-looking woman, heavily made-up with black cosmetics which evoke punk fashions and a certain perilous glamour, puffing voluptuously on a hookah; the camera then pans down to disclose the adult Caliban suckling greedily at her breast, in a formal tableau which deliberately constructs a perverse parody of a 'Madonna and child' painting (plate 1). Meanwhile, Ariel – who is as naked as Caliban and Sycorax – is gloatingly tormented by the latter, who holds him on a leash as if he were a recalcitrant household pet. This screen image, which I find both shocking and enthralling, does carry a powerful sexual

Plate 1 Jack Birkett as Caliban and Claire Davenport as Sycorax in Derek Jarman's film version of *The Tempest* (photo: Bridget Holm, from Derek Jarman, *Dancing Ledge*)

charge, which spills over into the way we consider the characters as they appear elsewhere in the film. Caliban's greed for his mother's breast echoes his first appearance, in which he was depicted gobbling raw eggs with lascivious gusto. And since the scene is the visual embodiment of Prospero's reminder to Ariel, heard in voice-over, of his mistreatment at the hands of Sycorax – a reminder which is designed to ensure Ariel's continuing servitude to Prospero – it must also underline the 'sado-erotic edge'[48] to their relationship. The absent, obscene Sycorax is thus given a compelling physical presence, yet she appears only in this brief segment, effectively as Prospero's puppet. He is manipulating Ariel's memory in order to ensure his continued service, appropriating Sycorax's power in order to enhance his own control over Ariel.

Jarman's depiction of Sycorax does nothing to query the misogyny and racism of Shakespeare's text in this respect. However, it is countered, at the end of the film, by the appearance of the veteran black singer Elisabeth Welch, in a blizzard of confetti, as part of the masque which ostensibly celebrates the wedding of Ferdinand and Miranda – though the camp glory of her performance, surrounded by prancing sailors who fully live up to their reputation as homoerotic icons, does nothing to enhance the appeal of institutionalised heterosexuality.[49] The heartbroken lyrics of 'Stormy Weather' are at odds with the delicious pleasures Welch's performance offers the spectator, underlined by the blissful expressions it summons to the faces of the other characters. There is nothing about either Jarman's comments on his intentions as director, or the racial and sexual politics inscribed elsewhere in the film, which leads me to believe that this celebratory recuperation of the black woman was conceived as a deliberate political statement; it could, indeed, be questioned as a tokenistic confirmation of the mythicised status of black women in Shakespeare's play, Jarman's film and the cultures which produced both. Nevertheless, the camera's loving attention to Welch in this most memorable and pleasurable scene does give the film's uneasy engagement with questions of racial and sexual difference a redemptive quality which is virtually unique among male-authored reconstructions of *The Tempest*. I am uncomfortably conscious that in offering a rather downbeat account of *The Tempest*'s handling of the question of magic and power, and then critiquing the film's uneasy relationship to questions of colonial and post-colonial representation, I have failed to convey anything of the huge pleasure I have derived from my repeated viewings of it. This is in part, I think, because the critical vocabulary of pleasure and celebration remains distinctly underdeveloped – it is difficult to do more than reiterate Miranda's inarticulate delight at the masque. But it is also, I think, the case that the aesthetic and political dimensions of the play are not reducible to each other: the magical pleasures of Jarman's film remain stubbornly resistant to my attempts to force political correctness on it.

'Marlowe outs the past': *Edward II*

Edward II has a counterpart to Elisabeth Welch's appearance in *The Tempest* in the form of Annie Lennox's performance of Cole Porter's 'Ev'ry Time We Say Goodbye' as Edward and Gaveston bid farewell to each other before the latter goes into exile. Since the making of *The Tempest* and of Jarman's second Shakespeare film, *The Angelic Conversation* – in many ways his gentlest and sunniest work – the upheavals of the intense campaign against Clause 28 and, on a more personal level, the diagnosis of the filmmaker's HIV+ status had intervened. The changes these events forced on the cultural and personal context in which Jarman works inevitably had a marked effect on the overt politics of the film, and Lennox's performance is a poignant symbol of this changed context for the representation of gay sexuality. She first recorded the song as part of the 'Red Hot and Blue' project, which sought to raise funds and awareness around the issue of HIV and AIDS by producing recordings and videos of cover versions of Cole Porter songs. In the context of AIDS, the song's elegiac quality is intensely poignant, and this is enhanced by the circumstances in which the video was made. Lennox had asked Jarman to direct the video for 'Ev'ry Time We Say Goodbye', but he was himself unwell with HIV-related problems when they were due to shoot. Rather than treating this painfully apt circumstance as an inconvenience or a distressing irrelevance, the video memorialises his absence by projecting home-movies of his childhood across Lennox's body – as one critic puts it, 'the home-movies are the projection of memory; the literal source of the memories, Jarman's past, allows him to be recalled in his absence'.[50]

Jarman once remarked

> I don't think there will be any satisfactory [artistic] response to the AIDS epidemic until it is over … What I don't want is for it to be in the realms of banality. You need Beethoven's *Ninth* to deal with AIDS adequately, not auctions of Keith Haring tea towels.[51]

To some extent, his participation in the 'Red Hot and Blue' project may thus appear contradictory, since it worked within the terms of popular culture in order to address an audience of sexually active young people who perhaps stand most in need of developing cultural forms which will enable them to make sense of the social impact of AIDS. Jarman's point here is not merely one about cultural hierarchy, however, and not just a value judgement about the enduring merits of classical music versus the graffiti-derived forms of Haring's streetwise artwork. Rather, the point he is making is one about the banality of the explicit, and the inadequacy of language and illustrative, representational systems of signification to express what is at stake in the struggle to represent AIDS. Hence the last cinematic project he initiated, *Blue* (1993), combines an entirely blue screen with a first-person voice-over recounting Jarman's own experiences with AIDS, and effectively abandons the construction of visual meaning through difference, structure or narrative as inadequate and irrelevant to the physical and emotional experiences he is trying to convey. This is of a piece with his aesthetic in all his films, in that, as I have noted, he seeks to work by suggestion and indirection, minimising text and leaving the work as open to multiple interpretations as possible in order to elicit each spectator's personal emotional engagement with the film.

In both the films under discussion, the fragmentation of text and image is echoed and intensified by the dislocation of space. Thus the claustrophobic, spatially disorientated setting of *The Tempest* is reinflected by the dank gloom which pervades the setting of *Edward II*, making it difficult to distinguish between throne room and dungeon – aptly enough, the film was shot in the old Hammer Horror studios at Bray. Jarman points up the figurative significance of this visually powerful setting: 'The set became a metaphor for the trapped country, the prison of our lives, "the closet of our heart", in Edward's words.'[52] Making a virtue of the film's extremely restricted budget, Jarman uses a few props – a hospital bed, a throne, a vast boardroom table – to delineate specific locales within the cavernous, shadowy set. The monumental quality of the setting and the use of lighting which centres the action in a pool of light surrounded by deep shadow combine to produce an effect which underlines the public significance of the most intimate acts, evoking a sense that the entire court is constantly under surveillance.

This collapse of the distinction between public and private has important consequences for the sexual politics of the film. The regulation of gay male sexuality often turns on attempts to extend the law into the bedroom; here, though, gay men 'flaunt it' in spaces which are neither private nor public, and thereby claim the right to determine for themselves where it is appropriate to assert their sexuality. Conversely, also in question is Isabella's freedom to move in the public domain as a woman. Sometimes she is made to seem intensely vulnerable, as when she teeters on her high heels down a narrow, steeply sloping corridor, where she is cornered and sexually tormented by Gaveston; or when she is being measured and fitted for additions to her wonderful wardrobe, standing, exposed and isolated, in the middle of the cavernous set wearing only a low-cut plain white undergown, while Edward humiliates her in front of her female attendants. As her power increases, however, she becomes more assertive in claiming and using space – the scene where Isabella uses a suspended deer's carcass for target practice is a neat image of the way brutality is used to regulate space and thereby exert social control throughout the film, prefiguring Edward's subsequent use of a still bloodier carcass as a scaffold to expedite the brutal murder of a young police officer. Finally, though, Isabella's attempt to master the social space available to her is thwarted, and she is confined in a cage with Mortimer, the two of them reduced from ruling a nation to this simultaneously lonely and spectacular imprisonment.

Like many gay film directors, Jarman has often been accused of misogyny in the representation of female roles; these complaints have become increasingly frequent in recent years, with *The Garden* and *Edward II* coming in for particularly severe criticism.[53] Such criticisms sometimes appear to be generated by a confusion of Jarman's critique of what has been called compulsory heterosexuality with an attack on individual heterosexual women.[54] Certainly, it is true that his films problematise the social institutionalisation of heterosexuality – this is, indeed, one of the key aims of his work as a political artist – and that they sometimes achieve this by making heterosexual relationships appear foolish or repugnant, as in the somewhat clichéd scenes depicting Mortimer's taste for bondage with prostitutes. Jonathan Romney argues that the imaginative failure which he finds in this aspect of the characterisation of Mortimer is related to the problematic nature of the film's use of 'heterophobia' as a polemical strategy (*'Edward II'*, p. 42). Romney objects strongly to the film's problematisation of heterosexual identity, although he does acknowledge that such a reversal may have a certain tactical legitimacy in bringing the nature of gay oppression home to heterosexual viewers – a concession which implies that Jarman's depiction of a homophobic state does not reflect the reality of life for many gay men and lesbians, but merely represents a kind of dystopian role-reversal. Jarman, in fact, has repeatedly stated that he considers the carnivalesque use of strategic inversion to be a useful way of prompting people to reconsider assumptions which are normally so taken-for-granted that they effectively become invisible, and that in adopting this tactic his aim is precisely to shock and provoke;[55] the published script of *Edward II* ends with the defiant declaration

HETEROPHOBIA
liberates
HOMOSEXISM
empowers.[56]

While there is, then, a specific political rationale for Jarman's playful use of 'heterophobia', the question of misogyny does remain problematic, as I noted in my discussion of *The Tempest*, and it cannot be denied that there are relatively few strong roles for women in most of his films. Yet it would be easy to list heterosexual mainstream Hollywood directors who equally focus their films on male characters, excluding women or representing them via a narrow range of stereotypes. In Hollywood movies, moreover, this marginalisation of women is not accompanied by the critical perspective on the politics of gender and sexuality which is central to Jarman's work, and from which in many ways women, whether heterosexual or lesbian, stand to benefit as much in the long run as do the gay men who are his principal concern. The spectacle of heterosexual men rushing to vindicate their own sexual politics by criticising Jarman's misogyny is not an edifying one, and in the case of *Edward II* it leads to less than careful readings of the film. Colin MacCabe, for instance, states that Jarman makes 'Edward's passion for Gaveston a consequence of his inability to be roused by the queen's body in a truly chilling scene' ('Throne of Blood', 13). This sounds suspiciously like the reactionary notion that homosexuality is the pathological refuge of failed heterosexuals. But Edward's love for Gaveston is already established by this time, and though the scene is certainly painful to watch, I would suggest that this is because it sympathetically registers the distress of the two people who are trapped in this disastrous marriage; Isabella's pain is not presented as negligible.

The casting of Tilda Swinton as Isabella is a crucial element of the film, although at an early stage of the planning Jarman had considered having a boy play the role (*Modern Nature*, p. 233). Swinton is known for her recurring roles in Jarman's films, in which she has considerable influence on how her performance is to take shape and mesh with other aspects of the film. Like Annie Lennox, she has an androgynous quality, most powerfully realised in her performance in the stage and TV productions of Manfred Karge's *Man to Man*, in which she plays a woman who re-creates herself in the image of her dead husband, and in the title role of Sally Potter's recent film of Virginia Woolf's *Orlando*. Swinton has spoken publicly on many occasions about both her rebellion against the upper-class military background she shares with Derek Jarman, and her commitment to radical politics, exemplified in her work in roles which engage with questions of class, gender and sexuality.[57] Both her androgynous quality and her strong political stance endow her with a distinctive appeal for a feminist/lesbian audience.

In *Edward II*, all aspects of the *mise-en-scène* conspire to make Isabella the spectacular object of the gaze whenever she is on screen (plate 2). But the logic of the high phase of feminist film theory which followed from Laura Mulvey's influential theorisation of the gaze as male must have an uneasy relationship to this film.[58] Analysing classical Hollywood cinema, Mulvey placed film as a reflection of social structures which control 'images, erotic ways of looking and spectacle' (p. 22):

Plate 2 Nigel Terry as Mortimer, Jerome Flynn as Kent, Tilda Swinton as Isabella and Jody Graber as Prince Edward in Derek Jarman's film version of *Edward II* (photo: Liam Longman)

> In a world ordered by sexual imbalance, pleasure in looking has been split between active/male and passive/female. The determining male gaze projects its phantasy on to the female figure which is styled accordingly. In their traditional exhibitionist role women … can be said to connote *to-be-looked-at-ness* (p. 27).

The pleasures of film thus reinforce the social construction of man as desiring subject and woman as passive object, serving to maintain asymmetrical relations of power between the sexes. Mulvey therefore advocates the 'destruction of [cinematic] pleasure as a radical weapon' (p. 23). In art cinema, however, the problematisation of the kinds of visual and narrative pleasure offered by Hollywood has always been at issue. By using forms and practices which owe more to the art cinema tradition than to Hollywood, Derek Jarman's films seek to problematise the relationships between viewer and film, and film and society, with the explicit aim of unsettling the power relationships identified by Mulvey. For Jarman, it is not the destruction of pleasure, but the production of pleasure for gay viewers that is radical, and to this extent his work forms part of the 'politically and aesthetically avant-garde cinema' (p. 23) which Mulvey places in counterpoint to Hollywood – a cinema which dares 'to break with normal pleasurable expectations in order to conceive a new language of desire' (p. 24). The language of desire which Jarman's films articulate is undeniably homoerotic, and as I noted above, the critical response to his work has amply demonstrated that this is productive of 'unpleasure' for viewers who bring to his work Hollywood-derived expectations of narrative closure, coherent characterisation and lavish production values. Complaints by such critics that Jarman's films are exclusive, aimed at a self-selecting gay audience, are in a sense precisely to the point – his project is to make cinematic pleasure available to people whose desires and identifications have never fitted the heterosexual schema Mulvey finds in Hollywood cinema.

If the male gaze by which the films are to be seen is a gay one, this necessarily gives the question of Isabella's 'to-be-looked-at-ness' a very different inflection than it would have in the context of a Hollywood movie. This question can most usefully be addressed with reference to the notion of masquerade. The psychoanalytic concept of masquerade, which has been much used in feminist film theory, equates feminine social identity with the wearing of a disguise, implying that conventional femininity is a performance which masks the essential lack which characterises the state of being a woman in patriarchal culture. The notion of masquerade has been used both to critique the processes by which women are compelled to submit to men's desire for a certain presentation of femininity, and, by insisting on the perception that femininity is itself a performance, to create a space in which alternative constructions of femininity can be put into play. In an influential essay, Mary Ann Doane suggests that masquerade is useful for the feminist film critic because it 'generate[s] a problematic within which the image is manipulable, producible, and readable by the woman'.[59] At the time when this essay was first published (1982), Doane – like many feminist film theorists – basically accepted Mulvey's presumption of universal heterosexuality, and used the concept of masquerade to negotiate with this framework, carving out a space within it for the subjectivity of the heterosexual female spectator. However, I would argue that the notion of masquerade meshes more productively with the theoretical presumptions which inform the sexual politics of the 1990s lesbian and gay communities, at least to the extent that they are typified by the characteristics of the 'new queer cinema/politics', and by Judith Butler's enormously influential theorisation of all forms of gendered and sexual identities as performative, enacted in an improvisational theatre of shifting and provisional identifications.[60] The dizzying speed at which sexual politics have changed over the last twenty years or so has awkward implications for the historically specific moment of feminism which is inscribed in Laura Mulvey's theorisation of the misogynist male gaze. In the 'queer nineties', Tilda Swinton's performance as Isabella incarnates an understanding of the simultaneous excess and lack of femininity as it is constructed in a patriarchal culture which, I would argue, is easily and pleasurably intelligible to the polymorphously perverse gazes of the dykes, queens and queers who make up a typical Jarman audience.

Theoretically, Mulvey's formulation of the sexual dynamics of cinematic pleasure is in no way dependent on a notion that the gaze of the camera enacts the controlling gaze of a heterosexual male auteur; yet this quite often seems to be presumed in applications of her work. In the case of *Edward II*, such a presumption must be further troubled by the disjunction between the filmmaker's declared homosexuality and the tendency – according with some feminist extensions of Mulvey's theory[61] – to analyse Jarman's films within a distinctly auteurist framework. Analysing the complex and uneasy relationship between *Edward II*'s political focus on homophobia and the sins of Heterosoc on the one hand, and the representation of the isolated female figure of Queen Isabella on the other, Jonathan Romney suggested that

> Jarman overlays the play's complexities with his own thematic obsessions, producing a contradictory film which is readable less in terms of sexual politics than in terms of the code of the 'Jarman film' as a genre in itself ... [in which] quintessentially Jarmanesque images add up to a contradictory surfeit of meaning that the text cannot accommodate (*'Edward II'*, 42).

However, the anxiety about coherence and consistency which runs through this review rests on problematic assumptions. For example, Romney brings to bear on the film a demand for psychologically coherent characterisation, complaining that if in their treatment of the bishop who offends them, Edward, Gaveston and their thugs are allowed to 'embody a sado-masochistic "rough trade" fantasy' and be 'celebrated as glamorous hoods', that makes it difficult to accept them as also being 'heroes and martyrs' (*ibid.*). There are two possible responses to this criticism. First, this apparent contradiction could be made intelligible by setting the representation of Edward and Gaveston within a gay tradition of glamorising deviance and criminality, which recently includes films like *Swoon*, Todd Haynes' *Poison* and Gregg Araki's *The Living End*, but which finds its most celebrated exemplar in the life and work of Jean Genet. Second, Romney's assumption is symptomatic of the liberal belief that gays are only entitled to tolerance when they are nice, kind, well-socialised people, preferably in search of a virtuous martyrdom. Jarman has explicitly dealt with this issue in an interview, conceding that Edward and Gaveston may not come across as the nicest of people, but stressing that this is part of the polemical point of the film: 'you don't have to like somebody to accept their right to have a love affair'.[62] Arguably, this is one element of the film which sticks fairly closely to Marlowe's original: discussing the play, Claude J. Summers proposes that by representing the relationships of Edward and his lovers as complex and ambiguous, it resists appropriation to the liberal defence of sexual freedoms and 'redefin[es] received ideas about both sex and politics … resonat[ing] with implications that transcend neat categories and question[ing] comfortable assumptions'.[63] Jarman has also compared his gay lovers to Shakespeare's Antony and Cleopatra, craftily playing on the liberal humanist notion that love knows no distinction in order to bathe Edward and Gaveston in the reflected glow of those archetypically tragic lovers; while Kent's declaration that 'the mightiest Kings have had their minions', described by Jarman as 'a great outing speech' (*Queer Edward II*, p. 84), constructs, in this context, a militant genealogy of men's love for each other. *Edward II* firmly rejects the possibility of legitimising homosexuality by inserting it into that effeminised conservative culture which I discussed earlier, but plays on the values and icons of that culture in order to insist defiantly that 'queerness' is its own legitimisation.

Though it is by no means the overt project of either film to do so, Jarman's different uses of Shakespeare and Marlowe in his films of *The Tempest* and *Edward II* do speak to the differing cultural status of the two playwrights and the diverse investments which English literary culture has at stake in the question of their sexual identity. It is curious that the 'fact' of Marlowe's homosexuality is far more taken for granted than Shakespeare's, although the historical evidence seems to me to be tenuous in both cases – Richard Baines's accusations imputing sodomitical leanings to Marlowe scarcely offer reliable evidence.[64] Indeed, since there is at present no consensus as to what – if anything – might have constituted a homosexual identity in the early modern period, it is almost impossible to decide what might count as evidence for its existence in individual cases. It is, I think, fair to suggest that Marlowe's plays demonstrate relatively little interest in women – certainly much less than Shakespeare's – but, as I suggested above, this is by no means a reliable indicator of homosexuality; discussing the politics of gender in contemporary drama, Michael Billington recently took the virtual absence of roles for women from David Mamet's plays to be a sign of the playwright's healthily robust heterosexual masculinity.[65]

Baines aside, anxieties on the part of critics and scholars about Marlowe's sexuality seem to be relatively belated, and I would argue that they have less to do with a concern for delineating the historical varieties of sexual identity and more to do with the institutionalisation of literary studies in the last century or so, and thus with the processes of value judgements and affirmation of cultural hierarchy that it entailed. Tracing the recent critical history of Marlowe's plays, Simon Shepherd has cogently argued that 'Marlowe the homosexual' partly explains the status of 'Marlowe-who-isn't-Shakespeare', the immature predecessor, working in a less aesthetically subtle form, who is 'always eventually to be understood as a flawed writer because of this [sexual] obsession which he could not control'.[66] For Jarman, however, the reverse is true, and Marlowe's sexuality is what endows the play of *Edward II* with its enduring significance, particularly for the modern gay community – in the gay press, reviews of Jarman's film, and indeed of the 1990 Royal Shakespeare Company production of the play, with the out gay actor Simon Russell Beale as Edward, invariably assume the relevance of Marlowe's imputed homosexuality. This critical reception, combined with its more explicitly homosexual subject, means that *Edward II*, to a much greater extent than *The Tempest*, is a film for and about the contemporary gay community. This difference is partly a factor of Marlowe's different cultural status, in so far as that is bound up with the assumption of homosexuality; but I think it is also a product of the changed social context in which the later film was produced. Jarman has ruefully acknowledged, in interviews and his autobiographical writings, that in the decade which separated the making of these two films the party atmosphere which characterised gay men's culture in the 1970s was effectively brought to an end by the combined onslaught of the HIV epidemic and an increasing social mood of intolerance towards sexual diversity, endorsed by political measures such as Section 28.[67] *The Tempest*, with its visual hedonism, political unselfconsciousness and low-rent mixture of cheerful camp and fragments of punk culture, is in many ways a product of the 1970s; *Edward II* speaks of a much darker and more fraught cultural moment. And yet, though the film does not flinch from depicting a violent, oppressive fictional world shaped by divisions of class, gender and sexuality, it does finally offer a fragile hope, remaking the literary past in a gesture of defiant affirmation of cultural diversity in the face of the violence and oppression which equally characterise the present. Instead of assassinating Edward in a brutal parody of anal sex, Lightborn – played by Jarman's companion, Kevin Collins – flings aside his poker and embraces him tenderly; and in the closing shot, the camera pans slowly across a crowd of silent lesbian and gay activists, while Edward, in voice-over, speaks lines of courage and loss whose poignant relevance is by no means restricted to gay experience in the 1990s:

> But what are kings, when regiment is gone,
> But perfect shadows in a sunshine day?
> I know not, but of this I am assured,
> That death ends all, and I can die but once.
> Come death, and with thy fingers close my eyes,
> Or if I live let me forget myself.

The juxtaposition of Edward's words with the image of the patiently determined activists endows his elegy with overtones of resistance and hope. Colin MacCabe has suggested that in rewriting the ending of Marlowe's *Edward II*, placing the brutal execution of the king under erasure and offering the alternative of Lightborn's tender kiss, Jarman 'transforms Marlowe's bitter and cynical play on power and desire into a film which also affirms the possibility of both difference and reconciliation'.[68] What makes this affirmation so powerful is that it is asserted in the context of a clear-sighted analysis of the complex realities of the interplay of power and desire in the world which the film represents as well as the world in which it was made. 'Without our past,' wrote Jarman, 'our future cannot be reflected, the past is our mirror.' The reflection of itself which the present finds in the mirror of the past is not a fixed image of loss and oppression, but also a form of acknowledgement, recognition and inspiration which may just enable the construction of a better future.

Notes

1   This phrase is used by Jarman in an open letter to *The Independent*, 20 May 1993, protesting against the planned closure of Bart's hospital, where he was being treated for HIV-related conditions: 'Without our past our future cannot be reflected, the past is our mirror.'

2   London, Vintage, 1991. I shall also discuss Jarman's earlier autobiographical work, *Dancing Ledge* (London: Quartet, 1984).

3   *At Your Own Risk: A Saint's Testament* (London, Vintage, 1993), p. 23.

4   Quoted in Simon Fraser, 'The Jarman Collage', *Rouge*, April–June 1991, 28–30 (30).

5   Hugo Davenport, 'Making the Most of his Gifts', *Daily Telegraph*, 6 August 1991, 10.

6   Jarman describes the *Sonnets* thus in the TV documentary on his work *Know What I Mean* (YoYo Productions for Channel 4, 1988).

7   See Paul Burston, 'Saint Derek', *City Limits*, 17 October 1991, 14–15.

8   For an account of the campaigns which led to the 1967 Act, its specific provisions and its immediate impact, see Jeffrey Weeks, *Coming Out: Homosexual Politics in Britain from the Nineteenth Century to the Present* (London, Quartet, 1977, revised and updated 1990), pp. 168–77.

9   Unsigned news report, *Gay Times*, May 1993, 4.

10 Alan Sinfield, 'Queers, Treachery and the Literary Establishment', Chapter 5 of his *Literature, Politics and Culture in Postwar Britain* (Oxford, Basil Blackwell, 1989), pp. 60–86.

11 See for example Chris Baldick, *The Social Mission of English Criticism* (Oxford, Oxford University Press, 1983); Brian Doyle, *English and Englishness* (London, Routledge, 1989); Hugh Grady, *The Modernist Shakespeare* (Oxford, Oxford University Press, 1991); and Terence Hawkes, *That Shakespeherian Rag* (London, Methuen, 1986).

12 *New Statesman and Society*, 18 January 1991, p. 8.

13 The comment was made in the documentary *Know What I Mean*.

14 Catherine Bennett, 'Lesson of the Gay Guru', *The Guardian*, 9 April 1992, 21.

15 See for example Richard Dyer, *Heavenly Bodies: Film Stars and Society* (London, British Film Institute, 1986), especially the chapter on Judy Garland; and Andrea Weiss, *Vampires and Violets: Lesbians in the Cinema* (London, Jonathan Cape, 1992).

16 On the question of entitlement, exclusion and cultural power, see Maia Ettinger, 'The Pocahontas Paradigm, or Will the Subaltern Please Shut Up?' in Linda Garber (ed.), *Tilting the Tower: Lesbians Teaching Queer Subjects* (London, Routledge, 1994), pp. 51–5.

17 Jackie Stacey, 'Promoting Normality: Section 28 and the Regulation of Sexuality', in Sarah Franklin, Celia Lury and Jackie Stacey (eds), *Off-Centre: Feminism and Cultural Studies* (London, HarperCollins, 1991), pp. 284–304 (pp. 293–6). For a comprehensive account of Section 28 and its contexts, see Martin Durham, *Sex and Politics: The Family and Morality in the Thatcher Years* (Basingstoke, Macmillan Education, 1991). No local authority has been prosecuted under Section 28, but its impact has nevertheless been considerable; for a persuasive assessment of its 'symbolic rather than juridical' effectiveness, see Anna Marie Smith, 'Which One's the Pretender? Section 28 and Lesbian Representation', in Tessa Boffin and Jean Fraser (eds), *Stolen Glances: Lesbians Take Photographs* (London, Pandora, 1991), pp. 128–39 (p. 128).

18 'Section 28 and Education', in Carol Jones and Pat Mahony (eds), *Learning our Lines: Sexuality and Social Control in Education* (London, The Women's Press, 1989), pp. 79–128 (p. 102).

19 The entire sample consists of less than one hundred men, from culturally homogeneous backgrounds; all of them had died of AIDS-related conditions. No control experiments have been carried out to ascertain whether or not the segment of DNA which appears to be associated with their homosexuality also appears in heterosexual men or women of any sexual preference. I am grateful to Dr Chris Coles for discussing the implications of the Human Genome Project and this particular piece of research with me.

20 Quoted in *The Pink Paper*, 23 July 1993, p. 6.

21 Reported in *The Pink Paper*, 30 July 1993, p. 3.

22 Quoted in *The Pink Paper*, 23 July 1993, p. 6. The historical connections between homosexuality and eugenics are traced in Frank Mort, *Dangerous Sexualities: Medico-moral Politics in England since 1830* (London, Routledge & Kegan Paul, 1987).
23 *The Normal Heart* (London, Eyre Methuen, 1987), pp. 76–7.
24 *The Epistemology of the Closet* (London, Harvester, 1991), p. 51.
25 *Homosexual Desire in Shakespeare's England*, p. 28.
26 Jarman queried the political validity of McKellen's acceptance of the knighthood in 'An Offer Sir Ian was Honour Bound to Refuse?', *The Guardian*, 4 January 1991, 34; the controversy which followed resulted in the publication of numerous letters and articles, in the *Guardian* and elsewhere, in the following two weeks.
27 *Manifesto for New Times*, quoted in Mark Perryman, 'Introduction: The Remaking of the Political', in Perryman (ed.), *Altered States: Postmodernism, Politics, Culture* (London, Lawrence & Wishart, 1994), pp. 1–19 (p. 2).
28 Quoted in Marianne Macdonald and Stephen Ward, 'Gay champion dies on eve of vote', *The Independent*, 21 February 1994, 1.
29 See Walter J. Ong, 'Latin Language Study as a Renaissance Puberty Rite', *Studies in Philology*, 56 (1959), 103–24.
30 Manuscript notebook containing treatment notes for *The Tempest*, June 1976, item 13 in the British Film Institute's Jarman archive.
31 'Skin Head Sex Thing: Racial Difference and the Homoerotic Imaginary', in Bad Object Choices Editorial Collective (eds), *How Do I Look? Queer Film and Video* (Seattle Wash., Bay Press, 1991), pp. 169–222 (pp. 170, 214).
32 Quoted in Fraser, 'The Jarman Collage', 28.
33 B. Ruby Rich, 'New Queer Cinema', *Sight and Sound*, September 1992, 30–9 (32). It is no accident, of course, that although there are many 'queer' shorts by lesbians, most of the feature films which have been identified as part of the NQC are the work of gay men; in terms of gaining access to the resources needed to make a feature, lesbians have far more in common with heterosexual women than with gay men – another angle on the question of gay men's ambiguous position in relation to cultural power. The work of lesbian film-makers who might associate themselves with NQC, such as Monika Treut and Sadie Benning, is not preoccupied with 'reclaiming the queer past' so much as envisaging a possible queer present and future for women.
34 Quoted from the BFI Jarman archive, item 13.
35 Quoted in Simon Field and Michael O'Pray, 'Interview with Derek Jarman', *Afterimage* 12 (1985), 40–59 (46).
36 Interview in *Film Directions* 2, (1979), 14–15 (15).

37 'Innocence and Experience', *Afterimage* 12, 30–35 (33).

38 'Prospero with a Day-glo Banner', *Daily Telegraph*, 4 April 1992, xxv. The 'shack' is Jarman's cottage at Dungeness in Kent; pebbles and plants seem distinctly un-exotic accoutrements for a garden located on the edge of a shingle beach.

39 In the press release announcing Jarman's canonisation, the Sisters of Perpetual Indulgence are described as 'a worldwide order of gay nuns whose mission is to expiate homosexual guilt from all and to replace it with universal joy'. The event is described in *At Your Own Risk*, pp. 131–3. I am indebted to Janey Stevenson for the notion of Jarman as magus.

40 In 1976 Jarman had drafted scripts for both *The Tempest* and a film about John Dee (*Dancing Ledge*, p. 162). Several modern scholarly accounts of Dee also represent him as a Prospero figure; see Peter J. French, *John Dee: The World of an Elizabethan Magus* (London, Routledge & Kegan Paul, 1972), p. 19, and Frances A. Yates, *The Occult Philosophy and the Elizabethan Stage* (London, Routledge & Kegan Paul, 1979), p. 160.

41 'Throne of Blood', *Sight and Sound*, November 1991, 12–14 (14).

42 David L. Hirst, *'The Tempest': Text and Performance* (London, Macmillan, 1984), pp. 54–5.

43 In the documentary *Know What I Mean* Jarman repeats this statement, emphasising that it sums up the essence of the film.

44 For a brief but thorough overview of this issue, see Nigel Smith, 'The Italian Job: Magic and Machiavelli in *The Tempest*', in Linda Cookson and Bryan Loughrey (eds), *Critical Essays on 'The Tempest'* (London, Longman, 1990), pp. 90–100.

45 Quoted in Burston, 'Saint Derek', 14.

46 Mike Sutton, untitled article, *Time Out*, May 1980, 33.

47 'White', *Screen 29* (1988), 44–64.

48 The phrase is used by Mike Sutton in his *Time Out* interview with Jarman, who accepted its validity.

49 For many viewers, the queerness of the sailors' dance will be underlined by its evocation of two other outstanding moments of cinematic camp, the 'There is nothing like a dame' number from *South Pacific*, and Quentin Crisp's epiphanic encounter with a group of sailors at the end of *The Naked Civil Servant*.

50 Bette Talvacchia, 'Historical Phallicy: Derek Jarman's *Edward II*', *Oxford Art Journal*, 16 (1993), 112–28 (117).

51 Derek Jarman, 'Rudi, Art and the Matter of Life and Death', *The Independent*, 8 January 1993, 21.

52 Interview with Mike O'Pray, 'Damning Desire', *Sight and Sound*, October 1991, 8–11 (11). The anachronistic play on words implicit

in 'closet' is a recurring feature of the film's reshaping of Marlowe's language.

53 See for example Bennett, 'Lesson of the Gay Guru', and Jonathan Romney, '*Edward II*', *Sight and Sound*, November 1991, 41–2. Bizarrely, one reviewer has complained that Jarman's films focus on women at the expense of gay men: see Stephen Bourne, 'Controversial, Decadent, Provocative ...', *Gay Times*, January 1990, 68–9.

54 The key essay on heterosexuality as institution is Adrienne Rich's 'Compulsory Heterosexuality and Lesbian Existence', in Ann Snitow *et al.* (eds), *Desire: The Politics of Sexuality* (London, Virago, 1984), pp. 212–41.

55 E.g. in an interview on BBC2's *Edinburgh Nights*, 27 August 1993.

56 Derek Jarman, *Queer Edward II* (London, British Film Institute, 1991), p. 168.

57 See Lizbeth Goodman, 'Subverting Images of the Female: An Interview with Tilda Swinton', *New Theatre Quarterly*, 6 (August 1990), 215–28.

58 The article by Mulvey which inaugurated the feminist debate about the gendering of spectatorship was 'Visual Pleasure and Narrative Cinema', first published in Screen in 1975 and most recently reprinted in Screen, *The Sexual Subject: A Screen Reader in Sexuality* (London, Routledge, 1992), pp. 22–34. All page references are to this reprint.

59 'Film and the Masquerade: Theorizing the Female Spectator', in her *Femmes Fatales: Feminism, Film Theory, Psychoanalysis* (London, Routledge, 1991), pp. 17–32 (p. 32).

60 See Judith Butler, *Gender Trouble: Feminism and the Subversion of Identity* (London, Routledge, 1990).

61 See for example Tania Modleski, *The Women Who Knew Too Much: Hitchcock and Feminist Theory* (London, Methuen, 1988).

62 Quoted in Jeff Sawtell, 'Unabashed Queer and Artist', *Morning Star*, 26 October 1991, 6–7 (6).

63 'Sex, Politics, and Self-Realization in *Edward II*', in Kenneth Friedenreich and Constance Kuriyama (eds), *A Poet and a Filthy Playmaker* (New York, AMS Press, 1988), pp. 221–40 (p. 223).

64 The relevant phrases are, 'That St John the Evangelist was bedfellow to Christ and leaned alwaies in his bosome, that he used him as the sinners of Sodoma' and 'That all they that love not Tobacco & Boies were fooles'; but they come in a long list of variously atheistical and anti-social claims, which include assertions that 'the woman of Samaria and her sister were whores & that Christ knew them dishonestly', and that 'the Angell Gabriell was baud to the holy ghost', so that ripping them out of context in order to 'prove' Marlowe's

homosexuality is a suspect activity – leaving aside the question of how far Baines's honesty is to be relied on. The full list of accusations is quoted in Millar Maclure (ed.), *Marlowe: The Critical Heritage* (London, Routledge & Kegan Paul, 1979), pp. 36–8. Alan Bray argues that Baines's combination of heresy, treachery and sodomy is merely stereotypical propaganda in *Homosexuality in Renaissance England* (London, Gay Men's Press, 1982).

65 'Man Trouble', *The Guardian, Weekend* supplement, 12 June 1993, pp. 6–9.
66 *Marlowe and the Politics of Elizabethan Theatre* (Brighton, Harvester, 1986), pp. xii, xiii.
67 See *At Your Own Risk, passim*.
68 Obituary in *The Independent*, 21 February 1994, 14.

Index

Index

PR 3024 .C48 1995
Kate Chedgzoy
Shakespeare's Queer
Children